SAINT
JOHN
NEUMANN

*His Writings
and Spirituality*

Other Titles in This Series

SAINT
JOHN
NEUMANN

*His Writings
and Spirituality*

Richard Boever, C.Ss.R.

Liguori
LIGUORI, MISSOURI

Imprimi Potest:
Thomas D. Picton, C.Ss.R.
Provincial, Denver Province
The Redemptorists

Published by Liguori Publications
Liguori, Missouri

To order, call 800-325-9521
www.liguori.org

Library of Congress Cataloging-in-Publication Data
Boever, Richard A.
 Saint John Neumann : his writings and spirituality / written and edited by Richard
Boever ; foreword by Justin Cardinal Rigali. -- 1st ed.
   p. cm.
 ISBN 978-0-7648-1980-3
 1. Neumann, John, Saint, 1811-1860. I. Neumann, John, Saint, 1811-1860. II. Title.
 BX4700.N4B64 2010
 282.092--dc22
   [B]
                                                    2010036307

Liguori Publications, a nonprofit corporation, is an apostolate of the Redemptorists.
To learn more about the Redemptorists, visit Redemptorists.com.
Printed in the United States of America

14 13 12 11 10   5 4 3 2 1
First edition

CONTENTS

PART II
Writings and Documents 113

FOREWORD

FATHER BOEVER has creatively written a biography of St. John Neumann in the first person as if the saint were speaking to the reader. Father Boever's desire to focus on the humanity of St. John Neumann rather than on his accomplishments is achieved in a unique way. Direct quotes from St. John Neumann throughout the text provide a moving context for the experiences of his life rooted in a deep trust in God.

In Part I, the chronology of St. John's life includes the development of his deep faith from the early years to his death while bishop of Philadelphia. The reader is privileged to peer into his heart during the discernment of a priestly vocation and his perseverance in traveling across the ocean to the United States where he is ordained. St. John's letters to his family in Bohemia are both tender and stirring in describing his challenges and joys of serving in the developing Church in America. His life as missionary and bishop convey the holiness and humility that attracted so many souls to being disciples of Jesus Christ.

In Part II, historical documents such as the letters to his family and pastoral letters to the clergy and faithful of Philadelphia enable us to ponder our own current day in the context of his life and times.

This book invites each of us to accompany St. John Neumann along his path of faithful discipleship, deepening our own commitment of discipleship in living out our unique vocation in Christ.

Justin Cardinal Rigali, Archbishop of Philadelphia
July 15, 2010

PREFACE

WHO IS YOUR favorite saint? The Catholic Church offers the witness of many men and women who have followed Jesus Christ in extraordinary ways. The first saint that comes to my mind is Mary, the Mother of Jesus. No human being played a greater role in the history of salvation. As a young woman her *yes* to God brings the living God into her womb. Her request at Cana leads Jesus to perform his first miracle when he changes water into wine. We find Mary, ever faithful, under the cross as her flesh and blood dies an agonizing death. Mary also is in the cenacle on the first Pentecost with the apostles awaiting the outpouring of the Holy Spirit promised by the risen Jesus.

I love St. Joseph, the husband of Mary. He taught his foster son the Jewish faith and how to be a carpenter. The impetuous Peter, the doubting Thomas, and zealous Paul all inspire me. The story of Mary Magdalene rushing from the empty tomb on Easter to announce the good news of the risen Lord also moves me deeply.

In the days of the early Church, we had heroic martyrs who shed their blood for the faith, learned teachers who possessed great insights into the mystery of God, and soul-searching mystics who went into the desert to find the Lord. From the Middle Ages come some of our greatest saints: the beloved Francis of Assisi, the soldier Ignatius who founded the society of Jesuits, Catherine of Siena who courageously challenged a pope, and Theresa of Avila, who eventually became the renowned reformer of her Carmelite community. I also want to mention the founder of my own Redemptorist community, St. Alphonsus Liguori, who is the patron saint of moral theologians.

I love the story of Thomas More, a lawyer and political figure, who chose to hold onto his principles even in the face of death. Katherine Drexel, a wealthy woman of Philadelphia, spent her fortune to educate the poorest in society. The courage of early American martyrs who died while bringing the faith to the New World also come to mind.

Recent stories in the media have focused on Mother—now Blessed—Theresa of Calcutta and her diaries, which detail the hope she held onto despite trials, doubts, and questions. Her struggle to hold onto her faith despite these powerful temptations demonstrates her humanity and makes her all the more inspirational to me. I also think of two saints who lived in modern times: Maximilian Kolbe, who died at the hands of Nazi guards so a married father could live, and Edith Stein (St. Teresa Benedicta of the Cross), a Holocaust victim.

While I admire the great saints who founded religious communities, who died heroic deaths for Christ, and who wrote weighty books on theological discourse, the ones who resonate with me the most are those who faced the same day-to-day challenges that I do in my own life. When St. Thérèse of Lisieux died at the age of twenty-four, she was known only to her family and friends. She struggled with health issues, felt the sting of rejection by others in her religious community, had doubts about God's existence, and even wondered about taking her own life. She loved what she called the Little Way: being faithful to Jesus in ordinary matters. Today, she is one of the most popular saints in the world.

I first heard about St. John Neumann in 1968 when I was in my year of novitiate as a Redemptorist in Ilchester, Maryland.

During our novitiate, we were introduced to the holy men of Redemptorist history. We learned about St. Alphonsus Liguori, St. Gerard Majella, and St. Clement Hofbauer. These men were giants in the Congregation, and they did great works for God and the Church. Novice master Father Leo Henighan, C.Ss.R., also had us read about Blessed John Neumann, who was not yet canonized. Neumann was one of the early pioneers of the Redemptorists in North America. He landed in New York from Prachatitz, Bohemia, eager to serve the many immigrants who were moving to the New World. Neumann was ordained a priest for the Diocese of New York, and he labored zealously for the souls in his care. Eventually, he felt a deep yearning for community life and this led him to join the Redemptorists in 1840. In fact, he was the first man to join our Congregation in America. And with a great sense of reluctance on his part, Neumann became the Superior of the Redemptorists in the United States. With even greater trepidation, he obediently accepted the pope's command to become the fourth bishop of Philadelphia.

When we asked the novice master why Neumann was being considered for canonization, he spoke to us about some of the significant works that Bishop Neumann performed throughout his life. He was the first vice provincial of the Redemptorists in America. As bishop of Philadelphia, Neumann worked to develop what eventually would become the modern Catholic school system. He also was instrumental in successfully increasing devotion to the Eucharist by organizing the 40 Hours eucharistic practices. And he was zealous about reaching out to new immigrants pouring into the United States from Europe. But what I remember most from the novice master's talks about Neumann more than forty years ago was this simple phrase: "He did ordinary things in an a extraordinary way." These words recall what Jesus said in Luke

16:10: "The person who is trustworthy in very small matters is also trustworthy in great ones; and the person who is dishonest in very small matters is also dishonest in great ones." The hallmark of sanctity is not necessarily doing great things for God. Rather, holiness is doing the will of God in our daily lives like St. John Neumann did in his. Neumann's commitment to prayer, to his vocation as a religious and a priest, to the love of God, and to the love of his neighbor are the hallmarks of St. John Neumann's spirituality. This is a path to God that all of us can follow.

Certainly, Father Richard Boever, C.Ss.R., has written a timely book. The anti-Catholicism that Neumann experienced in his lifetime was very public. And in our modern age—particularly in some media coverage—people of faith are sometimes dismissed or ridiculed in subtle ways. St. John Neumann was an immigrant who came to the United States, and became an American citizen. In fact, he was the first male American citizen to be canonized by the Catholic Church. This good saint spent a great deal of his ministry caring for many European immigrants. In our society today, immigration is a topic of continuing debate. We pray that the example of St. John Neumann will lead us to a just and compassionate policy toward those seeking to enter our nation, a land of immigrants. Many parents today are looking for alternatives to some aspects of the educational system. Charter schools are on the rise, and some parents home-school their children. St. John Neumann fostered the development of the Catholic school system—a system that continues today. And in spite of many challenges, the Catholic school system continues to provide a quality academic education for students as they grow in the knowledge and practice of their faith.

As you read this very fine book, you will come to know an outstanding man who has much to teach us today. The use of

Neumann's own writings—especially his letters—brings the reader into a very close relationship with the saint. It is clear from Father Richard Boever's commentary that he is most learned about John Neumann. Even more important, it is very apparent that Father Richard Boever loves this saint.

May all readers who enter into the life of St. John Neumann through this book receive inspiration as they come to know this American immigrant saint. And may all readers be moved to follow Jesus the Redeemer in doing ordinary things extraordinarily well—just as St. John Neumann did throughout his lifetime.

Patrick F. Woods, C.Ss.R.
Provincial Superior
Baltimore Province

INTRODUCTION

MY BROTHER has a farm about eighty miles southwest of St. Louis where he raises Angus cattle for the market. On the property, he has built a cabin in an isolated place farther from the main house—a place I often use as a hermitage. A wind chime hangs there.

Wind chimes like this one are rather simple constructs. Five or six aluminum tubes of varying lengths emit a note when they are struck by a wooden disk hanging in the middle of them. Each has a unique tone and, I am told by a man who knows music much better than I, that the breeze rings a perfect A-minor chord. Most of the time when I look at the wind chime, I notice little more than the aluminum tubes. The tubes are the most evident visual, but the wooden disk that makes them chime is actually the heart of the instrument.

Much has been written about John Neumann—his heroic virtue, his development of a school system, his devotion to the Eucharist, his untiring energy when it came to visiting distant places where his ministry was most needed. These are monumental accomplishments. They are much like the aluminum tubes of a wind chime that ring the notes. And the heart of the saint is like the wooden disk that chimes the work of his hands—much has been written about the works of St. John Neumann.

I began my study of St. John Neumann when I was a doctoral student at St. Louis University in search of material for my dissertation. I knew that the Redemptorists of the Baltimore Province were responsible for collecting primary sources for the recently canonized (1977) John Nepomucene Neumann—the first male American citizen to receive this honor. St. John Neumann became the focus of my dissertation. That was thirty years ago. Since then, I have remained "in contact" with St. John Neumann by praying with him, writing things about him, and admiring him from afar. This recent adventure—the evolution of this book—has been a different experience.

One day I wrote the archivist who safeguards the Neumann material in Brooklyn and told him that I found myself deeply touched by Neumann, and crying as I was researching. This response to the saint was unfamiliar to me. I admired Neumann, questioned him, and imitated him. In his response, the archivist congratulated me, and then said that perhaps I had finally fallen in love with this saint. The archivist told me that there were some wonderful historical biographies about St. John Neumann, but that the authors who had written about him were simply presenting him to the public—they did not seem to convey a love for the man himself. Perhaps, the archivist said, this book will finally touch readers and show them that the saint is not only worthy of imitation, but also of friendship. I certainly hope so.

In this book, you will find materials that are intended to help you get to know the saint better—not only for his accomplishments, but also as a person. Some of the material will simply present the facts, as is the case with the chronology. But some material takes a bit more liberty and poetic license. I wrote this biography in the first person—as if St. John Neumann was telling his own story. The book is not a historical document as such, but it is historically sound. Whenever possible, I also used the words from Neumann's journal, letters, and ecclesiastical instructions to tell his story. His words are not footnoted, but I have placed them in italics to distinguish them from my own interludes to help carry his story.

Following this biography, the reader will find an article about Neumann's spirituality; heartwarming excerpts from Neumann's funeral; words from a letter sent back to Europe by one of Neumann's confreres describing the funeral; a sermon given the day before his funeral by his vicar general; the funeral eulogy of Archbishop Francis Patrick Kenrick of Baltimore; and a memorial poem given to Neumann by the citizens of Prachatitz. These help bring some facets of Neumann's personality to fuller light.

The remaining items, which include letters Neumann wrote to his family and friends from America and his pastoral letters to the clergy and the faithful of Philadelphia, help reveal his personality. I'm hopeful that this material will help readers understand Neumann more fully and recognize him as one of the great saints of heaven.

A special thanks to the Redemptorists of the Baltimore Province who have preserved so much excellent material from the life of St. John Neumann and who continue to treasure these materials as a patrimony of the province. Special thanks also to two Redemptorists who read and commented on this book, Fr. Ray Corriveau of the Toronto Province and Fr. John Murray of the Baltimore Province. Their comments were most helpful.

Finally, thanks is merited by the Redemptorists of the Denver Province for establishing the wonderful publishing house at Liguori, Missouri, and to the men and women serving this apostolate now for their attention to the many details of publishing this book.

Pope Benedict XV said of Neumann, "The merits of an active man are measured not so much in the number of deeds performed, as in their thoroughness and stability. For true activity does not consist in mere noise, it is not the creature of a day, but it unfolds itself in the present, it is the fruit of the past and should be the good seed of the future. Are not these very characteristics the mark of the activity of Venerable Neumann? Bearing all this in mind, no one will any longer doubt that the simplicity of the work performed by our venerable servant of God did not hinder him from becoming a marvelous example of activity. Their very simplicity has forced us…to impress on our children…the proclamation of the heroic virtues of Neumann, since all find in the new hero an example not difficult to imitate."

Richard Boever, C.Ss.R.

CHRONOLOGY

1811	**March 28**	Born and baptized
1818		Began school in Prachatitz—First Confession
1819		Confirmation
1821		First Communion
1823–29		Studies at Gymnasium in Budweis
1829–31		Studies on the philosophy level in Budweis
1831–33		Seminary studies in Budweis
1832	**July 21**	Tonsure and minor orders
1833–35		Seminary in Prague
1835	**July 8**	Finished studies, but ordination delayed
1836	**February 8**	Left Prachatitz for America
1836	**April 20**	Set sail on the *Europa* for America
1836	**June 2**	Disembarked at New York City
1836	**June 19**	Ordained a subdeacon
1836	**June 24**	Ordained a deacon
1836	**June 25**	Ordained a priest, Old St. Patrick's Church in New York City
1836	**June 26**	First Mass at St. Nicholas Church, New York City
1836	**June 29**	Set out for ministry north of Buffalo
1836	**July 12**	Arrived in Buffalo and served parishes north of that city
1839	**September 25**	Wenzel Neumann joins his brother in parishes in New York State
1840	**October 18**	Left Buffalo and the Diocese of New York to join the Redemptorists
1840	**November 30**	Neumann becomes a Redemptorist novice

1842	January 16	Profession of vows as a Redemptorist (first C.Ss.R. to do so in North America)
1844–47	March 5	Named superior and pastor of St. Philomena's Parish, Pittsburgh, Pennsylvania
1847	January 27	Called to Baltimore to rest after exhaustion
1847	February 9	Appointed vicegerent of the Redemptorists in North America
1847	Summer	School Sisters of Notre Dame arrived in Baltimore
1849	January 9	B. Hafkenscheid appointed vice provincial of North America Neumann named consulter of the vice province and rector of St. Alphonsus Parish, Baltimore
1852	March 28	Ordained Bishop of Philadelphia by Archbishop Francis Kenrick of Baltimore
1852	April 28	First meeting forming the Catholic School Board of Philadelphia
1853		40 Hours Devotions inaugurated
1854	October 21	Went to Rome for the Solemn Declaration of the Immaculate Conception
1855	February	Visited family and friends in Bohemia
1856	May 26	First Sisters of St. Francis profess their vows before Bishop Neumann
1857	April	James F. Wood appointed coadjutor Bishop of Philadelphia with right of succession
1858	Sept 13	Exterior of cathedral completed, cross and keystone placed on structure
1859		Sisters of the Third Order of St. Francis begun in Philadelphia by Neumann
1859		Immaculate Heart of Mary Sisters came to Diocese of Philadelphia from Monroe, Michigan
1860	January 5	At 3 PM, St. John Neumann died while on an errand
1860	January 10	Neumann buried in crypt at St. Peter's Church, Philadelphia

PART I

John N. Neumann

A Biography in the First Person

SETTING THE SCENE

THE DAY I ARRIVED in New York City was the center point in my life. It was Trinity Sunday, 1836, when the ship the *Europa*—which sailed out of Havre—arrived in New York Harbor. As we approached shore, everyone on board pressed up against the railing, gazing through the mist at the welcome sight of our new home. *In spite of the heavy rains, we all stood on deck as long as anything could be seen and took delight in the beautiful green of the shore, in the light red houses and the landed estates which could not be painted more beautifully....What happiness may not the just man feel, when on his*

St. John Neumann sets foot on American soil.
(Window in Neumann Shrine, Philadelphia)

deathbed he sees the end of his misery approach and the land of his yearning lie before him.

I came to America to be a minister. And much like the Lord's desert experience, my journey also began in a kind of desert—the desert of the high seas. For forty days I sailed, sometimes tossed mercilessly by towering waves, other times with hardly any movement in the sails, a frightening stillness to endure. I could not help but think how these experiences were like the spiritual life—sometimes in mortal combat with the powers of evil, and other times fighting a battle with an overpowering stillness. Time and time again, I asked the captain to allow me to go ashore. We were quarantine on board due to illness among some of the passengers on the ship. I was well and wanted to get on with my journey, even though I had no idea what was in store for me. I only had one dollar left to my name, and I had not yet received word from Bishop Dubois of New York about whether he needed a German priest in the diocese. I did know that the bishop of Philadelphia no longer was in need of a German-speaking priest and I was worried about whether I would be able to minister to people after spending so many years preparing for this work. In the years to come, I would know firsthand the very real need for priests in America. In fact, I often found myself wishing that I could duplicate myself several times over! *The need of Catholic priests and the spiritual desolation of the faithful (were) increasing day by day. Judging from a human standpoint, the disproportion would have lamentable results, only God alone is the support of His Church.* Finally, after asking the captain of the *Europa* for several days if I could go ashore, he wearied of my supplications and permitted me to go to Staten Island where I caught a ferry to the city itself. I breathed a sigh of relief and said a prayer of gratitude once I landed on shore.

Obviously, there was no one to meet me in New York; neither did I know the layout of the city nor any destinations to find once I arrived there. Nevertheless, I found great solace in walking through the city, looking for clues about where to go next. I wanted, of course, to find a Catholic church and I walked down endless blocks in the rain all day. It was a good thing that I was already accustomed to walking long distances at a quick pace. But by the end of the day, I still had not satisfied my quest. That night, I stayed with a Swiss family, and they were able to point me in the direction of a Catholic church the next morning. The church unfortunately was an English-speaking parish. This should not have surprised me as I now was in an English-speaking country. The people at the church directed me to the cathedral, where it just so happened a German-speaking priest resided with the bishop. An hour later, I found my sanctuary. Father Raffeiner greeted me like a long-lost brother. I found out that he also traveled to North America back in 1832 to join the Redemptorists after hearing about the need for priests. He was, however, delayed in New York City by inclement weather. And as it turned out, he never left the city. He saw the great need for priests after getting involved with the German-speaking immigrants who lived there. So Father Raffeiner remained as a priest in the diocese, in the same place where he first arrived in North America.

As it turned out, my anxiety about being ordained was unnecessary. Father Raffeiner told me that three weeks prior, a letter was sent to Europe saying that I had been accepted into the diocese of New York! Since I had already set sail by the time the letter was sent, I did not receive the correspondence. The bishop informed me that I would be ordained as soon as he returned from a pastoral visit to a remote area in the diocese. What a wonderful bishop!

Thanks, a thousand thanks to Thee, my Jesus, for having prepared a place for me in Thy sanctuary. Now free from anxiety, I can enter into myself. This I do the more gladly as I know it to be my duty. O, what emotions were mine when, on the Feast of Corpus Christi, I set foot on American soil!...My God, how can I thank Thee for Thy goodness in sending me to so paternal, so pious a man! Here I am at last! Doubt and uncertainty have vanished like mist before the rays of the sun. I may now look forward with confidence to the speedy attainment of my hopes. Silently, O my Jesus, silently but surely have You disentangled the knot which once appeared to me so difficult....My God, I am seized with fear when I consider the sanctity of the office that awaits me and compare with it my own unworthiness. Lord, punish me not in Your anger! Take from me the burden, or dear Lord, increase my strength and faith, my hope and charity, a thousandfold! Enkindle in my heart charity toward my neighbor. In such sentiments I would be willing to die; I would not care what might happen to me....O Jesus, I must henceforth labor for the salvation of others. Do Thou strengthen my weakness! Be Thou forever praised, dearest Jesus, my Lord and my God! Behold, my life, my strength, my whole being, all that I have, all that I am, I devote to Thy greater glory.

MY EARLY LIFE

I WAS IN MY TWENTIES when I knew that I would dedicate myself to the North American missions. But this knowledge and determination did not spring up overnight. The seed was planted in the earliest days of my life when I was still living with my parents, Philip Neumann and Agnes Lebis. My father was born on October 16, 1774, in Obernburg, a town in Bavaria. He moved to Prachatitz, my hometown, in 1802 when he was twenty-eight years old to ply his trade as a stocking weaver. At that time, commerce between Bavaria and Bohemia was common, and German was the language we normally spoke at home. My mother was Czech, but I would not study the language until years later when I was in the seminary. My classmate, Krbecek, helped me learn Czech grammar and vocabulary; in exchange, I lectured him in Italian, a language he admired for its beauty. This study greatly helped me master other Slavic dialects which were useful to me during my pastoral ministry in America.

My father and mother married in 1805, and I was the third of six children. Catherine, the first-born, later married Matthias Berger and had one son, John. This nephew of mine later became a Redemptorist priest and missionary in America like his uncle and gave me great joy. He would be the man who wrote my first biography using his sources both with family in Bohemia and Redemptorist confreres with whom he lived. Veronica, my second elder sister, married Anthony Kandl, but they had no children. I

was the third child of the Phillip
Neumann family, born March
28, 1811, which fell on Good
Friday that year. My baptism
took place on the very day of my
birth in the parish church of St.
James and I was given the name
of the protector of Bohemia, John
Nepomucene. The three children
of the family born after me all
became religious. Joanna entered
the Sisters of Charity of St. Charles
Borromeo and became known as
Sister Mary Caroline. My sister

Young John Neumann
(Baltimore Province Archives)

Aloysia followed in Joanna's footsteps, joining the Sisters of Charity
after caring for my father until his death. Then there was Wenzel,
my dear little brother who came to join me in New York. In 1841,
he became a Redemptorist brother in my own congregation and
became known as Brother Wenceslaus.

The family tree of my parents did not survive beyond two generations but their accomplishments as Christian parents surely will
bring them great reward. *We were brought up in the old-fashioned
school. Our parents were both deeply Christian. While our father from
morning to night supervised the apprentices and workers, of which
there were at times five or six in our house, our mother never missed
a day hearing Mass. She always took with her one or the other of the
children who was not yet in school....In my case there was needed
at times the promise of a penny or something similar to bring me to
Mass, rosary and Stations of the Cross.* I received my first confession
when I was seven years old, confirmation when I was eight, and
First Holy Communion when I was nine.

As I grew in age, I found myself becoming more intrigued with the wonders of nature, which is not to say that I did not also love my religion and the life of the parish. I was always fervent in my devotion and did have a dread of sin. At age seven, I entered the local school and did well in my studies during those first six years of schooling. My love of books began in these early days—a love that sometimes tended to lend itself to a bit of extravagance later in life. The entire culture surrounding me during my upbringing was in tune with my family's deeply held beliefs—there was never a contrast or division between religion and intellectual life. This allowed me to pursue my curiosities without a great fear of violating my religious convictions. *I had acquired from my father, who was a great lover of books, a decided passion for reading. As a result, the time that others spent in sports or bird catching, I spent in reading all the books I could get hold of. This is the reason why my mother often called me the little book-worm. I was accustomed to fill up the many idle hours and days with nothing else but the reading of all sorts of books that I could get my hands on, without thinking of being selective.*

Parish Church at Prachatitz *(Author)*

In my seventh year, I made my First Confession and in the summer of 1819, I was confirmed by The Most Reverend Bishop of Budweis. For as long as anyone could remember, no bishop had ever visited our remote mountain village. As a result, the huge crowd and the solemnity were indescribable and the memories remained so vivid in my memory that I can recall the smallest details of the occasion.

If I recall correctly, I was not yet ten years old when I mastered the *Larger Catechism*. As a result, I was admitted to First Holy Communion with the older communicants at the school. I have no particularly strong recollection of the day; in Bohemia, it was not the custom to observe the day as solemnly as in other countries. Thereafter, we received Communion every three months.

During my school years, I was taken by the wonders that surrounded me. One night, I was unable to sleep because I was fascinated by the moon's ability to float in space without falling into the vast expanse of the universe. My told mother me to go to bed, and to let the moon float on its own. During my last year in the local school, I was tutored in Latin, along with ten or twelve other students. This was the custom for boys who intended to enter the study of science in the upper grades. I also began to study botany with the parish catechist in the church gardens. This interest continued into adulthood, and I often would collect botanical specimens from the forests of New York. *I have made use of the opportunity thus afforded to extend my knowledge of botany. I gather the flowers on my way, many of them unknown in your country. Had I an opportunity I would send to Bohemia specimens of the rare and curious plants I everywhere meet.*

At age twelve, I finished schooling in Prachatitz and entered the gymnasium in Budweis under the direction of the Piarist Fathers. Budweis was a day's journey from home. I boarded with three others students. *Room and board were very cheap and the cost no more than sixteen florins for the ten months. Actually, I had very little studying to do. The catechist at home, during our few lessons each week, made us learn so much that with little preparation we could have been immediately promoted into the third class. That, however, was not permitted. I used the many idle hours and days in more and more reading—all kinds of books, whatever I could indiscriminately get my hands on.* In my third year at Budweis, however, I ran into a problem. We had a very old, good-natured professor who had an unfortunate addiction to liquor. As might be imagined, we made no progress in our studies. In fact, I forgot much of what the catechist at home had taught me. During that third year, our professor, intoxicated as usual, came to our examination which was presided over by the reverend superintendent. The unfortunate man was, of course, compelled to withdraw. Soon

Budweis Gymnasium *(Baltimore Province Archives)*

after, he died by his own hand. His successor was as strict as he was learned, and he wanted us to crowd into six months the studies that should have been done in the previous two and a half years. This required too much of most of the pupils—especially after developing bad habits under his predecessor. As might be expected, this caused many students to be left behind.

In these years of gymnasium, I was dissatisfied with the teacher of Christian doctrine. He was the very personification of dryness, and a stickler for verbatim recitations. I had no memory for words, so the two hours of religious instruction were very irksome to me. When at the end of the gymnasium years of school, I was exhausted and some of my grades were not as good as they should have been, my father figured I was finished with my studies and that I was ready to exchange my books for a trade. It would have been an appropriate time to end my formal studies, and I even resolved to discontinue them during the vacation. But my mother, brother, and sisters persuaded me to change my mind. My father consulted with the dean, who allowed me to take the exam a second time, and, after successfully passing it, I returned to school. This time, I did not have to share my room with other students, which allowed me to concentrate more on school—and my studies improved as a result.

During the two years of study following gymnasium, which we call philosophy, many changes took place in me. There were at least a dozen students who showed a great aptitude for the sciences. We employed all of our free time—even our days of recreation—communicating with one another about what we had learned in our studies. While improving ourselves in this way, we were greatly assisted by the good Cistercians, our teachers. They received us kindly and answered all of our questions. *During these two years I followed perhaps a little too much my inclination for the natural sciences. Natural history, geography, physics, geology, astronomy kept me busy, while algebra, geometry, trigonometry, which I had formerly disliked, were now my favorite studies.* At one point, artillery Commander Joseph Juttner helped me apply my mathematical studies through the practice of aiming a canon. I studied hard, and looked for opportunities in daily life to apply what I had learned. Still, there were times when I applied myself only enough to pass a test. One day after a history test, my classmates saw me shaking my head. You see, I wanted to rid myself of the material that I had studied just for the test. Some of the material included information about Josephism, an anti-Roman bias that I could not accept. I have always been pretty straight-laced in church matters. Later, in the seminary, I was even accused once of being too orthodox in my theological beliefs but it seemed to me that during controversy, the safer position was to follow the teachings of Rome. This seemed to be a reasonable approach.

During my time as a student, I never abandoned my spiritual life. With the course of study, I not only remained faithful to my prayers, but I also read and studied a number of works like The *Imitation of Christ* by Thomas a Kempis, and *The Sinner's Guide* by Venerable Louis of Grenada. I did my best to practice virtue and avoid sin. A fellow student once asked me if I experienced any difficulty with my living arrangements. I roomed with a widow who had a lovely daughter. I told him *that girl occupies my thoughts no more than any other woman. To me they are all beautifully bound books which I know not how to read.*

At the end of the philosophy years, the time came when I had to declare my field of future study. I cannot say that I was aware of any definite inclination for the priesthood during my childhood. I did own a little altar made of lead, and I served Mass nearly every day. Yet my ideal of a priest seemed too high to be attainable by me. At home, I was accustomed to reciting the prayer before meals. One day without thinking about it, I blessed myself in the Latin style instead of making three crosses on my forehead, mouth and breast. An old woman servant at our home who enjoyed a reputation for strict fasting, saw me do this and remarked: "Look at that—our little Johnnie is going to become a priest." My mother often mentioned this incident because she wanted me to become a priest someday. Despite all of this, the idea of becoming a priest did not cross my mind until I was older. The possibility of getting accepted into the seminary seemed slim—only twenty of the eighty or ninety applications were accepted. Besides, I had great interest in the sciences, so my inclination was to enter medicine. While grappling with uncertainty about my choice of a profession, I returned home during the autumn holiday of that year. To my surprise, my father was not opposed to the idea of me going to Prague to study medicine even though such a step would involve considerable expense. My mother, however, was saddened at the thought of me pursuing this profession. I told her about my inability to procure recommendations for the study of theology from influential people, as I was not acquainted with anyone who would be able to make such a recommendation on my behalf. But she refused to listen to my reasoning. She urged me to send a petition to the Episcopal Consistory, and firmly believed that God would guide me. Honoring my mother's wishes, I drew up a petition for admission to the seminary and sent it by special messenger to the council. Without any recommendations, and simply at my own request, I was admitted to the seminary. From that moment on, the temptation to devote myself to the study of medicine disappeared. Without regret, I also gave up physics and astronomy almost entirely, even though they were among my favorite pursuits. I then began my studies of the sacred science on All Saints Day, November 1, 1831.

THE SEMINARY

THE SEMINARY for the diocese was located in Budweis, the town where, except for my earliest education in Prachatitz, I had attended school up to that point. The small seminary had been established in 1804 and numbered 140 students. This number of students was more than sufficient to supply the diocese with the clergy it needed in the ministry.

I was happy in the Budweis seminary, surrounded by good friends and good spiritual advisors. *Because of the limited space in the seminary, only the two highest classes were permitted to live there. I therefore boarded outside. I studied Old Testament, Hebrew, Church History, and my other subjects to my own satisfaction and to that of the professors who were diocesan priests. With the exception of the professor*

Budweis Seminary *(Archive Postcard)*

of Church History and Canon Law, who was by and large a Josephist, a good spirit prevailed among the professors, and with great ease they taught us much useful material in a short time. At the end of the first year of theology I was one of the few who were allowed to receive the tonsure and the minor orders. This occurred on July 21, 1832.

In the second year of theology, we had to study the New Testament both in Latin and in Greek, along with hermeneutics and Canon Law. I found most interesting the epistles of St. Paul, which the professor interpreted expertly. About this time I also began to read the publications of the Leopoldine Foundation—especially the letters of the Reverend Frederic Baraga and other missionaries working among the Germans in North America.

Frederic Baraga was born June 29, 1797, in Slovania and had gone to America in 1831 to minister to the Ottawas at Arbre Croche, Michigan, and later with the Chippewas at La Pointe.

The Leopoldine Society, which published his letters to Bohemia, had been established by Father Reese, a priest who was sent by Bishop Fenwick of Cincinnati to Austria in 1827 so that he could collect funds for the American missions. Beginning in 1828, he published accounts of this missionary work in *Abriss der Geschichte des Bistums Cincinnati in Nord-America*. The publication spurred a tremendous interest in the

Missionary, Bishop Frederic Baraga
(M.H. Weltzies & Co., 1900)

work of the missionaries in the New World. It also led to the eventual organization of the charitable society established to support mission work with prayer and money for the spiritual good of the contributing members, and to help in the spread of the faith. The members committed themselves to one Our Father and Hail Mary daily with the invocation, "St. Leopold, pray for us." They also pledged to give one kreuzer per week in alms to the missionary effort. In later years, the Ludwig-Mission Verein would serve a similar function in Bavaria.

In those days, I was profoundly influenced by the letters of the American missionaries and by my studies of the missionary journeys of St. Paul. I found myself thinking more and more about the missionary life. I kept these thoughts to myself until I found out that one of my dearest friends was thinking along similar lines. *In this way there developed in one of my fellow students, Adalbert Schmid, and myself, on the occasion of a stroll along the Moldau, a sudden resolve to betake ourselves to North America as soon as we had attained our desired goal of ordination and had acquired some experience.* Adalbert would continue to be a very special person to me but he later decided not to pursue the life of a missionary after ordination. Years later, I tried to persuade him to reconsider the missionary vocation. *Since my ordination on the title of the American Mission, my life has received a direction from which I can no longer turn aside...Now I can hope to see you in America, in this country whose name after the name of Jesus, used to transport us into the sweetest dreams during our student years. We had learned to love it to such an extent that time never grew heavy in our conversation about it although we exchanged every day the same thoughts in its regard. The thought of the American Mission was so interwoven with our understanding of the love of God and our neighbor that since then every other way thereto, even if it seemed friendlier and perhaps more secure, appeared narrow and sad.*

The resolve made the theological studies all the more important to us. Next to Scripture, I enjoyed the study of dogmatic theology the most. I kept a copy of Peter Canisius' *Summa Doctrinae Christianae* next to my textbooks, and came to know it as my own. The practice of supplementing my formal studies with solid literature would remain with me throughout the seminary. I knew that I would have to be well-grounded theologically if I were to leave the settled environment of Bohemia for the wilds of America. I began to keep notes about many of these works and the intellectual roots that I nurtured in Europe never failed me.

Beyond the foundation of solid theology, my decision to go to America would require me to speak languages I had not yet mastered. I knew that English would certainly be necessary, and I was sure that being able to speak French also would come in handy. As it so happened, each diocese was allowed to send two seminarians to the larger archepiscopal seminary in Prague every year. For me, Prague was full of promise. There, I imagined that I would experience a cosmopolitan atmosphere, which would help me prepare for America. It also seemed that Prague would provide me with more opportunities to learn foreign languages. So I contacted the Most Reverend Bishop of Budweis, Ernst Konstantin Ruzicka, and applied for one of these positions. My request was granted, and I transferred to the much larger seminary in Prague for my last two years of seminary.

Unfortunately, going to Prague was not an easy move for me. Theological differences presented me with conflict in Prague. I dreamed of bringing the spirit of my faith to a foreign land, only to witness the attack on it in my own country. Only after I had been active in the ministry in America would I come to understand that the esoteric discussions of the professors at the university had little effect on the rock-solid foundation of the simpler faith apparent in my parishes. The needs in America were much more basic and foundational.

While in Prague, I imposed a discipline on myself that I thought would serve me well in the wilderness of North America. For a small-town boy, my faith would be my consolation in the big city of Prague, and it would continue to serve as a refuge throughout the years. Eventually, I discovered that the discipline I imposed on myself in Prague would become the natural condition of my life while serving in the missions. *It was gratifying and very consoling for every Catholic in America to learn that only his Faith alone is the same everywhere and with all nations. My Germans, as also the Irish, have often told me that they now felt themselves more strengthened in their faith, since they, especially the former see the most perfect unity of faith with all Catholics, whether they come from Italy, Germany, Ireland, France or America, amid the indescribable confusion of the Protestants.*

Neumann's journal *(Baltimore Province Archives)*

During my years in Prague, I began writing my unguarded thoughts and feelings in *Mon Journal*. The writings were not a diary as such but afforded me the opportunity to externalize my deepest longings and feelings and frustrations. It often became a discussion with God, his Mother, or one of the saints about various issues. I figured they were my principle companions in Prague, as they would be in the New World. The *Journal* served as a mirror for my beliefs and my weaknesses. I wrote entries in it for most days when I was living alone. I began writing in it during my final years of seminary in Prague and I continued to write in it during the years when I served alone as a parish priest in western New York.

During this time, I tried to find a spiritual director who would help me navigate my course in life. Instead, I finally realized that

I would have to initiate my own dialogue with the Lord and let him direct my pen. With his guidance, I would include only what would help me correct my faults and obtain eternal life. So keeping my journal became a kind of prayer, and a way to understand the movements of God in my life. In it, I recorded what I now consider the most difficult time in my life. Before Prague, life seemed to unfold on its own, and all I had to do was to cooperate with the movements of God's grace as it presented itself in my daily routine. But when I felt isolated, I sank into an introspection that touched my tender conscience. And in this state, I became ruthless with my thoughts. The trials I endured during that time forced me to articulate what I truly believed about my life and my life in God. In Budweis, life was less complex. *Oh, inexplicable labyrinth of life! Who would manage to find his way, if he read the history of my life. The Lord began to call me to Himself by consolation; He put up with my deafness for three years, I turned to Him half-heartedly. To what a beautiful way did the Lord point. He gave me milk because I could not have digested any other food. It was mother's milk, which strengthened me.* But at Prague, I came to learn a desolation that I now believe was necessary for me to grow in virtue. I was particularly sensitive when I felt unappreciated, and I easily became vain when praised. Granted, these traits might not be so unusual for a young man. But in my case, life circumstances exaggerated these responses. It was difficult for me to be fervent when I suspected someone might scoff at me—others' perception of me was important. I often went to great lengths to avoid the derision of others.

I would never be known as an orator. In fact, I was very self-conscious about my ability to deliver a good sermon. *In my homiletics class, this tension was well known to me. So that we would get more practice, our professor informed us that he would be increasing the number of homilies that students would have to deliver so that we would get more practice. I soon became preoccupied with the task and the new schedule. What I have done so far is not very good. I am quite beside myself in my anxiety and discouragement.* The prefect confirmed my worries. He told me my sermon needed more work, and he pointed out my mistakes. I prayed in my *Journal* for guidance. *You are aware of my weakness, my inclination to discouragement; my lack of skill in preaching worries me so much. I would readily turn to You in prayer, Lord, but so many of my prayers, marred by my sins, go unheard, that I no longer have the confidence to approach the throne of Your mercy.*

When my turn came to deliver the sermon, my fears were realized. *I was doing fairly well as they say, when of a sudden my memory went blank. I paused and finally had to leave the pulpit. Without any great need, I tried to make excuses that really had nothing to do with my lapse of memory. Though no one pressed me, I lied in saying I knew the text in Latin but not in German—which was not true. My conscience was, by Your grace, was telling me not to lie; nevertheless I repeated the lie several times without any need to do so, because no one was asking me about it.* My embarrassment pushed me around like a torrent against which I had no footing. Such experiences showed me my human weakness.

I became aware of what I would consider a great number of character defects. These defects often made me feel uncomfortable, and I found myself going to extremes to avoid the feelings that were associated with them. Loneliness was especially difficult for me. I never realized how important my companions in Budweis were to me. So when I experienced the isolation of Prague, the absence of these companions grew in intensity. *Dear God, everybody is displeased with me. How can I evoke their affections? I am so fainthearted and timid!…Thinking about my friends today made me feel so disconsolate, especially after supper, that I started to cry!*

Here I am, with all my carelessness and indifference while my friends in Budweis are surrounded by remarkable people and enjoy wise and holy spiritual direction! They don't even think of me anymore. In my loneliness and grief they have forgotten all about me.

For some reason—probably because I am not gregarious—I did not experience the comfort of family or friends during the last two years of my seminary or while I was working as a young priest in the wilds of New York. This affected me profoundly. My old friends seemed so far away. Schmid decided to enter the monastery at Hohenfurth rather than accompany me to America. I had so looked forward to going to America together. Still, Schmid held a special place in my heart and when I received correspondence from him, it made my day. *I received a letter from my friend Schmid today! O my Jesus, You do indeed hear my prayers to strengthen me in Your love and in my trust in Your providence and to restore my hope.*

I experienced the inclination toward sin that was part of my fallen nature. Sometimes I felt incapable of virtue. Everywhere I failed. I found it terribly difficult to endure all of these trials without a spiritual guide or a worthy companion. *There is a terrible void in my soul, I am completely discouraged, I cannot pray, to whom shall I turn for help? Then arises an embittered spirit and hate against my Creator and Jesus in my soul. Pride and unbelief, animal and devilish desires want to engulf my tortured, abandoned soul. And to such blasphemous thoughts I feel a great inclination, despair offers me suicide as a desirable means to free myself from my torturing doubts, and this means even seems allowed because all regard also for his phantom laws has left my soul.*

I did read the great spiritual authors to seek direction and counsel for my life. I read works by St. Teresa of Avila, St. Augustine, St. Francis de Sales, and St. Alphonsus Liguori. I also read *The Sinner's Guide* by Venerable Louis of Grenada, *The Spiritual Combat* by Father Dom Lorenzo Scupoli, *The Dolorous Passion of our Lord Jesus Christ* by Anne Catherine Emmerich, and *Meditations* by Jean Croiset. Though I was often inspired by these readings, they also made me all the more aware of the inadequacies in my own spiritual life. Some days, my vainglory disturbed me the most; on others, my impatience with other people was more troublesome.

It was very easy for me to make a long list of my weaknesses. *I was worse than lax most of the day, for I often actually took delight in the impure thoughts that occurred to me. I was glad that I had them and maybe even coddled them! I also let myself be roused to anger once, though briefly. I was lazy and careless about my work. I no longer value humility or make an effort to acquire it because of my tepidity, lack of love, wavering faith and my despair of recovering God's grace. Indeed, the condition of my soul is simply astonishing. Right now I would gladly quit this particular path of salvation I have trod for so long! Oh, Jesus, is it possible that You may still comfort and console me? Come to me! I am Yours. Do come to me, my Jesus.*

As the time of my ordination approached, my anxiety increased with each passing day. When I reflected on the expectations I had regarding my own improvement, I became discouraged and wondered about my decision to enter the priesthood. *For what sort of a priest would I be with all the sins I have, with all my bad habits, my inflexibility and stubbornness, with my host of spiritual and bodily frailties?* It was during one of these times that I wrote: *Lord, I am beginning to feel that awful state of depression coming over me again! I lose all yen for prayer because you seem to have turned a deaf ear to my cries. My distress grows from day to day. My own weakness overwhelmed me, and I feared distance from God. In my writings, I implored God to lift me from despair. My God, do not let this despair of mine continue…it could lead me to suicide. This faintheartedness and lack of faith is frightening.*

I felt so despairing and alone during this time in my life. I feared that the center of my life—my love of God—had vanished. I was well aware of my own imperfections, and I had to rely on faith and God's love for me to carry me through my weaknesses. So often, I felt alone, disliked, and unappreciated. If others felt that way about me, why would God view me any differently? *My immense wretchedness moved my soul so that I neither was able at all to stem the flood of my tears nor did I wish to do so, there is no longer any consolation for me here on earth. Jesus, my delight, is lost and I cannot find him. He cannot or will not hear my cry. I stretched out my hands to him, he did not take hold of them; I have cried my eyes dim, he is not moved; my voice is hoarse from praying, he does not show himself....If I pray, the fruitlessness of my striving and the fear that my prayer is a lie and will increase my punishment hovers threateningly before the eyes of my soul. If I begin to pray, my conscience becomes still more restless; if I stop praying, I clearly see the abyss to which I am hurrying. Lord, mercy! Or else!*

The depression I experienced caused my greatest suffering, and it seemed that so many things triggered this tendency within me. In spite of my recognized gifts, what I felt most was a great weakness. I did not feel strong. I did not feel resolved. I did not feel loved. So it was difficult for me to believe that it would be any different with the Lord. I came to realize that a deep, abiding faith was the only way to quell the horrors that secretly raged within my spirit. Oh, how hard this was to embrace! Knowledge did not hold the answer for me—it was faith. Knowledge would have been much easier. Around the time that I came to a realization. *I stand before You, my Savior; You have not spurned my sincere offer to become Your obedient disciple. I no longer look for comfort from either heaven or earth. You, divine Master, can judge whether such are necessary for me. I propose to worry no more over the aridity You send me. You, my God, are the font of both aridity and grace. I am grateful to You for letting me learn this.*

A new awareness grew out of these experiences. Even so, I continued to chastise myself for my weaknesses. My path slowly became one of surrender. *O, purify my motives, my thoughts and my desires! Of myself, I can do nothing. Tell me what to do to be worthy of Your grace which I so need if I am to seek perfection. Holy Spirit, Sanctifier of my soul, dispel the darkness that hovers over me.* I had reached a point where I knew experientially that I could trust only in God. My own efforts were not only inadequate, they were complete failures. *When I beg your grace in order to practice virtue, You grant it to me and it does help me accomplish something worthwhile. But then I become conceited and proud. When I ask You to send me misfortune so that I may learn the path to salvation, I then bear it with little resignation. I even ask You to deliver me from it. If You remove it, I get depressed and desolate and I feel miserable. Behold me, dear God at the foot of Your throne. Give me whatever You will. Spare me from whatever You will. Let me know Your will without a doubt, for that must be my law.* It was during this time that I learned the true meaning of poverty of spirit.

I sometimes have to step back and find some humor in my struggles to improve my spiritual life. I have realized that only God can make this happen. *In this knowledge, I find peace. True, I feel but little devotion; my soul is dry and sluggish; but yet, O Lord Jesus, I believe in You, I hope in You, I love You, and I grieve for having ever offended You! Behold my resolution to live entirely for You, to be patient in sufferings, diligent in the fulfillment of my duties, humble before You and my neighbor, and devout in Your service. O my God, accept the sacrifice of my lowliness! Holy Immaculate Mother of my Jesus, pray for me, a poor sinner, that I may worthily receive my God!*

Aside from my inner spiritual struggles, I also experienced other challenges while I was in Prague. My decision to go to Prague mostly had to do with my desire to learn and practice English in preparation for living in North America. But this preparation was not to be. At the same time, I found the theological studies much more liberal than what I had experienced in Budweis. This should not have surprised me—I should have expected this liberal approach in a university setting and in a bustling capital city. Nevertheless, I found myself badly disappointed.

I had barely attended a few classes in French when there appeared a decree of the Reverend Archbishop of Prague (Andreas Alois Graf Ankwicz) that no seminarian should attend these lectures. I had even more difficulty learning English since this language was not taught at the university. Similarly, I was very displeased in Prague with the professors of Dogmatic Theology, Moral Theology, and Pastoral Theology. The first was more against the pope more than for him; however, he offered such ridiculous objections that he lost our respect and could do no harm. The second man was too philosophical for any of us to understand him. The third was an out-and-out Josephist. It took a lot of effort and self-control to bury myself in the study of subjects and ideas whose foolishness I had come to realize.

So I resolved to do the best I could in the situation that resulted from my transfer to Prague. I had to learn languages on my own; and in this I succeeded. Eventually, I approached the French professor, and requested a language exam. Initially, he refused my request because I had not attended his class, but eventually I was able to take the test. I passed it with distinction. I suppose I wanted to prove something to myself, but I found learning English a bit more difficult. I struggled with my own private study of the language, and for a while, I supplemented my studies by conversing in English with some factory workers I met in the city. After this, I wrote in my *Journal* in three languages—English, French, and German. My English never improved enough to please all the people who listened to me, and this became increasingly apparent to me in later years when I was living in Philadelphia. My coadjutor bishop once told another bishop that I should have submitted my pastoral letter to him for editing before it was published. I would have to agree with him.

During this time, I also continued to develop my familiarity with Italian by translating *The Way of Salvation*, by St. Alphonsus Liguori. I read the works of St. Teresa and the letters of St. Francis Xavier in Spanish. And I had to learn Greek, Latin, and Hebrew as they were required for scriptural studies. With my native tongues of German—and later Czech—I became comfortable with all eight languages. So while my academic setting in Prague made it difficult for me to learn these languages, I learned enough to feel prepared for the missionary work I intended to do. As the time for my ordination approached, I was even offered an office job in the Church because of my language skills. But I wanted to accomplish other things through the ministry, so I refused the offer. A few chided me for passing up this opportunity to have such a bright future in the Church.

As the time of my seminary drew to a close, our class that year received sad news. After all the preparation for missionary life and for the priesthood, we found out that we would not be ordained at the end of my seminary. We were informed that there would be no ordinations in the Diocese of Budweis because no new priests were needed. At this time, I had not yet approached American bishops about ordination because my original plans involved ordination in Bohemia with my family present, and then the start of my missionary work. My family did not yet know of my desire to go abroad.

I continued to worry about my future, but a subtle change had taken place in my life. I realized that I was only expected to do God's will. My desire was to do his will with all my heart, without any expectation of consolation or worry about my own comfort. Still, I was heartily glad to return to Budweis in August, 1835, after the successful completion of my examinations. I was going home again! *I am a lost sheep who can't find the Good Shepherd. You, then, O Good Shepherd must search me out and lead me to the proper path from which I have strayed. I am persuaded that I am not worthy, for I have declined this grace so many times. But we have the good fortune to know the God who pities the sinner who sincerely wants to find Him.*

Departure From Home

AFTER MY TIME at the seminary—when normally I would have received the Sacrament of Holy Orders—I returned home. It was July, 1835. I remained firm in my resolve to emigrate to America. I would wait, still anticipating that ordinations would be scheduled and hoping for word from a bishop in North America who might be looking for a priest to serve the people of his diocese. I still hoped that I would be ordained in Bohemia, so that I could give my dear parents my first blessing before leaving for my missionary work.

While waiting for ordination and the unfolding of providence, I decided to set up a regular routine. I began rising at 4:30 am to recite Lauds; at 6 am I would pray Prime, study English, and do some translation work; at 9 am, I stopped for Terce, studied the Psalms, and went to Mass. Afterward, I would take a walk, and visit relatives or friends. At noon, I said Sext, had dinner, and studied the *Catechism*. In the afternoon, I continued my study of spiritual writers, did more translation work, and read aloud before and after supper. At 8 pm, I said Vespers, examined my conscience, wrote in my journal, and retired at 10:30 pm.

I also used this time to make pilgrimages to the small shrine churches that surround Prachatitz. I visited Gojau, the sanctuary of the Blessed Mother, Krumau, Goldenkron, Podsrp, Strakonitz's Chapel to Our Lady of Victory, the chapel of Our Lady of Help in Skocic, Our Lady's Shrine at Klattau, and Our Lady's Shrine at

Nepomucene—the birthplace of my namesake. On these pilgrimages, I confessed my sins and received communion.

The pastor at Chrobold offered me an invitation to preach in the church on the Feast of the Nativity of the Blessed Virgin. *Tomorrow I shall preach at Chrobold my first sermon in honor of the Blessed Virgin Mary. No doubt curiosity will attract many. Thy will be done, O Jesus! If success will not elate me, help me worthily to announce the praises of Your Mother! But if failure be more conducive to my spiritual advancement, may Your will be done! My sermon was not so successful as I had hoped it would be, but I bore my failure with passable resignation.*

Since business often called me to Budweis, I walked the journey without hesitation. I usually took care of business, visited

Philip Neumann, John's father
(Baltimore Province Archives)

with friends, consulted with the bishop, or stopped to see Father Dichtl. This was how I spent my days, waiting for word on my ordination.

After three weeks at home, I finally found the courage to tell my parents and other family members about my intention to go to America as a missionary. *I am certainly in a most embarrassing position, and to disclose my resolution to my parents seems almost impossible. I detest this delay to my eager wishes, and I doubt if my application for the needed traveling funds will be successful. My parents and family will surely oppose my project, and my own heart sinks at the thought of separations. I had not mentioned my intentions to them earlier*

*because I knew my plans would be cause for concern. But I could
no longer keep my plans a secret.*

*When the day finally came, and I disclosed my plans to them, I
could not help but wonder whether my mother had suspected all along
that I had such a plan in mind. My mother talked to me about the
dangers and hardships that such a life would entail, and also of her
fears as a mother. My sisters were more direct about their concerns,
and not easily won over. But I had to summon all my courage before
talking to my father. July 26th, before setting out for Budweis, I made
known to my father the project I have in view. I could see that his
distress was intense, though he tried to conceal it by a smile. Later,
my father gave his consent in writing, which was needed to obtain
permission from Budweis to leave the country.*

Months later, I was granted a passport in December. Upon
hearing about my plans, one of my friends told me that he thought
all my learning would be wasted in America. I asked him: *Why do
you ship your good to foreign markets? Because, in foreign markets
they command higher prices. For the same reason, I intend to go to
America.* The payment I was hoping for was eternal life.

After eight months passed and no word came about ordination, I realized that it probably would be postponed indefinitely
and that I would have to make my move. And even though I had
continued to solicit funds for my travel from the Leopoldine
Foundation, I was unsuccessful. It was through the private efforts
of Father Dichtl that I would have a minimal amount of funding,
which would require me to be very frugal to afford the journey to
America. I also had continued to write to the bishops in America,
but by the time I set sail for America, I had not heard from any
of them. I would have to make my journey anyway, and trust in
divine providence.

On February 8, 1836, I left home and began my travels across

Europe. I could not say goodbye to my family face to face. It was simply too hard for me, and I knew it would be too difficult for them. So I wrote a farewell letter instead. *My very dear parents: By my sudden and unexpected departure I designed to lessen our mutual pain of separation, as much on your account as on my own. Convinced that your parental blessing will follow me wherever I go, I forebore for the reason stated to ask it before leaving you. I feel assured also, that the thanks I owe you for so many and so great benefits, and which I now express in writing, you will accept as if tendered by word of mouth. I am persuaded that the career in which I am about to embark, and which with God's blessing, I shall faithfully pursue, will be conducive to your spiritual good also.*

You have, my dear parents, the right to lay claim to whatever return my affection could possibly make you, and, God knows, I would have done my duty in this matter! But the unalterable resolution cherished for three years, in spite of so many hindrances, and which was so near being fulfilled; the ease with which I acquired the knowledge necessary for my future career, with many other circumstances, combine to assure me that it is God who calls upon me for this sacrifice, however painful, in behalf of the ignorant and abandoned. These considerations, added to the conviction that my sacrifice will be beneficial not only to my own soul but to yours, likewise determine me not to relinquish the end in view. My dear parents, may you bear patiently and resignedly this trial imposed upon us by God! The greater the sorrows now, the greater our joys in the hereafter! God would not demand such sacrifice did He not deem it salutary to us and were He not willing to impart the necessary strength. May His holy will be done!

I thank you for all you have sent me. You have furnished me too abundantly; less would have been sufficient. In a few days I shall set out by way of Linz. Tomorrow, I call on the bishop. I embrace you with all my heart, and beg you to present my regards to the Reverend Dean and the other priests of my acquaintance. My heartfelt thanks to the charitable ladies of Prachatitz for all their very acceptable gifts. From Nancy, I will write soon again. And it was in this way that I set out on my journey to America. *Ah, my Jesus, You must tear my heart from this world that it may be healed! O Jesus, be my Savior!* After visiting with the bishop, who was slow to lose me to a foreign land, I traveled through the snow-covered Bohemian Forest. My friend Schmid accompanied me for some distance. *At Eisiedeln my dear Schmid and I parted. But few words had been interchanged by us in the stagecoach, for we had little to communicate.* In Linz, I first visited the Blessed Sacrament and then went to the seminary where I stayed overnight. The next day I was presented to the bishop who was honored to meet me, a young missionary. At that time, there were not many Bohemian priests going to America, and the fact that I was made an impression on him.

I arrived in Munich on February 20 where I visited my cousin Janson there, and I also met Father Henni who already was a missionary in Cincinnati, and who would later become the Bishop of Milwaukee. He told me that Philadelphia no longer needed a German-speaking priest, but mentioned that Detroit, Vincennes, or New York might be in need of one. Archbishop Brute of Vincennes happened to be in Rome at the time, and I wrote to him to find out if he might be in need of a German-speaking priest. But I never received a reply from him. Father Henni told me that it was unwise to sail to the United States without word from one of the bishops regarding open positions in the ministry. What was I to do? It took a long time to send and receive communications, and I did not have enough money to remain much longer. It was a disheartening, and discouraging time. *What is worse than all else is that in these trials I cannot encourage myself with the thought that my heart is pure. Perhaps God has forsaken me on that account. Prayer has grown irksome; my efforts seem vain and fruitless. O Jesus, have mercy on me!* If I could not find a bishop to ordain me in the New World, I was resolved to go live simply in the woods, perhaps as a hermit.

I continued on to Strassburg by way of Augsburg, where I was cordially received. For my mission, I received prayer books and religious works. Still, I was filled with anxiety. *I have indeed arrived thus far safe. But I feel dejected, owing in part to the state of my soul, the delay in my journey, and the visits I have been obliged to pay. O my Jesus, truly present in Your Blessed and Most Wonderful Sacrament, help me!* I trusted he would help me but when I arrived in Strassburg, I was told that the funds promised to me had been given instead to missionaries from Alsace and Lorraine. I then was told about a generous man in Paris who I might contact. Since my means were slim, I was encouraged to go to Paris and await a reply from one of the American bishops. Now, my future seemed all the more uncertain. *But no evil shall befall me, for I am Yours, my Jesus, and You are mine! Men cannot injure me, for You are omnipotent! Out of my poor purse I have to pay the freight of other people's books. But if they only serve to glorify Your name, dear Jesus, I am willing to hunger and to pay, for I love You in my poverty!*

I stopped in Nancy on the way to Paris, and wrote home again. I was supposed to meet up with a certain Father Schaefer, who also was supposed to travel to America. But after four days, I could no longer afford to stay in Nancy. During my time there, I did have the opportunity to visit with the Sisters of St. Charles Borromeo, who Father Dichtl was bringing to Bohemia. This was the Order my sisters would enter at a later time. The sisters gave me a booklet called Novena to St. Francis Xavier, which I planned to use at the first opportunity. The confessor at the convent gave me some relics of a martyred missionary from Cochin China. While he approved of my undertaking, he thought that I was foolish to leave Europe without a written discharge and recommendation from my bishop in Budweis. What was I to do? These things were beyond my control. Finally on March 11, Father Schaefer did arrive in Nancy and we traveled to Paris that very afternoon. Once we arrived there, we had a difficult time finding a place to stay. We were turned down at the seminary of St. Sulpice, and went instead to the house of the "Foreign Missions." After repeated entreaties, we finally were provided a room, and charged twenty francs a month for the lodging. I was unsuccessful in my search for the gentleman who had a reputation for being a generous benefactor to missions. I never received a letter from Bishop Brute and my slender purse of 200 francs was rapidly dwindling from all my travels.

I arrived in Paris about the middle of Lent, and the first walk I took showed me this city in glaring colors. I met a procession of masked fools. Carnival clowns, I cannot call them; for, as I said, it was mid-Lent, and Lenten clowns would be an appellation not only quite inadmissible, but among Christians altogether unchristian. Some were on foot, some on horseback, and others in chariots. Their behavior was simply scandalous. I marvel that the earth did not open and swallow them alive. However sad this picture, the great devotion in the churches was consoling. I was indeed surprised to see in this so-much-decried city the crowds that filled the sacred edifices. Not only are the poor and the aged there to be seen, but multitudes of the higher classes. This proves that the apparently impossible is possible with God. He can cause a camel to pass through the eye of a needle. He can harmonize riches and piety. During Holy Week, especially, the churches presented the sublime spectacle of divine life in God. Here may be seen the faithful of every condition in life kneeling dur-

ing the consecration, kissing the floor, frequenting confession and Holy Communion, etc. In short, Paris can display the two extremes of piety and wickedness.

As much as possible, I tried to use my time well in Paris. I visited many of the great churches for prayer and devotion, and I went to communion several times a week. On the feast of St. Joseph, I found fervent prayer. St. Joseph was always a special patron for me. I often heard the sermons of Abbe Lacordaire. And again, I was impressed with the Sisters of Charity. The presence of these saintly religious in a church, in their modest demeanor on the street, enkindles in my heart the love of Jesus. I visited the Louvre but found it difficult to look at the beauty of the art without being distracted from my purpose; I was more at home in the zoological and horticultural gardens. I also found the many bookstores a place of danger. I purchased some books that I truly treasure. But my funds were so meager that I had to make sure I disciplined myself when it came to buying more.

During this time, I also bought a small, ivory crucifix. The cost was not great, but due to my limited funds, I had to be prudent. I found that it was easier to deny my body food and rest than it was to forgo the temptation to buy wholesome books and objects of sacred art. *My little crucifix has given me the greatest pleasure. I have long wished for such a one. Seven francs do not seem so much for what affords such gratification.*

On March 22, I was almost two hundred miles away from Germany. My purse had dwindled to one hundred and twenty-five francs, and there was no promise of financial help from other sources. Even more unsettling was the fact that Father Schaefer received a letter from Bishop Brute, but no mention was made of me. *I yielded to the bitterness of my soul. I had not the strength to control it, though it would have been better for me had I done so.*

Worn out with the struggles of the day, I fell toward evening into a deep sleep, from which I awoke refreshed and somewhat comforted. I had been afraid to pray; it seemed to me so utterly useless. But now I must say my Office and other prayers and await better times.

My birthday fell on Palm Sunday that year. I was 25 years old. *O my Lord, I thank You for the love You have begun to plant in my heart! I will cultivate the precious germ; I will cherish it as coming from You, my Heavenly Spouse! I will guard it day and night that nothing may injure it; that its delicious fragrance may greet You on Your entrance into my heart. But do You, O Lord, water it with the dew of Your grace; do You cause it to flourish, else it will wither and fall to the earth. O Mary, Mother of my Lord Jesus Christ, in union with all the saints and angels, pray for me that I may become a perfect disciple of Jesus!*

I spent Holy Week in prayer in France, and celebrated Easter. I noticed a difference in the ceremonies I experienced in Paris compared with the Roman Ritual of ceremonies I knew. My pro-Roman bias surfaced; the difference in the ceremonies made a very disagreeable impression upon me. It can scarcely be the spirit of Christ that has introduced such changes; consequently there is wanting, even in the hymns, that simple, tender, elevating character so noticeable in the Roman liturgy. *I prefer in obedience to accomplish something less perfect than, through self-seeking and vanity, to attain greater perfection.*

Eventually, I knew I could no longer wait for a letter from Bishop Brute, so on the Tuesday after Easter, I packed up to leave Paris and surrendered my future entirely to divine providence. When I arrived at the station for the stagecoach, I discovered that it had left five minutes earlier. I had to hire a cab to catch up to the stagecoach, and that cost me an extra five francs. I was having to count each penny by that time, but there was no turning back on my journey. I had to get to the harbor for the final part of my voyage to America, and I could not afford to wait any longer. It was not until the next day that I was able to catch the stagecoach to Havre. I was very frustrated, but resigned to God's providence. *My God, I now near the term of my journey in this part of my native land. Soon I shall leave it. O Jesus, forgive the sins I have committed here in the Old World!…While crossing a marshy tract today, I lost my crucifix. I certainly regret my little treasure, but what does it signify, provided I lose not You, My Jesus!*

I arrived in Havre on April 7, 1836. After a visit to the Blessed Sacrament, I got my first glimpse of the Atlantic Ocean. It was exactly as I had imagined it. The next day, I found the ship *Europa*, and learned that a couple days later, there were two other ships sailing for America. Fortunately, this reduced the price of my passage on the *Europa*, and I secured a second-class ticket for the April 12 sailing date. We did not sail, however, until April 20. It had been a long journey across land from Prachatitz to this harbor, and I was about to commence another 40 days' journey at sea. As I boarded the ship, I was filled with so many feelings—the sadness of leaving home, the anxiety over what waited ahead. I knew that when I arrived in New York I had neither an address to find nor any person to meet me to show me the way. But I was on a journey, which would take me to a new life. It would be 19 years before I would see Europe again.

PRIEST OF THE DIOCESE OF NEW YORK

FEW BOHEMIANS had considered missionary life in America in 1836. But what I found especially difficult about leaving the Old World was the unknown that awaited me in New York. Had that not been the case, I would have suffered much less anxiety.

The *Europa* was a nice enough ship. It had three masts and it was 210 feet long. There was one traveler for each foot of the length of the ship. Needless to say, there was not much privacy. And at times, I was quite repulsed by the manners and scurrilous talk among some of my fellow emigrants. Some of these passengers mocked my piety, so I kept to myself. I knew I was quite unskilled in conversation about daily matters, so I journaled (in Latin to avert curious eyes) and read from the *Imitation of Christ* and *Philothea*. The trip was a long 40 days, but like Christ in the desert before his ministry began, I thought of the voyage as a gift from God. All things considered, my journey passed off very well, only somewhat slowly.

Already on the vigil of Trinity Sunday (May 28, 1836), *we sighted America as a fine mist and on Sunday evening we anchored at quarantine about one hour from Staten Island. It is indescribable how good it is for human eyes when one sees land again after wandering about for 40 days. All who could only stand on their feet a little came and as if by magic lost all sickness and weakness. There was no end to the rejoicing and singing. But the rejoicing soon ended. The captain announced that the wind was unfavorable and as we had some sick aboard, we would have to remain some days yet, perhaps a week even at sea, which was all the more unpleasant as the drinking water was stinking already for 14 days and full of worms and the provisions had disappeared to a great extent. Besides that, there was a strong contrary wind and entering the harbor was dangerous. So we waited...*

I repeatedly asked the captain to allow me to disembark, but he refused until the Feast of Corpus Christi. What a momentous feast to mark my calendar of arrival into the New World! I had one dollar in my pocket, but was filled with such joy that it did not concern me. *With the captain's permission, I crossed over to Staten Island in a rowboat and from there, I rode with the steamer Hercules to New York City, which was about three hours distant by boat....My first care was to find a Catholic church. I walked along the mile-long streets of the city until evening. I found*

Old St. Patrick's Cathedral in NY *(Catholic Churches of NY City, 1878)*

a large number of churches, chapels, etc., but no Catholic church wanted to show itself. I had to put all my philological knowledge together to explain to myself from the inscriptions of these buildings, often decorated with ideal beauty, whether and in which Christ they believed. Often there was nothing on the top of the church roof, often a weather cock, sometimes a cross indeed, but over the cross a weather-cock. I thought to myself that the devil may present himself ever so beautifully but still he must let his cloven-foot be seen a little. I spent the night with a Swiss innkeeper who pointed me in the right direction. Even though I was disturbed that I could not find a church right away, I wrote: Now that I am here, all uncertainty has disappeared as a mist. I see the goal of my wishes, the dear aim of my resolutions before me. Quietly and naturally You, My Jesus, untie the knot which seemed to me too intricate than that I could think of the time of its solution without worry.

The city of New York numbered 300,000 inhabitants and stretched along Broadway about one mile from the Battery to Twenty-Fifth Street, which was out in the country. Most of the city's population was below 14th Street. On the second day, I found Father Raffeiner the Pastor of St. Nicholas German Parish, who lived at the cathedral. Father Raffeiner was delighted to meet me, and told me that I had already been accepted in the New York Diocese for ordination three weeks earlier. Of course, I never received word of this in my travels. He brought me immediately to the grand old Bishop Dubois, who was unconcerned about the standard paperwork and said that he needed me right away. *As soon as he had seen my testimonials, he told me at once that he was determined to receive me into his diocese. I was to be ordained a sub-deacon on the 19th and a deacon on the 24th and finally a priest on the 25th of the month under the title of the American Mission. I celebrated my First Mass in*

St. Nicholas Church *(Catholic Churches of NY City, 1878)*

the German Church of St. Nicholas; it was as solemn as it could possibly be here. After the Gospel, Father Raffeiner preached the sermon before a crowded assembly of people. Oh, how I wished that my dear ones were here in body. At the end, I gave 30 children their First Communion for which I had prepared them since my arrival a couple weeks back.

My ordination had the simplicity of Jesus' presentation in the temple, though the Catholic paper included the event with a couple

Bishop DuBois *(History of the Catholic Church, 1890)*

lines, misspelling my name: "Father John Newman was ordained on June 25 at the 7:30 am service by Bishop Dubois." But to me, the ceremony was much more than that—it was an event that marked the beginning of a new life that I felt confident was providentially directed by God. *Oh Jesus, You poured out the fullness of your grace over me. You made me a priest and gave me the power to offer You up to God. Ah! God! This is too much for my soul. I will pray to You that You may give to me holiness, and to all the living and the dead, pardon, that some day we may all be together with You, our dearest God!* I wished only that my dear parents and family could have shared the profound happiness I felt in the solemn ceremony.

My assignment would take me to the region between lakes Ontario and Erie, near Niagara Falls. In that location were several German congregations north of Buffalo, about 500 miles from New York City. The first twelve hours of my trip to Buffalo took me up the Hudson River to Albany. It was a pleasant enough trip, and I was met there by the Father John Urquhart, the pastor of St. Mary's Church. The next day I celebrated Mass, and then boarded a train to Schenectady. From there, I took a canal boat to Rochester. The Erie Canal was completed four years before I headed west, and "Clinton's Big Ditch" as it was known in some parts, became the road to my new parish. Along the way, in Rochester, was a German-speaking community in the process of forming and building the parish of St. Joseph. They were delighted to have a priest who spoke their language, and the Bishop instructed me to spend some time with them. I immediately began teaching catechism to the young people. Some of the people wanted me to remain in Rochester so that I could minister to the needs of the parish, but the arrival of the Father Joseph Prost, C.Ss.R., and the other Redemptorists made it possible for me to move on to Buffalo. I was very impressed by the priest and his other colleagues. I stayed for a week in Rochester, and then boarded another canal boat for the day's journey to Buffalo.

Twenty years prior to my arrival in America, there were few Catholics in the U.S. population. As a result, not much attention was paid to them. But during my years in the United States, 4.37 million other immigrants came to the country, and nearly 1.5 million of those spoke German. For these immigrants who were often isolated as a result of language and culture, the Church became the center of their social lives. By 1860, the Catholic population had grown so much that it was the largest denomination in the country. This increase in the Catholic population worried some of the so-called native people of the United States.

I was among those who believed that language helped keep faith alive, and that German-speaking priests were needed in great numbers in the United States. Almost immediately, I proposed that seminaries be established in Europe to train priests for the American missions. Like many priests who came to the New World, I had thought of working among the Indians. But a common belief among American missionaries was that for every Indian converted, ten Germans fell away from the Church for lack of parish life. I soon found this to be true as well. As with most clergy, the circumstances of life around me determined the course of my ministry. And there was no time to waste.

The town of Buffalo was rapidly growing, and due to the many arrivals from the Erie Canal, it had a population of about 16,000 people. Thousands of other immigrants passed through the town, usually on their way farther west. There was a horse-drawn omnibus, which provided the public with transportation on a set of rails. And there were kerosene lampposts that lit up the streets. Father Pax, the resident pastor in the city, was overjoyed to see me. Because he had been the only priest working in that region at the time, he was near

Church at North Bush (now Kenmore), NY *(Baltimore Province Archives)*

exhaustion. He offered me the parish in Buffalo, but I decided to take the outlying areas under my wings. I traveled eight miles northeast of Buffalo to Williamsville, which had the beginnings of a stone church. At the time, the building still was not under a roof, but the town was centrally located in the larger area where I would begin my ministry. The town had a settlement of four houses, and I took up residence with a Catholic family there. My new parish radiated out from this central church about ten to fifteen miles in distance, encompassing a 900-square-mile area. There were 400 families, and of those, 300 spoke German. The parish included the communities of North Bush and Lancaster, and eventually included the towns of Transit, Sheldon, Batavia, Pendleton, and Towanda. My nearest out-mission was two hours away, and the farthest was twelve.

For the most part, the children had not been in any school, know German badly, English just as badly; besides that they very seldom have an idea of the supernatural world. With the scant cultivation, many weeds have grown up and there is no thought of a German school. Now, as long as they are small and weak, they are not in the best mood to receive religious instruction and when they have grown stronger, they will have to work and there will then be no thought of religious instruction. Ah God, my God, how is thy Kingdom regarded!...My Jesus, I am poor, but see, tomorrow I will pray to Thee, O Jesus in the Most Holy Sacrament, for the spiritual welfare of the German congregation here. Thou hast given Thy life and blood for us, oh let it not be lost in our regard.

Like an old German emperor followed everywhere by his court, do I carry with me all needful church articles when visiting my three parishes of Williamsville, North Bush, and Lancaster. From an American citizen here I have received two acres of land for a church; the large number of French and Irish Catholics at Niagara Falls renders a church, or at least a chapel, necessary. Do you remember our examining together a fine steel engraving of the Falls? You little imagined then that I would one day establish a parish in the neighborhood. I am so near to them that I can hear the roar of the cataract in my room. It sounds like the noise of a distant hailstorm. I have not yet visited the Falls.

I lived at North Bush with a native of Lorraine who, in consid-

eration of payment in his next life, furnishes me with board and lodging. My furniture consists of four chairs lately purchased with some money I had laid by, two trunks, and a few books. For your consolation, I will tell you that the timber for my future residence has already been cut, and my people are rejoicing in the prospect of supplying me with corn, potatoes, etc. I have never yet suffered from hunger; and as for clothes—when one garment grows too shabby for wear, someone or other of my good people provides me with another. So you see, my dear parents, things fare well with me. If it were otherwise, this wandering life that I lead would soon become impracticable; but as it is, every house is my home.

What joy would be yours could you see the affection entertained for me by my good parishioners; and again would you rejoice at the sight of our holy religion planted and cultivated, with the help of divine grace, in the midst of these dark forests.

In the forests which I had to roam while going from one parish to another, I was intrigued by the vegetation I noted as I walked. I always had a keen interest in botany and these journeys afforded me a wonderful opportunity to gather specimens of flora that was not known back in Bohemia. At one point, I sent a wonderful collection of rare and curious plants back home. The roads from one place to another are swampy, especially in the forests; and where the roads have been made by felling the trunks of trees, it looks just like it used to long ago on the road of Pfefferschlag between Kubinberge and Schwarzberge. The country round about is undiversified, very level, and the horizon is limited by the tall woods nearby.

In the forests, beech, oak, ash and linden trees abound, and in some places are also found the finest cedars. The sugar maple provides the sugar in ordinary use here. At the beginning of spring the trees are bored, and a single tree will yield about a bucketful of maple sap a day. This is then boiled down to about 1/30 of its bulk, and the result is a sort of sweet syrup, which is here called molasses. If the mass is still further boiled down to ½, the residue is a brown sugar, which is still capable of further refinement. The taste of the sugar thus produced is a combination of the sweetness of honey and white sugar, this latter being a product of the Southern States derived from sugar cane.

Apple, pear, and cherry trees succeed here very well, but they are all young; the land has been cultivated only during recent years. Plums do not thrive at all; they dry up, or die out entirely, or do not bear. They are entirely unknown to the American people. It is also to be remarked in connection with the apple and pear trees that we hardly ever find them attacked by worms.

There are no white butterflies here and only a few colored ones. The fruit is, as a general thing, not so sweet as in Europe. Snails and rain worms are seldom met with. But we have here a great abundance, especially in the woods, a species of insect which they call mosquitoes. Their bite produces a violent swelling and causes the greatest suffering to both man and beast. Even during the sermon, I must constantly use my handkerchief to drive them off. In the beginning I was frequently annoyed while preaching and my hearers distracted in their attention by the attempts to fight them off and the smart and oftentimes resounding blows which those present dealt themselves. At night one is obliged to make a big fire near the house and stables, if one wishes to get any sleep; for with their constant buzzing about, all thought of rest is impossible. But the smoke from the fire drives them away.

The plants and flowers here are for the most part strange, but very beautiful. Lilies grow wild in the woods, as do likewise red currants, gooseberries, raspberries, and bromberren. Black strawberries are not to be found but only the red sort....

Of the birds known at home, I found only the crows and night owls; the other kinds seen here are much more beautiful but rarely have I heard any of them sing. Beautiful yellow canaries with black *wings, hummingbirds, the smallest among the birds, and various parrots are most in favor. There were bears and wolves in this neighborhood until quite recently, but it seems now that they have been entirely exterminated by the Indians who still roam the forests here. Deer one meets with more frequency. Quite common are the beautiful skunks, whose odor is so dreadful that the stench of a decaying animal compared to it is incense. The rabbits are smaller, more rare and in winter they are snow white. Poisonous rattlesnakes are still sometimes met with, but the Indians have shown the immigrants different plants which counteract their bite.*

Among the very commonly occurring poisonous plants there are especially two species which are so dangerous that they cause painful swelling of the members in persons of weak constitutions even without coming in contact with them. The farmer with whom I am living walked barefoot upon some of these and for three months suffered terrible pains in both feet in consequence. Some persons, however, can go about among them with impunity. These plants are called rhusto-hydodendron and radicans. Both grow in swamps. The weather here if very changeable; rarely does rain, fair weather, heat or cold last longer than three or four days together. The heat, however, has frequently been as high as 94 degrees Fahrenheit. This causes much sickness. The greater part of the settlers are attacked when they come into the low lying districts by a fever of which not rarely two or three persons, especially children, of the same family die.

The place from which I am writing you these lines lies between Lake Ontario and Lake Erie and is somewhat more healthy by reason of the continual wind. These two lakes, like all the others in North America, contain the purest fresh water. These lakes likewise abound in fish, a matter of great advantage to those who live here.

Ministering in my parishes among people of various nationalities, I noticed the cultural differences among these immigrants—particularly between the Irish and the Germans. By the grace of God, these differences did not cause religious division in the Church since they were cultural, rather than concerned with doctrinal matters. The handbook of all Catholics is the *Catechism*, which transcends national borders.

While my parishioners were united under the *Catechism*, there still were times when disagreement endangered the ministry. What may be the reason that the Irish so despise the Germans? In the religious respect at least, one has no advantage over the other. Drinking saloons were a part of the landscape, and it seemed that wherever a church was established, a saloon was sure to follow.

Once, a saloon owner announced that he would be sponsoring a ball on the next holy day. I preached against the event at Mass, and told the parishioners that if they participated, I would leave the church. They did not believe that I would stand by my word, so they continued with their preparations. On the day of the ball, they learned not to test a stubborn Bohemian. I packed my bags to leave, but the parishioners begged me to stay. The saloon keeper asked that I allow just that one ball since everything for it had already been purchased. I refused, telling them they had fair warning. The event was canceled. I felt bad about this, but I also knew the importance of standing my ground and letting the folks know that I meant what I said.

There were times when I was frightened. On one occasion, I was walking through the woods on a ministerial visit and decided to stop and rest on a fallen tree trunk. I noticed shadows nearby, but could not figure out what they might be. Eventually, I figured out that I was being observed by a band of roving Indians. I prayed. But when the Indians found out that I was a "black robe," they spread out a buffalo skin and carried me to my destination. Another time, I was confronted and ordered to stop by a drunken man with a pistol. I continued walking without a word. By the grace of God, I am still alive. Still another time, I got lost. It was terribly frightening to be lost in the woods in an area with so few people around. Getting lost like that in the woods could mean death. As it turned out,

An encounter with Indians. *(Window in Neumann Shrine, Philadelphia)*

it meant that I was able to help one of my parishioners. I came upon an Irish settler deep in the woods. He was quite sick, and I was able to revive him with my altar wine. Eventually, the man recovered and told me how to get to my original destination. He never forgot my visit, and neither did I.

One problem I discovered shortly after my arrival was the existence of the trustees, who caused me and others problems throughout my ministry. In the United States, the Catholic Church was not allowed to own property as a separate entity. It was not recognized as an institution, so it could not own property. As a result, leaders in parish communities had to become owners of church properties. For Protestants, this model worked much more comfortably than it did for Catholics. In and of itself, the arrangement did not present a problem. But the trustees sometimes got too big for their britches, as they say. Once, while I was living in a parishioner's house in Williamsville, the trustees stirred up some controversy because my residence was situated above a tavern, and I had to pass by the room of a servant girl to get to mine. So they wanted my benefactor to dismiss the servant girl. I became aware of this situation through North Bush parishioners, who had heard about it in Buffalo. Gossip did travel! When the trustees met and called me in to speak to the situation, I remained calm and said little. It eventually became apparent to those present that the matter had little substance. The origin of the whole situation stemmed from the jealousy of one of the trustees, who apparently thought that I should have stayed in his house. The "case" finally was dismissed. Shortly after the incident, I decided to move to North Bush where another parishioner offered me a place to stay. Though North Bush was not nearly as well developed as Williamsville, and the house was a mile and a half from the primitive church, I relocated to avoid any perception of scandal. I did not want to have anything to do with a decline in faith of any parishioner. *My God, my God, sanctify me, that I may become a fit instrument of Thy graces and mercies to the souls Thou hast confided to me! If Thou seest that success will make me vain, do not, I beseech Thee, on that account to allow me to fail. Humble me in some other way, but do not punish me through my parishioners.* The move resolved the problem, but throughout my ministry, I would continue to experience occasional difficulties with trustees.

Beyond the Catholic community, there existed an anti-Catholic/ant--immigrant sentiment in the general population. Any time the status quo is threatened, a negative reaction is seldom far behind. The great influx of so many Catholic immigrants was changing the population and resulting ownership of land. Upon my arrival in Williamsville, and before we had a roof on the church building, some of the local residents threw rocks over the walls during Mass. One time, one of the rocks actually fell on the altar! A few men ran outside to confront the perpetrators, but they were never caught. Harassment of Catholics happened everywhere, and many incidents occurred in which the perpetrators were seldom found. These antagonists became known as the "know-nothings," because no one owned up to the prejudice. Anti-Catholic prejudice sometimes was referred to as Nativism. It was as if some people thought they were the only true Americans. How quickly they had forgotten where their families or ancestors had come from!

After I left Bohemia, life continued in a regular fashion for my family in Bohemia. My two older sisters, Veronica and Catherine,

both married—Veronica with John Kandla, and Catherine with Mattias Berger. John Berger, the only child to come from these marriages, later would come to America and become a Redemptorist priest. But before John came to the United States, my little brother Wenzel joined me in New York in 1839. He took me by surprise two days before the feast of his holy patron. The good news and loving messages he brought me dispelled all un-

Brother Wenceslaus Neumann, John's brother *(Baltimore Province Archives)*

easiness and carried me back home in my imaginings. He was a godsend, and acclimated quickly to his new surroundings. *In my absence, he conducts the German Catholic school for the parish in North Bush. For the rest, he is also cook, housekeeper, and stableboy. It is already much easier for me to fulfill my mission duties. It strengthens my faith and hope very much when I consider how within a few years, churches and schools amid woods and swamps, even if they are poor and without any pretensions externally, have often been erected and are also not the less frequented. The sight of a poor Catholic church, at least on Sunday in the country and in the woods, is very consoling. Groups of Alsatians, Lorrainers, Badenser, French, etc. come from all sides out of the woods; often from places 5–10 miles distant; the wealthier ones on horseback or wagons in the peculiar dress of so many countries.* In time, Wenzel would follow me into the Redemptorists as a Brother of great reputation. Many called him a true saint! My other two sisters spent their lives as religious Sisters. Louise looked after my father until his death and then joined the religious community. Eventually, the homestead was transferred to the Sisters of St. Charles Borromeo for use as a residence for the elderly. God blessed my family with religion. I missed my family terribly, and with the poor mail delivery, I did not receive any correspondence from home. You may easily imagine how much I yearned for news from my dear fatherland.

I continued to put the word out back home that we needed German-speaking priests! There were too many immigrants with spiritual needs, but too few priests to help them. I was convinced that a special seminary was needed to address the issue. My own mission district could support 2 or 3 priests as well as me alone. The Bishop granted me permission to seek more candidates and I told the people back home that *I am sending in writing the authority of Bishop Dubois, which assures two or three priests or finished theologians the reception into the Diocese of New York. Nothing is wanting now except that God the Holy Ghost inspire some of his faithful to devote themselves to the service of our Holy Church in North America. The need of Catholic priests and the spiritual desolation of the faithful is increasing day by day. Judging from a human standpoint, the disproportion would have lamentable results—only God alone is the support of His Church. When I arrived here in America three years ago, it seemed as if the Germans in America would soon have sufficient priests. But the results taught otherwise. The Most Reverend Bishop*

Hughes, the coadjutor of this diocese, declared not long ago, that he would receive 7–8 if they were to be had. It is not necessary that they speak English and French because they can learn both more easily here. English I have learned very easily from an American whom I taught astronomy in recompense. Through frequent intercourse with the French, I have also learned their language and so I understand everything perfectly and can also converse with them without much trouble. Should any of the confreres in Bohemia have his heart set on devoting himself to the missions of the northern Indians, he could find no better preparation for that than in the temporary ministry among the Germans here first. The body becomes hardened by fasting, by travelling and by frequent exertions; one also gradually becomes acquainted with the country, its customs and in many sections, also with the Indians themselves. It would be good for a priest destined for America to have health and a strong constitution on account of frequent journeys, fasting and preaching; still the lack of these ought not to frighten anyone because where human powers fail, the heavenly ones come to one's aid.

I suggested establishing a seminary in Germany that would focus on training future missionaries to serve in America. *In reality, however, only poor priests can thrive among the Germans here. The priest is forced to be travelling all the time; a few good Catholics settle in the villages, most look for some stretch of woods, build there a block-house in 2 or 3 days and then begin the burning and felling of trees to prepare fields for potatoes and oats and in 6 or 7 years be ready for wheat. These folks live at a distance of two or ten or twenty miles from the church and often several miles from each other in the midst of the woods. The heart of the pastor can have pleasure in nothing else other than in the salvation of the souls. If he loves comfort, honor or money, he loses in a moment patience and with it all confidence. His effectiveness is then at an end.*

The character of the German also gives the priest work. A foolish love of freedom has brought a large part of them to this country. Now they are free and their own masters but are actually slaves to their own ambitions. They would like very much to control spiritual matters as they find independence in temporal matters and to choose for themselves a God, or at least a way of honoring Him, which suits their inclinations. The example of Americans surrounding the German makes an impression on him. As these are usually wealthy, and he tries above all to become so also, he believes that he must imitate them also in unbelief. In addition, here everyone is called upon to contribute to the support of the church, the school, the pastor, the teacher. By their contribution ever so small, the German believes that by it he has bought the right to speak like a dictator in everything. Still, with the sincere Catholics of character, all attacks of heresy, which here are very fanatical, are mostly fruitless. Apostasy from the faith is very rare, in spite of many and strong inducements. If any danger threatens the Church, it is the lack or the insufficiency of Christian education. The education of our growing youth takes up much of the missionary's time; but God's help shows itself here in a most wonderful way. The desire for knowledge and the ardor of the young Catholics is often astonishing. When I was preparing the children in Williamsville for First Communion last year for three months, many came daily five and six miles, even in the worst weather to attend the instruction and in this short time, not only the main chapters of Christian doctrine and morals had been sufficiently learned but greater progress had also been made in reading and writing than, according to my experience, is made often in several years with hard work.

Not to forget the hardships of the missionary, I must say that they are many and considerable, but just for that reason, this calling will be welcome to those who like myself, seek an occasion to propitiate the Divine Justice for sins committed; the violence which the mis-

sionary must do to himself is, for him, a consoling pledge of heaven. It is gratifying and very consoling for every Catholic in America to learn that only his faith alone is the same everywhere and with all nations. My Germans, as also the Irish, have often told me that they now felt themselves more strengthened in their faith, since they see the most perfect unity of faith with all Catholics, whether they come from Italy, Germany, Ireland, France, or America amid indescribable confusion of the Protestants.

The number of Catholics is almost beyond number, people are beginning to notice them and in some places they predominated. The religion is increasing here more and more, not so much through conversions as through immigration; but the former also are not very rare. Many Catholics live in extreme poverty, especially the Irish. They live in very low cottages of boards, often without windows, chairs or beds. When I visit them to prepare them for the reception of the holy sacraments and to hear their confession, I sit down on the floor beside them. Children and adults make the sign of the cross at the entrance of the priest and their greeting of welcome sounds more consoling from believing hearts than the stereotyped compliments of vain Frenchmen. Even if various national vices are blamed on the Irish, this comes from bad treatment which they received in their fatherland.

As the ministry continued in New York, I eventually reached the decision to enter religious life. The matter of vocation is mysterious, and if I tried to explain this decision in a logical manner, I would not make much sense of it. When I was still in the seminary in Prague, and after I first made the decision to become a missionary to North America, I jotted a thought in my journal that perhaps I should consider entering the Jesuits or the Redemptorists. It was just a passing thought, and was not a serious consideration at the time. The reason for the initial thought stemmed from the fact that I knew both communities had missionaries in North America, and at the time, I was still concerned about how I was going to fulfill my dream. My dearest friend John Schmid, with whom I had discussed missionary life and who also had a longing to go to America, joined a religious community, the Cistercians in Bohemia. I was disappointed at the time because I had hoped that our deep friendship would accompany me across the ocean, but that was not to be.

Later on my way to my first assignment in Buffalo, I met the Redemptorist Joseph Prost in Rochester, New York. The Redemptorists were planning to serve the German community there, and he had arrived to begin the good work. I encountered Father Prost again one year later. *In the summer of 1837, Bishop DuBois came to my parish on his episcopal visitation; he was accompanied by Father Prost. The latter would have liked very much to get the bishop to give over Buffalo and my parishes to the Congregation of the Most Holy Redeemer. To facilitate this project, he exhorted me often and at great length to enter his Congregation. His reasons were all very good and true but they did not impress me because at that time I did have a spark of a vocation.*

After the visitation, I had to find from Fr. Prost the procedure for enrolling candidates into the Confraternity of the Scapular. He responded and in the letter spoke words that echoed in my mind about the difficulties of a solitary life like mine on the frontier. *Vae Soli*, he wrote. Beware of living alone! In reality, I was experiencing a spiritual reality similar to the poem of St. John of the Cross in his book, Ascent of Mount Carmel. *Jesus, my delight, has fled; alas, I seek for Him in vain! I have lost my Beloved. He hearkens not to my sighs, He heeds not to my voice. My eyes are blinded by tears, my voice has grown weak from lamenting; but He is not moved. He does not show Himself to my poor soul. Jesus, Jesus, where art Thou?*

Because thou has followed Baal, O thou priestly soul, thy Spouse has separated Himself from thee, He has wedded another. And Behold! Baal wretchedly repays thee. He mocks thee, he repulses thee with scorn, and thou wonderest faintly and hopeless, tormented by thy reawakening love and fruitlessly sighing after thy Savior. Oh Heavenly Father, see my poor heart opens up to Thee, touched by a ray of Thy divine grace. Drive from it, I beseech Thee, the evil one, for, of myself, I am unable to do so.

In the context of my spiritual aridity, I considered the words of Father Prost and eventually resolved to become a Redemptorist. *For four years now I had spared myself no pain to bring the parishes under my care to fervor similar to that which I had observed at St. Joseph's Parish in Rochester. But things would not go that way. This, as well as a natural, or rather supernatural, desire to live in a community of priests where I would not have to be exposed alone to the thousand dangers of the world, made me suddenly resolved to request from Father Prost…admittance into the Congregation of the Most Holy Redeemer…and received from him acceptance in a letter of the 16th of September from Baltimore.*

Bishop Hughes was hesitant to grant me permission to join the Redemptorists. Father Prost appealed to Canon Law, however, and the bishop was obliged to yield. The departure from my confessor and friend Father Pax in Buffalo, and the good people of my parishes, was difficult for me. But I was filled with the assurance that taking this step was the will of God, and that gave me consolation.

Quite simply, I had become exhausted on the frontiers of New York, and for several months, I needed to step out of my ministerial routine. Wenzel took care of me and of the details of pastoral life. I used to tell myself that God often permits me, for my greater humiliation, to fall into despondency. *Then rise up before me all the sins of my past life, my hardness of heart, the thought of God's justice, etc., and I feel as if I should die of grief.…God enlightened me. He has taught me how pleasing virtue is to Him, and how hateful vice,…O Lord, my God, have mercy on me! Break the hard rock of my heart,* Young Wenzel stayed behind in New York and gathered our things. I arrived in Pittsburgh on October 18, 1840, and Wenceslaus in November of the same year to become Redemptorists.

The Redemptorist Years

The Sons of St. Alphonsus Liguori began in 1732, one hundred years before the first Redemptorist missionaries arrived in North America. The saint had met some poor sheepherders in the countryside outside of Naples. In need of the solace of their religion, the first Redemptorists gathered and eventually established a religious community to work with those who were most in need, the most abandoned. The poor immigrants in North America certainly fit into this vision. So in 1832, the Redemptorist vicar general in Vienna, Father Joseph Passerat, sent three priests and three religious Brothers to start a ministry in America.

A rare portrait of St. John Neumann in his Redemptorist habit *(Baltimore Province Archives)*

Orders were formed early, and as long as the spirit of their holy Founders was not entirely blown away in their sons and grandsons, they did an extraordinary amount of good. Even if the Rule of the founder did seem strict, well rounded out and so determined, human shrewdness, or rather the deceit of the devil, always found openings, by which communication with the children of this world was open to the religious. If the head of the Order is not of the spirit of the Founder, abuses, defects and scandals irresistibly creep in, which make out of an asylum of godliness, a refuge for the basest passions of mankind. How unfortunate was the interference of the state in the internal government of the Orders! Rules of an Order ought not to be changed by individuals of a community, much less by the State. Holy things must be treated holily. Why is the spiritual life, the striving after perfection known so little? Even not at all in monasteries (convents) that are destined before all to send missionaries of heavenly character among the people of the world? Oh how bad do not things seem around the confessionals! Who enters the convent to become perfect? Ease, inordinate ambition are most frequently the motives. But how did they do it, or rather, how does it happen that the Order of the Jesuits, the Redemptorists, the Sisters of Charity and of the Carmelites, almost alone contain for the most part devout souls? But they are most despised with all their poverty and all their strictness, as they almost alone maintain humility!

Long before joining the community, I had a good opinion of the Redemptorists. These men were a great blessing for the local Bishop, Edward Fenwick, O.P., of Cincinnati, in 1832. The missionaries were scattered throughout the area to help care for the many German immigrants, and for seven years, the early Redemptorists searched for a foundation that could support a community. This would not happen until 1839 at St. Philomena's in Pittsburgh. In the face of an upheaval caused by trustee problems in what was referred to as the "factory church," it was felt that these German missionaries were better equipped to deal with German personalities throughout these difficulties and they were invited to assume the pastoral care of the parish.

In the next few years, other foundations were entrusted and, at one point, Archbishop Eccleston of Baltimore was ready to turn the entire ministry to the German people in the United States over to the Redemptorists. This would have been impossible, of course, considering the number of immigrants who came to the United States in the first half of the nineteenth century.

I was the first person invested with the Redemptorist habit in America. That took place on November 30, 1841, when Father Prost—the superior of the Redemptorists in North America at that time—came to Pittsburgh for that purpose. There was no established norm for how a novitiate should be conducted. And at that time, there were too few priests and too much work to consider having an ordained person like myself not involved in apostolic work—even during the novitiate year.

On my first day, I was given the high Mass to sing in the church. Other assignments follow one after another. I had scarcely been in Pittsburgh two weeks when my novice master, Father Tschenhens, was called to Baltimore. This only left me with Father Czackert, who had to go to the many mission stations of the parish to serve the people in these districts. *I daily made two meditations and two examens of conscience with the community, spiritual reading in private, and a visit to the Blessed Sacrament. I recited the Rosary also, and that was all.* In the evening recreation period, it was common practice for one of the community to relate something edifying that had happened since the last conversation. I related a dream that I had about being in Baltimore. A bishop seized me in the dream in an effort to make me a bishop. I woke up during the part in the dream where I was trying to escape from the bishop's hands. Father Czackert told me that I had better get those kinds of thoughts out of my mind, that I was there for perfection, and that after vows, such foolish thoughts would disappear.

In March of 1841, the Redemptorists in Europe sent four additional priests and one student to America to join the mission. The additional men would prove to be a great help. But even more importantly, the commitment meant that the European superiors had not lost hope for a place for the Redemptorists in the New World. Later that year in May, Wenceslaus and I were ordered to join a new arrival, Frater Fey, in Baltimore to continue our formation. That sounded promising to me, but I would soon discover that the need for priests was just as great in Baltimore. As a result, I would not have a real novitiate there either.

I went to St. John's in Baltimore, but after three days, I was sent to New York to St. Nicholas Church, the place of my own first Mass back in 1836. Two weeks later, I was sent to Rochester to continue my novitiate under Father Tschenhens, but he was sent to Ohio to settle a dispute in the parish. So there I was again without a director for my novitiate. During this time, I began to have doubts about whether I had made the right decision to join this group of men! I remember thinking, what will my future be? *I am thinking of that continually without really wanting to. A year ago, I took a step forward indeed, as I believed, but perhaps without sufficient reflection.*

During my novitiate, Father Prost was relieved of his position as vicegerent in America, and was replaced by Father Alexander. I could only pray: *You know, O Lord and God, that in my way of thinking and in my will, I submit to Your Holy Will unconditionally and will ever persevere in this holy Order if it pleases You.* When John Berger, my nephew, entered the Congregation years later, I told him about my novitiate experience—or rather, the lack of one. *I myself was never a real novice, for when I entered our beloved Congregation, it had neither a novice master nor a novitiate in America. Notwithstanding this disadvantage, I am not without my*

share of experience. I passed through the numerous temptations with
which the evil spirit is accustomed to try the recruits of St. Alphonsus.

Finally, shortly before the time I took my vows as a Redemptorist, I was called back to Baltimore again. Along the way, I gave parish missions to the German people in various locations. Finally on December 8, 1841, I arrived in Baltimore and was granted time for quiet and solitude until I made my profession on January 16, 1842. I was the first Redemptorist to profess his vows in the United States. The chronicler of the house, who thought he was very clever, wrote that "a new man has entered the Congregation." I was now a member of the community, and knew that it was God's will for me to be a member. *The mutual bodily and spiritual help, edification and good example, which one has around him till his death in such a spiritual society, make my life and my office a great deal easier for me. I also confidently hope that death in this society will not be unwelcome to me, as is generally the case with seculars.*

The Redemptorists would continue to increase in numbers— some came from Europe and others from America. In 1843, Father Alexander returned from oversees with eight priests, one professed student, and five lay brothers. Frater Seelos was the professed student, and in the days ahead we would become confidants and fellow workers in the vineyard of the Lord in Pittsburgh. In fact, we shared a room there, separated by a curtain for privacy.

My first assignment as a professed Redemptorist was as an assistant priest at St. James in Baltimore. St. James was entrusted to the Redemptorists by Bishop Eccleston when the old St. John's Church was torn down to make way for St. Alphonsus, which became known as the German cathedral. Most of the time, there was only one father at home. The others usually were traveling to minister to various German communities. These missions included East Hartford, Shrewsbury, and Frederick in Maryland; York and

Cumberland in Pennsylvania; and Richmond in Virginia. There was no shortage of need for our ministry. It was a blessing to pray with members of the community, and to work so closely with them.

With donations from the Leopoldine Foundation back in Germany, the construction of St. Alphonsus was going well. Construction of another large Redemptorist church—St. Philomena in Pittsburgh—was also progressing but without the liberal contributions of Germany. As a result, progress on construction of St. Philomena was slower than it was at St. Alphonsus. The vicegerent was not pleased with this

St. Philomena in Pittsburgh *(Baltimore Province Archives)*

and he replaced Father Cartuyvels with Father Fey. But the task proved too much for him, too. Guess who got the job? In March 1844, I was appointed pastor and was on my way back to Pittsburgh.

The Diocese of Philadelphia was split off from the Diocese of Pittsburgh eight months before I was assigned there. Bishop Michael O'Conner was the first bishop of the diocese. The bishop was suspicious of the Germans, and also was closely associated in his mind the Redemptorists with this group of immigrants. At an earlier date, pernicious letters were sent to Rome decrying the care of the German immigrants in the United States. In these communications it was suggested that an Irish hierarchy in the United States was to blame. When I met the bishop, however, it seemed as thought things would be okay.

There were six thousand German immigrants in the city, and even more in the surrounding area. Despite the large population, they were short of money, and a large debt had accrued during the parish construction. In fact, the walls of the church were only half built when I arrived. I could do little more than establish the Church Building Society, and ask each parishioner to contribute at least a nickel every week toward the construction of the church. Later, Bishop O'Connor would claim that I had built the church without money. Little did he know how much anxiety this project caused me.

The real glory of St. Philomena was not the construction of the church itself, but the devotion that the parishioners showed throughout the process. For this, I credit the wonderful men who were stationed with me at St. Philomena—especially the wonderful Father Francis Xavier Seelos. He certainly exhibited the zeal and the holiness of his namesake. Living with him and Father Joseph Mueller was a blessing. We had a real community that was full of dedication and devotion. The community spirit among us inspired the same spirit among the parishioners. Confraternities and pious societies were established in the community, and through the involvement of the people, these groups helped increase the bonds among parishioners and strengthened the parish. The school also thrived. Our pastoral focus soon included the surrounding countryside, and the communities we served from St. Philomena eventually grew into fifteen separate parishes.

Unfortunately, I was not blessed with the strength to take care of all I wanted to in the parish. I did manage to develop a *Catechism* for teaching the children and a Bible history for teaching them salvation history. These works proved to be very popular among the German-speaking clergy over the years. But I wore myself out again! It seemed I would never learn. So much needed to be done, and I saw no alternative. My confreres grew concerned about my health, and wrote to our superior, Father Czackert—the man who succeeded Father Alexander as the American vicegerent. They had observed me coughing blood. Father Czackert ordered me to see a doctor, who subsequently gave a negative report about the state of my health. Since my three-year term of office was completed, I was ordered back to Baltimore. I was to be relieved of my duties as a superior, and would only be able to work as an assistant pastor so that I could recuperate and regain my strength. Things, however, did not work out that way.

I was at St. Alphonsus Parish but a few days when I received a message that totally surprised me. Not only did I receive more work, but the task was beyond my ken. I was appointed superior of all the Redemptorists in the United States! This was incomprehensible because Father Czackert had only held the office for half of his appointed term.

The American houses had long been under the direct authority of the vicar general, Father Joseph Passerat, for our Transalpine Redemptorists. In 1841, the Congregation in Europe was re-organized into six provinces to better respond to needs of the communities. The American houses remained under the authority of the vicar general in Vienna until 1844, when the Austrian government interfered with the vicar general's ability to direct men in non-Austrian lands. As a result, the American houses were placed under the authority of the Belgian provincial. Almost immediately he came to assess the strengths and weakness of the work of the Redemptorists in his new jurisdiction. He arrived in Boston in May 1845 with Father Bernard Hafkenscheid.

For the next four months, they visited all of the American houses. The Belgian provincial was shocked to see how liberal the culture was in America. But even more emphatically, he concluded that the rapid expansion that began in the 1840s had to be slowed. It was clear that the confreres were overwhelmed with work, and a large debt had accrued due to the construction of so many new churches. The provincial initiated a large number of regulations, demanded regular observance of prayer, and ordered a halt to new construction. Under the new regulations, the American superior could not grant permission to other confreres for expenses exceeding one hundred dollars without his expressed permission.

The American Redemptorists were to stop expansion efforts until more men were available to manage the volume of work in the places that were already established, and until money could be raised to lower the large debt. In the end, Father DeHeld did not trust Father Czackert, his former U.S. vicegerent, to follow his strict directives. So in 1847, I was appointed the new vicegerent. At the time, I was only thirty-five years old, and I had joined the Redemptorist community only five years earlier!

In all fairness to Father DeHeld, he did not make these new directives for Redemptorists in North America without a commitment to do more work in Europe to help the cause. He sent more Redemptorists from Europe to the American mission, and also worked to raise additional funds—particularly through the Ludwig Missionsverein.

My primary objective as vicegerent was to make sure that the provincial's regulations and plans were carried out. I was confident that this was what obedience demanded of me. I also was told to remove the Redemptorists from Detroit and Washington, and was expressly forbidden to send any Redemptorists to New Orleans as had been in the plans. Obviously, not all the men in America agreed with the Belgian provincial—especially the Austrians, who probably would have preferred to remain under Vienna's authority and jurisdiction. Many believed that the Redemptorists could not afford to stop expansion in the United States due to needs of the immigrants who were in dire need of our help. I understood their concerns, and appreciated their zeal. But I did not feel I had the freedom to chart the course for our mission. That was the responsibility of the provincial, and I was simply appointed to implement his directives.

Even my friend Father Seelos was not in complete agreement the provincial's perspective. I told him once that *your Reverence seems to think that it would be easy to keep the rule where even two Fathers are present; for my part I am convinced that it does not work out, since history shows that the spirit of observance is soon lost because the meditations, the conferences, etc. must be*

The Redemptorist Rule in Neumann's hand *(Baltimore Province Archives)*

omitted too often. Then little by little a spirit of self-sufficiency, independence and estrangement from our Holy Congregation takes possession of even the most zealous. This spirit must be hard to put aside because up to now it has led most of those imbued with it out of the Congregation.

I had the rules of the Congregation printed to ensure regular observance in our houses. It was the first time the rules were printed in the United States, and they were much needed—especially by those who were not experienced in our way of life back in Europe. I also copied by hand the rule for Redemptorist novices, and entrusted Father Seelos with the position of novice master. *The novitiate was moved to Pittsburgh where regular observance was observed in the house. To my great internal satisfaction, we began to see the arrival of men joining our wonderful community. The novitiate and the House of Studies are the seminaries of the Congregation; from them are our missionaries to go forth. If the students are educated according the spirit of St. Alphonsus, the Congregation will continue to correspond the end for which it was established.* Father Robert Kleineidam and seminarian Peter Steinbacher arrived first, and then they were followed by John Duffy and Peter McGrane. Gradually, the number of men joining our thriving apostolate increased. Father DeHeld took two clerical students—Isaac Hecker and Clarence Walworth—back to Belgium to study and learn the skills necessary to be parish missionaries. In addition to these new American students, more Redemptorists from Europe would be coming to join the American mission.

Incorporating the directives of Father DeHeld here in the United States proved to be more difficult. Father Alig in Washington was a good man, very zealous, and doing great work. But Father Alig was in Washington, and the provincial said that even if Father Czackert had granted approval to include this place, he had done so without authority. Bishop Eccleston could not see Father Alig leaving his post. In the end, Father Alig refused to obey my summons to return to Baltimore. Despite his disobedience, I did understand the zeal that Father Alig had for the souls he was trying to help in his ministry. I had other challenging situations to deal with as well. Bishop Blanc of New Orleans was under the impression that Father Czackert had agreed that we soon would be in New Orleans. But the provincial gave me directives to ensure that this did not happen. Only later was I able to authorize the Redemptorists to assume charge of the parish in New Orleans, but the delay was not to the liking of the bishop. And how was I to withdraw the Redemptorist from Detroit? While we tried to work toward retrenchment of the men in established ministries, urgent requests for Redemptorists came to me from a number of bishops. They were desperate for priests—especially German-speaking ones—to care for the needs of immigrants. Bishop Kenrick of Philadelphia, Bishop Bazin of Vincennes, and Bishop Henni of Milwaukee all wrote to me begging for priests. I received eight official pleas from bishops all over the United States—some from as far away as Texas and Oregon—to establish new houses. But I was not able to honor their requests.

We Redemptorists had ten communities in the United States. These were mostly located in large urban areas and from these houses the fathers and Brothers also served seventy out-missions. The need was immense! So many immigrants needed services in their native tongue! I had a few problems in these communities. Father Kannamueller in Buffalo bought property for a church without permission—and with money we did not have! There was little doubt that the parish needed improvements. But it was unsettling that Father Kannamueller made the decision on his own, despite our decision to pay down existing debts. Then there was Father Rumpler in New York who set out to establish St. Alphonsus Parish with great determination—even though the provincial had prohibited the expansion. Father Rumpler claimed that the Belgian provincial had granted him permission to proceed—a claim that I was unable to substantiate. Father Rumpler stubbornly completed the plan. Then there was the colony of St. Mary's in Pennsylvania. The colony absorbed many of the donations coming from Europe, but seemed to be making little progress. At one point, it was suggested that St. Mary's might be better suited for the Benedictines than the Redemptorists. I told Father Alexander, my consulter, that I thought the experiment was doomed to failure, but he did not agree and as vicegerent, I did not have the authority to decide the issue. So the project continued to absorb funds—a source of frustration to many of our men!

I sometimes think that the greatest accomplishment for me during the time as superior was not so much in the work that I was able to do for my own community, but in the way that I was able to help the women religious—vital to the life of the Church in America. In the summer of 1847, the School Sisters of Notre Dame arrived from Munich to aid the German immigrants in the colony of St. Mary's, Pennsylvania.

Neumann, founder of the Notre Dames in America
(Window in Neumann Shrine, Philadelphia)

In New York, Mother Theresa was informed that St. Mary's would not work well as a location for the motherhouse. When I met with her, I told her that I agreed with that assessment.

Mother Theresa went to St. Mary's to assess the situation for herself. She soon discovered that the location was too far away from everything for a motherhouse, and that it also faced terrible financial difficulties despite European support from the Ludwig Missionsverein. When the sisters arrived at St. Mary's, they realized their dream of establishing a motherhouse was in jeopardy. Dejected, Mother Theresa returned to Baltimore. I realized how much these women were needed, and decided to do everything I could for them.

I first offered Mother Theresa a building attached to St. James Parish that originally was used to house the Redemptorist novitiate. I sold the building to them for the price that we originally put into the building. Father Stelzig, my consulter, was critical of this decision and wrote about it in a letter to his mentor, Father Starck, back in Vienna. Father Stelzig believed that we needed to charge the market value of the building since it had increased in value from the original amount we paid into it. Father Stelzig wrote a lot of letters about me back home, and I sometimes wondered whether he was my consulter or a consulter to Father Starck back in Europe! In any case, the sale of the building helped the sisters establish a presence in the New World.

Before long, the sisters were teaching in all three of our German-speaking parishes in Baltimore—Sister Magdalena at St. James, Sister Caroline at St. Alphonsus, and Mother Theresa at St. Michael's. Bishop Henni of Milwaukee eventually visited Mother Theresa, and told her that the sisters were desperately needed in his diocese. At the time, Wisconsin had one of the largest concentration of German immigrants in the United States and the bishop wanted Mother Theresa to consider transferring the motherhouse to Milwaukee. There was logic to his rationale, so it was decided that a visit to Wisconsin was in order. I had to visit all the Redemptorist houses anyway, so I used that obligation as an opportunity to accompany Mother Theresa and Sister Caroline on their trip to Milwaukee. During our travels, I gave the two sisters English lessons. We also visited the Redemptorist houses along the way, and during those visits, I was able to get the sisters to agree to staff our parish schools in Pittsburgh, Philadelphia, Buffalo, and New York. Getting those commitments made the trip to Milwaukee very worthwhile. The sisters thankfully adjusted to their new life in America. We provided them with pastoral care, and our Redemptorist missionaries successfully directed many vocations to their community. It turned out to be a good exchange. I did what I felt was necessary for the sisters, and for the Church. Mother Caroline and the sisters eventually thought of me as their founder here in America. I could think of no higher honor!

The Oblate Sisters of Providence was another community of sisters that stole my heart. From their beginnings in 1828, they cared for children of color. But by 1847, the new archbishop had no one to serve as chaplain for the sisters, and as a result, he was on the verge of disbanding the community. I felt that I had to do something, so I sent one of our greatest men—Father Thaddeus Anwander—to talk to the bishop. While I was at home praying for his success, Father

Neumann befriends the Oblate Sisters
(Window in Neumann Shrine, Philadelphia)

Anwander was on his knees, begging the bishop not to disband the community. Ultimately, the bishop agreed. I took tremendous personal interest in the work of the Sisters and made sure they always had a priest to say Mass in their convent on the appointed day. These sisters had a unique charism for the American Church, and provided needed care to children of color, who were neglected by other communities.

My role as vicegerent took up a lot of my time, but I was still able to serve as pastor. My philosophy for parish ministry was simple enough—provide good church services with good preaching; ample opportunities for the sacrament of penance; establish a strong parochial school; and cultivate active parish societies. I enjoyed teaching catechism. It was something I had done since the start of my ministry in the woods north of Buffalo. My own *Catechism* seemed to be a great help in guiding the young boys and girls in their faith. But I think the love in my heart for these sons and daughters of God was what really carried the message to them. They seemed eager to learn.

Back in Europe, the Redemptorists were experiencing a number of problems. In fact, there were so many disturbances after the revolutions of 1848 that there was some doubt about whether the Congregation would be allowed to remain in Austria. Father Passerat, the vicar general, was exiled from Austria and separated from the rest of his government. Some time later, I found out Father Passerat had wondered whether all Redemptorists would have to immigrate to the United States. The biggest problem I experienced in my role as superior of the American Mission was that the office did not have the authority it needed to be effective. My opinion was shared by others as well. In November 1847, Father DeHeld informed me that he had recommended that the American houses be formed into their own province. It was during this time that jurisdiction for the American houses was removed from the Belgian provincial and placed back under the Austrian provincial, Father Starck. My consulter had written a number of letters about me to Father Starck, claiming that I was a man without prestige. It would not be the first or the last time that this charge would be made about me! But the transfer of power from Belgium to Austria was disheartening to me. I knew Father DeHeld's position well, but I was unsure about the direction that Father Stark might take with me. My concerns were soon laid to rest. Father Stark granted a *sanatio* for any difficulties I experienced with Father Rumpler over the second New York house. He also condemned Father Kannameuller's actions in Buffalo. And he confirmed the rejection of Washington as a new establishment. As vicegerent, he also granted me more authority. Father Starck was familiar with the American mission, but decided to make a visitation in 1847. Afterward, he changed four superiors and also accepted the foundations of Detroit and New Orleans—contrary to directions originally set by the Belgian provincial.

Father Czackert could not have been more pleased with Father Starck's visitation—it meant that a house in New Orleans would become a reality. Father Czackert set out immediately for the Crescent City. Since 1843, he had wanted to make that trip. Bishop Blanc had a small church waiting for him. With great zeal, Father Czackert assumed the care of 20,000 German immigrants in the city, and he won over the trustees of Assumption Church. By 1848, he was buying property for an English-speaking parish church across the street.

America never was made into a separate province as Fr. DeHeld suggested but Father Passerat did appoint me as vice provincial in 1848! This appointment, however, required the signature of his two consulters. Due to the upheaval in Europe at the time, Father Passerat's consulters were not in the same location. So I never knew whether my appointment as vice provincial was ever official or not! As it turned out, it did not matter. Not long after, a new man was appointed Vice-Provincial in my place. The appointment of Father Bernard Hafkenscheid was made official in January 1849. I finally was able to return to the apostolic labors I longed for. I was retained in provincial government as first consultor to the new superior but I was able to spend more time hearing confessions, preaching, visiting the sick, and teaching children as Rector of

St. Alphonsus Parish. Father Seelos told me he thought that we should partner in giving missions but I preferred to serve the mission parishes associated with the parish. *Much good is accomplished because of the ten to fourteen stations which we have here, only one or two could or would support a priest, if they could get one.*

Around the time that I left my position as superior of the Redemptorists in America, I made the following observation: *During the ten years which I have so far spent in the Congregation I have arrived at this conclusion: If a missionary is sincerely and honestly motivated by a desire for the glory of God and the salvation of our German people, he will do a lot of good, but more than that, he will prevent a lot of evil.*

Our great mistake is that we allow ourselves to be deceived by the spirit of worldly shrewdness, the desire for fame and the love of comfort. We ought to fight the temptation to make spiritual things a means of temporal advancement. Thus the things that we should and

Interior of St. Alphonsus Church *(Baltimore Province Archives)*

could do, become for many an occasion of sin and of unfaithfulness to God. The principles of faith fade out in our hearts in proportion as we allow the principles of the world to come in. We place our confidence, not in God but in our own intelligence, experience, and so on. We seek not what is least or most difficult or most despised, but what is easiest and what redounds most to our own glory. If only we loved God alone and from our whole heart, how easy it would be for our superiors to lead us according to the prescriptions of the rule. God would then urge us on and we would not resist.

I was happy to be out of the superior's position and serve again as a pastor. *How good it is to be in the Congregation and to live in America. Here we can truly love God, work much and suffer a lot for Him, and we do all this quietly and unnoticed by the world.*

Among the various duties I performed as a parish priest, I served as the regular confessor for our Archbishop who walked to our rectory for the sacrament. He frightened me when he told me one time that I might have to get myself a mitre one day.

My Life as
Bishop of Philadelphia

ONE DAY, I spotted a pectoral cross and a ring on the dresser in my bedroom! I had been out of the rectory. I asked who had been in my room, and was told that the archbishop had shown up for his regular confession. Oh, sweet Lord! I fell to my knees in prayer. In recent months, while I was busy about my ordinary apostolic endeavors, the bishops of the United States were writing back and forth, surfacing names so that Archbishop Kenrick could propose worthy candidates to Rome as his successor in Philadelphia. Three names eventually were sent to the Holy Father, Pope Pius IX, as candidates for the position of the fourth bishop of Philadelphia. I was second on the list, but the Holy Father chose me as the new bishop; he made the appointment to me under obedience to accept the position and without appeal. The Lord gives and the Lord takes away; blessed be the name of the Lord!

Archbishop Kenrick
of Baltimore
(History of the Catholic Church, 1890)

Philadelphia was considered the cradle of freedom for the United States. A prosperous and elegant society had emerged in that city, and the population there would expect a bishop who was able to mingle with them with ease. The diocese itself was very large. It spanned more than 35,000 square miles, and included half of Pennsylvania, all of Delaware, and a good portion of New Jersey. There were 170,000 Catholics in the diocese at that time, along with 113 parishes and 100 priests. The Know-Nothings and the Nativists had a strong presence in the city. In fact, they had burned St Augustine's Church eight years earlier. I was sure that my foreign accent would confirm their prejudiced belief that the papists were trying to take over the United States by sending millions of immigrants to America. All this, and I was only 41 years old!

I chose for my episcopal motto: *Passio Cristi conforta me*! As I told one of the confreres the night before my ordination: *If our Lord gave me the choice either to die or to accept this dignity, I should prefer to lay down my life tomorrow rather than be consecrated Bishop; for my salvation would be more secure at the judgment seat of God than it will be if I appear before it burdened with the responsibility of a bishopric.* On the day before my ordination to the bishopric, Fr. Hafkenscheid, the Vice Provincial, ordered me to pen my *Autobiography*.

St. John's pro-Cathedral
(Historical Sketches of the Catholic Church and Philadelphia, 1891)

So on Passion Sunday, March 28, 1852—my forty-first birthday—I was consecrated bishop by Archbishop Kenrick. When all was prepared and I was dressed in the bishop's colors, I told the confreres that *the Church treats her bishops like a mother treats a child. When she wants to place a burden on him, she gives him new clothes.* The dear people who I had served as Pastor at St. Alphonsus presented me with a beautiful chalice, a ring, and a pectoral cross and chain—all made of gold. The parishioners of St. Philomena's in Pittsburgh also showed their affection by giving me an ostensorium of great beauty. These were always my favorite episcopal trappings because the givers were so dear to me, and their sacrifices provided me with these things of beauty, given from their hearts.

As for the diocese, Philadelphia had a great history—not only as a symbol of American independence, but also as a diocese. According to William Penn, the first Mass was held in the diocese in 1686. And it is certain that Mass was celebrated publicly in the city of Philadelphia ever since. My mission as the fourth bishop of this immense diocese began immediately. In the first week, I conferred the sacrament of confirmation six times, and preached at each occasion. And in the first five years, we built fifty new churches. I sent my first pastoral letter less than ten days after arriving in Philadelphia. I felt it that it was important to ask for the peoples' support and prayer. Four weeks later, I sent a circular letter to all the clergy to spur the construction of our unfinished cathedral. I stated theological positions on learning in a lecture to the Philopatrian Institute, a Catholic literary society. I told them that all pursuit of knowledge should further the interest of God and be used in his service. I told them that the writings of the transcendentalists should not be found in any Catholic library and that I felt that romantic novels were a danger to morals. From the very beginning, I was a busy bishop without a support staff. I had no one to help me. As I told my relatives back home: *A bishop in America has to do everything himself and by his own hand.*

There were only two bishops at my episcopal ordination in Baltimore, but it wasn't long before I met most of them. Less than two months after the ceremony, I was back in Baltimore for the

First Plenary Council of Baltimore. All the bishops of the United States assembled for the first time in plenary session to consolidate the legislation and practices of Catholic life in America. During the session, the bishops addressed a number of topics and issues— trustees, parish schools, liturgical practices, the need to reduce the size of some larger dioceses, immigration, and the establishment of financial and administrative guidelines. During the session, I served on two committees: one that examined liturgical ceremonies, and another that addressed the need to establish Catholic schools in every parish. The Council urged each parish to set up schools without waiting for state help. It also was decided that a definitive catechism was necessary for religious instruction. As a result, I was asked to write or choose a catechism for the German-speaking immigrant population. And so it was that my own 180-page *Larger Catechism*, as it was known, was officially endorsed by the Council of Baltimore for German-speaking Catholics. I also was commissioned to write an official letter to the Leopoldine Foundation of Vienna to thank them for their generosity, and to urge their ongoing support. In addition, the council recommended the creation of eleven new dioceses. As a result, the New Jersey portion of my diocese became part of the Newark Diocese, which by this action then encompassed the entire state of New Jersey. Concerning trustees, the council insisted that the local bishop appoint these officers or give authority for the election of the trustees to the local faithful. Finally, it was decided that parishes should have boundaries, and that scrutiny was necessary when considering foreign clergy for the presbyterate.

Of note was the council's decision not to make a public statement about the issue of slavery. The bishops' stance on the morality of slavery was not in doubt—their position had been well known since the days of Gregory XVI. However, it was felt that making any statement at that time would be misconstrued as support for a political candidate rather than a faith-based statement about the issue.

The council helped me in several ways—it allowed me to get to know many of the bishops around the country, and it permitted me to see how my administrative challenges were similar to those in other dioceses. I believe that the council reached good decisions, and I sought to incorporate all of them in my diocese.

Founding of the Catholic school system
(Window in Neumann Shrine, Philadelphia)

Back home in Philadelphia, the first issue I tackled which was dear to my heart had was the Catholic school. We held three meetings on the issue, and adopted a Central Board of Education for the Diocese of Philadelphia. I served as the president of the board, which also included pastors and two representatives from the parish. We were charged with seeking funds for the expansion of schools throughout the diocese. A group known as the "Young Catholic Friends' Society" emerged, and helped to finance poorer parishes with funds that they collected for the school system. In addition, the board was charged with recommending a general plan of instruction for the local parish schools while the pastors continued to hire and pay the salaries of the teachers.

In my mind, it was important that the school be an independent building with its own space, equipment, and teachers to instruct the children. Makeshift structures do not provide the foundation necessary to make each school a permanent and vital part of each parish. For the schools, religious instruction was a vital part of the curriculum. *The school system of the United States is very liberal in theory; but in reality it is most intolerant toward Catholics. Everyone has to contribute to the erection and maintenance of the public schools, in which instruction is restrained to reading, writing and ciphering. As respects religious instruction which is excluded from those schools, parents are free to have their children reared in whatever religion they please. Notwithstanding these liberal concessions, it cannot be doubted that the young mind is influenced by the irreligious disposi-tions of teachers. Even the text books are nothing else than heretical extracts from a falsified Bible, and histories which contain the most malicious perversion of truth, the grossest lies against the doctrines and practices of the Catholic Church. Due to the prejudice against the faith that was infused in the public school system as we knew it, the determination that religious instruction needed to be part of the daily curriculum and to the conviction that Catholic values need to permeate even secular subjects, we will spare no effort in the establish-ment of a solid, Catholic school in every parish to guarantee, as best we can, that the gift of the faith continues into future generations.* A pastor of one of the largest parishes in Philadelphia continued to tell me that it was impossible for his parish to start a school. I finally told him that if it was impossible for him to establish a school, I would have to look for someone else to take his place. That was all I needed to say. A school began in that parish right away, and opened with a large student body!

I was pleased with the development of the school system, and wrote to my father letting him know of the progress. I told him that the number of children in the school system quickly increased from five hundred to five thousand. My goal at the time was to have another ten thousand children in the schools in Philadelphia before the end of that year. The sacrifices that the people made in their efforts demonstrated their love for the faith. And because of their help, my job was much easier and far more bearable than it would have been without their assistance.

I strongly believed in the need for children to become firmly rooted in their faith. I also was concerned about the need for uniformity in worship—particularly since the Church in America represented so many different nationalities and customs. This concern was shared by the Plenary Council of Baltimore. In my examination of this issue, I wrote: *During the past month I had all the priests of Philadelphia, who number over 100, gather for 10 days of the spiritual exercise which I gave and followed the time with a synod. I have reason to rejoice at the success of both. The later especially are very necessary in the United States to bring about unity and uniformity in the exercise of spiritual functions, because as missionaries meet here from all parts of Christendom and each bringing along the peculiarities of his nation, there is no more suitable means that these synods for arranging everything from the beginning according to the standard of the Eternal City. Besides several statutes about different points of church discipline, a beginning was also made to introduce the 40 Hours prayer to the Most Blessed Sacrament in all the larger churches so that in a short time there will not be a week in the year when the Blessed Sacrament will not be exposed on one or the other place of the diocese. I also had the pleasure of seeing how all the missionaries are striving to introduce into their respective districts the confraternities of the Scapular and of the Rosary and of the Immaculate Heart of Mary. All this will, with the grace of God, enliven more the spirit of faith and devotion which are perhaps exposed to greater dangers and difficulties in these states than elsewhere. During the coming month, I will begin the visitation of those parishes and churches in the country which I did not find time to visit last year.*

As these visitations here are at the same time Spiritual Exercises of 3–4 days for the whole parish, it will take most likely three to four months before I return again to the city.

The Forty Hours Devotion was not new to the diocese when I introduced the idea of initiating a schedule to incorporate it throughout the diocese at the synod of clergy. I wanted to give our people a chance to express their deep devotion in some special way. And I also wanted to make the exposition of the Blessed Sacrament a perpetual blessing to the diocese. The clergymen at the synod were cautious as the result of a recent surge in anti-Catholic sentiment from the Nativists. I did not take their reservations lightly. I shared their concern about the anti-Catholic sentiment, which was all too prevalent in our city. And I worried that this idea could open up the possibility of desecration of the Sacrament itself.

My love of the Blessed Sacrament inspired great devotion within me: I love the Most Blessed Sacrament, my longing for it is unspeakable. Why is that the case, my Jesus? That I, so near the overflowing fountain of love and grace, may not miss the moment for quenching

Neumann and the Forty Hours Devotion *(Window in Neumann Shrine, Philadelphia)*

the thirst of my soul, and, as a mediator between You, o my God, and Your redeemed, may inflame them to love and desire for this heavenly Bread. So I was particularly attuned to the need to take care that the Sacrament not be dishonored.

The Forty-Hour Manual
(Baltimore Province Archives)

Then something unusual happened—I seemed to receive a message from heaven to proceed with the idea. One night, I fell asleep at my desk while catching up on tasks that I was unable to complete during the day. Suddenly, I snapped awake by some strange intuition. I discovered that the flame from my candle had charred some of my papers, but had not caught them on fire. The candle still burned brightly, yet miraculously, no damage was done. The situation could have been disastrous. *I thanked God for his protection, and then I suddenly heard the voice of God in my mind. As the flames are burning here without consuming or injuring the writing, so shall I pour out my grace in the Blessed Sacrament without prejudice to My honor. Fear no profanation, therefore; hesitate no longer to carry out your design for My glory.*

How could I hesitate after receiving that message? So we started the devotion at St. Philip Neri Parish, whose namesake had started the Forty Hours devotion in Rome. I compiled the schedule of parishes, along with a booklet of rites and special prayers to be used during the devotion. Later, I received a special indulgence from Rome for those who attended.

Not all of my endeavors in the diocese were as successful as the development of the school system and the inauguration of the Forty Hours devotion. I was unable to stimulate the progress of the cathedral in the manner I had hoped, or in a way that some of my people expected. Financially, I took the same conservative approach that I had taken as vicegerent of the Redemptorists, and made the rule that the construction of the cathedral could progress only as rapidly as monies were collected. I wrote to the pastors, letting them know that it was their responsibility to solicit funds for the Chair of the diocese.

Cathedral construction
(Baltimore Province Archives)

This was not a popular reminder—especially given all the urgent needs for building facilities in the individual parishes. The first drive raised only $5,000, and the construction of the cathedral was almost suspended. The following year, I approached the subject at our diocesan synod. The pastors responded generously, and decided to increase the contribution four-fold that year. I wrote a thank-you letter to the people for their generosity, and had high hopes for the future. But I was not so lucky the following year, when collection of the money dropped.

Construction of the cathedral was slow, but building programs in the parishes progressed. By the end of my second year as Bishop, we had completed the construction of six churches that had started under Archbishop Kenrick's; we rebuilt six other churches, and we constructed thirty new ones for a total of forty-two parishes in thirty-four months. Eventually, a coadjutor bishop was appointed to assist me in the financial management of the diocese, due to my poor administrative abilities.

Much more difficult than the cathedral building project were the troubles that flared around one of our parishes—Holy Trinity. The parish's problems existed when Archbishop Kenrick was bishop in Philadelphia, and I was still vicegerent of the Redemptorists. Back in 1847, Archbishop Kenrick had asked the Redemptorists to start a new parish to serve the German-speaking parishioners of Holy Trinity due to problems with the parish trustees. I had to decline the invitation because of our retrenchment stance in those days, and as Bishop, I had to smile when I realized that my earlier decision was a problem that I later inherited.

In 1850, Bishop Kenrick had closed the parish. I told the trustees that for services to start again, the parish must cede property rights to the bishop. The trustees refused, took the matter to court and won the case. Afterward, the local papers hailed the trustees' victory, and referred to them as the "anti-bishop party." The saddest part about the entire controversy was that thousands of Germans were deprived of church services in their own language as a result of the church's closure.

Despite the court victory, I was determined to give the Germans of the area a place to worship and so I began construction of another parish in the vicinity of Holy Trinity. It would be named St. Alphonsus. Eventually, I also appealed the court decision in favor of the trustees of Holy Trinity on the grounds that the trustees had not acted in accordance with the Catholic understanding of parish, and as a result, could not be considered trustees of a Catholic parish. The judge asked a number of penetrating questions about Roman Catholicism, and the role that the Church's hierarchy played in determining what it meant to be a member of the church. Having made his point, the judge asked the jury to make its decision, keeping in mind that foundational issues of the United States Constitution were involved. Ultimately, the jury found this time in favor of the bishop, and the trustees were forced out of office. After some resistance on the part of the deposed trustees and arrest for contempt

Neumann's passport, American citizen
(Baltimore Province Archives)

of court, a new election was held and the issue was finally resolved. This court decision would prove to be a precedent for similar cases involving disputes between bishops and trustees—not only in Philadelphia, but throughout the nation.

In another parish, as a new church was being built, the Germans asked that the official language of the parish be German. The English-speaking people, of course, asked that the official language be English. I decided that the parish should be English speaking, but that a German parish could be established once all the bills were paid. The Germans complained that I had betrayed my own German people. I told them that I was not a disloyal German because I was actually Bohemian, not German. After I made this statement, they placed a railroad tie on the tracks in front of the train I was riding on—in an attempt to derail it. By the grace of God, the accident was avoided.

I set a goal of visiting every parish in the city of Philadelphia every year, and every parish in outlying areas every two years.

While on these visitations, I examined parish books, checked financial records, heard confessions, confirmed parishioners, preached, and visited the sick. It was a very tiring, but wonderful part of my year. To meet this goal, I spent nearly half my time on the road performing these duties in the country districts. Some of the people back in Philadelphia were none too happy about my absences and the attention I was paying to these country parishes. But regular visitation of all parishes remained a high priority for me

In my early years as bishop, I panicked when the Vincentian superior general in Rome, due to a shortage of men, withdrew priests as teachers in the seminary of St. Charles. My own priests were already so taxed, yet I knew that it was essential to provide educators for our future clergy. It was essential that we continued to have a seminary in the diocese. I asked Father William O'Hara from St. Patrick's Church to be the new superior of the seminary. Together, we recruited other capable clergymen to serve as professors. So by the grace of God, we averted the tragedy of having to close the seminary—especially at a time when native clergy were so needed.

Toward the end of 1854, a wonderful event was announced that filled my soul with great joy. The Holy Father announced that he was declaring the Immaculate Conception of Mary a dogma of the Catholic Church. I had always honored our Lady under that title and was delighted with Rome's decision. It also gave me the opportunity to make my *ad limina* report concerning the diocese to the pope and allowed me the opportunity to visit my family in Europe after nearly twenty years away.

On November 17, 1854, the Holy Father invited 154 cardinals, archbishops, and bishops to assemble in Rome for the declaration of the Immaculate Conception of the Blessed Virgin Mary. This would be a "new" teaching to be officially defined by the Church.

This did not to imply that belief in the dogma itself was new. When I told my father I was coming over to Europe for the declaration, he said: *Why do they have to bring American bishops to Rome to tell us that the most holy Virgin was conceived without sin when we have always believed it here?* I agreed with my father's assessment. More than a century earlier, St. Alphonsus had dedicated the Congregation of the Most Holy Redeemer to the special patronage of the Immaculate Conception. For the most part, the dogma was universally believed and was only going to be solemnly declared a doctrine in the ceremony.

After all the bishops and other learned churchmen had an opportunity to fine-tune the wording of the doctrine, 53 cardinals, 140 bishops, and 50,000 priests, religious, laywomen and laymen crowded St. Peter's Basilica on December 8, 1854. During the ceremony, Pope Pius IX stated loudly and publicly that he declared, pronounced, and defined the doctrine that the Blessed Virgin Mary was without sin from the moment of her conception as a singular favor of the Almighty! What a monumental moment! After the ceremony, I wrote: *I have neither the time nor ability to describe the solemnity. I thank the Lord God that among the many graces He has bestowed on me, He allowed me to see this day in Rome. I wrote a Pastoral Letter before and after the declaration on the wonder of the Virgin Mary.*

My voyage across the Atlantic was better than my first in 1836. Compared to that original forty-day voyage, this one only lasted for seventeen days, and I had privacy on the journey. I arrived in Havre and crossed France by rail. In Marseilles, I boarded a small vessel for the port of Rome, Civita Vecchia. For the two months I was in Rome, I was able to live in the Redemptorist community of Santa Maria in Monterone. There, I was able to live as a Redemptorist. I wore the habit every day rather than the regalia of a bishop, and attended all the community prayers. During my visit, I made the pilgrimage of the seven churches in the holy city on foot five or six times. It was a wonderful experience, and the confreres were so hospitable!

Private time with the Holy Father for my *ad limina* visit was a deeply moving experience for me. I was scheduled to meet with him on December 16 to report on the state of affairs in my diocese. Back in my time in the seminary, I wrote a letter to my friend Holba defending the infallibility of the pope—even though it was not a declared doctrine of the Church at that time. That's how dearly I reverenced Pope Pius IX. He was smiling when he asked me if being ordered to take the position as bishop under obedience was not better than sacrifice. I had to smile back.

The report of the diocese elicited high praise from the Roman officials. Being so close to the daily struggles of the diocese, I sometimes had a tendency to overlook the obstacles that I had already overcome during my time as bishop. I suppose that I have always considered the daily effort of putting one foot in front of the other as nothing special. But others were more impressed, and clearly saw the progress that had been made in the diocese.

While I had the pope's ear, I told him about my plans to start an orphanage for German immigrant children. Too often, they were either left without family or they were temporarily abandoned by parents who had to focus on getting their feet on the ground. We already had two wonderful orphanages in the diocese, but we needed one that specifically served German children. I shared with him that I wanted to ask sisters from the Third Order of St. Dominic to oversee this effort. Instead, the pope suggested that I gather women from America to do the work as I envisioned it, and that I form them into a Third Order of St. Francis of Assisi. My mind began to race because at that time, I knew of three women who were planning to form a religious community under the guidance of Father John Hespelein at St. Peter's in Philadelphia. The pope's counsel seemed so prophetic to me that I was able to meet with the Franciscan superior general in Rome who then gave me permission to receive and profess members of the Third Order of St. Francis. From that blessed moment, the new community of dedicated sisters began—at least in my own mind.

It seemed that God was with me in a special way on this European venture. Only on one occasion did I have reason for panic on the trip. After the Roman visit, I was able to return to Bohemia to visit my family and friends. On the road to Prachatitz, I suddenly realized that I had misplaced a large collection of relics that I had been gathering in Rome. I was heartbroken, and telegraphed every place I had visited. But the relics were nowhere to be found. Finally, I prayed to St. Anthony. I promised to promote devotion to the saint back home if he would only help me. Surprisingly, a young man showed up and gave me the missing package. I was unable to spot him afterwards to thank him. I was not dressed as a bishop, so I have no idea how he knew who I was. In any case, I kept my promise once I returned home and commissioned a large and lovely portrait of St. Anthony.

On January 13, I arrived in Austria where I stayed with the Redemptorists. During my stay, I was able to make contact with my dearest childhood friend, Father Adalbert Schmid. At that time, he was director of the seminary. It was a very happy reunion. So many times when I was studying in Prague and when I was studying in New York, I longed to receive his letters. His friendship was one of my greatest joys. During my stay, I also made contact with Father Coudenhove, the rector of Maria Stiegen in Vienna. He was the rector of St. Peter's when I first arrived in Philadelphia as bishop. It was good for this lonely prelate to see old familiar faces.

I had dinner with the former Emperor Ferdinand in Prague who had donated a large sum for the missions. He also made me a member of the Nepomucene Heredatat, an honorary title in the empire. I visited the Sisters of St. Charles Borromeo where my sister Joan (Mother Caroline) was the superior. God blessed me with one experience after the other of loving companionship. I could not have asked for a greater gift. On January 30, I traveled to the beloved Budweis to visit my alma mater and the bishop there. He wanted me to take his carriage to Prachatitz but I asked that my arrival back home be quiet and secretive. But my plans for a quiet arrival were not to be. As I neared Nettolitz, the church bells announced the arrival of the hometown boy who had made it big in America! People poured out of their houses and made me stay overnight in the small town. From there, I had planned to walk home the next day. It was only three hours away, and I had done it so often as a youth that I thought it might be just what I needed. The next morning, however, the magnificent sleigh of Prince Schwarzenberg was there to take me home. It had four horses and a coachman and the people assembled all along the way, ringing bells and welcoming me home with signs showing my own coat of arms. I was awash with laughter and tears all morning. I could not believe the reception they gave me all along the way. I wondered to myself what they would think if they only knew how some of the more sophisticated people of Philadelphia viewed me. My father could only say time and time again, "My son, my son!" My eighty-year-old father embraced me and lifted me off the ground in his hug. He had, of course, aged and I was so grateful to my sister, Louise, who cared for him so well. My mother had died while I was in America, and I would visit her grave. Even so, I knew she was also with us. For seven days, I stayed in my own home and said daily Mass in our beautiful parish church with a full congregation. I was only able to escape home without the fanfare of a glorious send-off by rising before daybreak, and leaving before anyone knew it was my day to depart. This was the second time I left home in secret. I just could not bear to do it any other way.

On the way back home to Philadelphia, I visited my teachers at the Cistercian monastery in Hohenfurth. I also visited the Redemptorists in Altotting, the place I had hoped would become a seminary to prepare missionaries for America—one project that never came to fruition. On February 21, I was in Munich where I visited with Mr. Stiessberger, a brother of one of our priests at St. Peter's in Philadelphia. He persuaded me to have a portrait made of myself, and said that the portrait could be sold in Prachatitz with proceeds going to the poor. His argument worked. The portrait was the only one taken during the years that I was a bishop. He told me kiddingly that some of the money should be given to me for new clothes—a reference to the day we had gone for a walk together and got soaked in the rain. On that day, when he suggested that I change my shoes, I told him that if I were to do so *I'd have to put the right one on the left foot, for I have only one pair of shoes to my name!* We both chuckled at that.

The trip to Europe was marvelous! I left the continent on the last day of February, and made it back to the United States in seventeen days. The night I arrived in New York Harbor, I headed back home to Philadelphia. Two days later, I had dinner with the Redemptorists at St. Peter's, filled them in on all the confreres I saw in Europe, and told them about all the happenings in the Congregation around the world. It was a very pleasant visit. In May, I issued a second Pastoral Letter on the Immaculate Conception, praising the Mother of God and her glories. The grind of daily work soon took over again, and the European trip seemed like a distant memory to me.

I have often indicated that our immigrants were unpopular with many Americans. These "foreigners" were characterized as a real liability for the nation. They also were mislabeled as carriers of disease, and instigators of riots and immorality. The truth of the matter was that sixty-two percent of the population that received alms were actually foreigners. There also were twice as many foreigners inhabiting

At home among the immigrants
(Window in Neumann Shrine, Philadelphia)

prisons as natives. This should not have been a surprise. Life for many new arrivals was difficult, and resources were so minimal that bad things sometimes happened. But because of this fact, the Church also suffered much abuse—so many of the new German and Irish arrivals were Catholic. These would be followed by waves of other ethnic groups who also were Catholic. For our diocese, the problem was even more pronounced because one-third of the German immigrants settled in Pennsylvania.

In spite of the bigotry, the Church grew rapidly, and we did all we could to help the Catholic immigrant. As I mentioned earlier, while in Rome I told the Holy Father that I wanted to establish an orphanage for German children. I had to do what I could to help. The St. Vincent Orphan Society was established with help from three German pastors of St. Peter's, Holy Trinity, and St. Alphonsus parishes. Property was purchased, and construction of the orphanage began.

In our works of mercy, success was directly related to the tireless dedication of our women religious. Many wanted to join their ranks despite the rigors of their way of life. The struggles that these sisters endured as a result of deep poverty, the overwhelming needs of the immigrants, and intimidation from some Americans who did not like Catholics inspired a number of women who wanted to join their ranks. This was a great blessing for the American Church.

Neumann's *ad limina* visit discusses founding of OSF Sisters of Philadelphia
(Window in Neumann Shrine, Philadelphia)

Male religious orders also came to our aid. We desperately needed these men to teach our boys, and serve in our parishes. As you can well imagine, the Sisters of the Third Order of St. Francis were like daughters. What great ladies! Although teaching would become part of the community's ministry, the care of those who were sick was at the root of their beginning. Mrs. Anna Bachmann, a widow, as well as Barbara Boll and Anna Dorn had started living like sisters long before they began wearing religious garb. These women were under the capable direction of Father Hespelein at St. Peter's Parish, and the religious vocations that swelled in their individual souls eventually expanded far beyond the small group into a wonderful community of Franciscans. I was able to be part of their history because of my position in the church and my interest in their religious life. In Rome, the Holy Father urged me to gather a new community under the patronage of the great St. Francis for our many works. The simple garb of the Third Order of St. Francis was first granted to these women on April 9, 1855, at St. Peter's Church in Philadelphia. After a year of novitiate and with great simplicity, the women professed their vows on May 26, 1856 in my private chapel. They officially began their monumental ministry by visiting the sick and by providing a place for poor, homeless girls to live. Their mission to help others eventually expanded to the care of girls who had contracted smallpox. The great spirituality of these sisters animated all their works so that their patients recovered both physically and spiritually.

Eventually, this seed would mature into the establishment of magnificent hospitals. Mrs. Anna Bachmann eventually was known as Mother Mary Francis, Miss Anna Dorn as Sister Mary Bernardine, and Miss Barbara Boll as Sister Mary Margaret. Three additional professions took place later that same year, so the new community was off to a good start. I tried to give the new community all the time my schedule would allow. I gave conferences on the duties of the religious life, and was anxious to establish the community on solid footing by providing the sisters with a rule written by my own hand. The lives of these women were austere and penitential, and their spiritual happiness radiated from them.

In 1857, after a meeting with Sister Mary Francis and Sister Mary Bernardine, I gave them a bag of books. They assumed that they were ascetical books for their library, but they actually were books for the schoolroom. It would not be long before the gesture became obvious to them and the sisters began another one of their ministries as teachers.

On another occasion, I visited the Sisters of St. Joseph, who also were active in the diocese. These women lived in great poverty—so much so that they often had no coal for the fire to heat their house, nor enough food to eat. I told them to study the cross as the answer to their problems. But I also had a real concern for their physical needs. It was customary for me to give medals to the Sisters after meetings like the one we had just completed. This time, however, I gave them Yankee medals—fifty dollars in gold pieces to help them survive their crisis.

I continued to make visitation of the vast area under my care in the diocese. I had to be gone for long periods of time, but the prosperity of the faith was evident. The local editor of our Catholic paper correctly wrote that the faith was spreading far and wide throughout our ancient forests. The pastoral needs of the many people flooding our countryside demanded vigilant care. I decided to learn Gaelic because the Irish needed the consolation of the sacraments in their own language. I had to laugh when one of the ladies exclaimed after her confession that there was an Irish bishop in the area. Perhaps my accent was not as pronounced in Gaelic as it was in English!

Building churches and schools was a never-ending project due to phenomenal growth. Through God's favor, more religious men and women took up ministry in the diocese, while those already present increased their efforts. There are too many religious communities to add them all, and there is a danger of forgetting one or the other.

The diocesan pastors were essential to the life of the church and I made myself available to them whenever it was convenient to them. They were essential in the parish and in the schools. *In order that our parochial schools may truly produce Christian virtue it is necessary that the children advance in the knowledge and love of God at least with equal pace as in the knowledge of human sciences. Therefore, we exhort the pastors to stress particularly, in their direction of these schools, religious instructions and the cultivation of good morals and not to confide these matters to the teacher alone, especially the secular teachers. Indeed, if it can possibly be done, the pastors themselves should catechize and instruct the pupils and instill into them the simple truths of Christian Doctrine.* The pastors were charged with teaching students that God wanted them to obey their parents in a spirit of humility and filial fear. The pastors also were to teach pupils about the importance of living chastely, and loving God with true meekness and charity. Wayward children were not to be expelled from school too quickly. The pastors were charged with watching over these troubled students more carefully and strictly to prevent them from negatively influencing others. But they also were tasked with helping these students find a happier state of mind through patient instruction. If students remained incorrigible even after pastors had taken these extra steps, only then were they allowed to be dismissed.

Managing a diocese the size of Philadelphia's was tough. To help alleviate the strain, I proposed that the diocese be divided in two—one portion would cover the metropolitan area of Philadelphia, and the other would cover the surrounding countryside. There was some discussion about this proposal, and I suggested that I take over the portion that covered the surrounding countryside because I thought I would be better suited for that territory. *Because of the great distance from the episcopal see, it is very difficult to watch over the priests who are often only slightly known to me and who come from various parts of the old and new world with different customs. From the 11,600 baptisms of the year 1853, we estimate that there are 250,000 Catholics in the 26,000 square miles of the territory comprising the Diocese of Philadelphia. Although I have been occupied every year for at least five months on holy visitation, there still remains missions which I have been unable to see....The City of Philadelphia, which has more than five hundred thousand inhabitants and (if you will pardon the statement) a very worldly character, needs someone else instead of myself who am too plain and not sufficiently talented; besides I love solitude. For more than fifteen years I was occupied on the North American missions; I have loved corporal labors and journeys to the mountains and through the forests. Visiting Catholic families separated from one another by long distances and preaching to them, etc. has been my greatest pleasure.* So I figured that I would assume responsibility for the part of the diocese that covered the surrounding countryside, while the other person could serve as bishop for the metropolitan area.

Neumann as bishop
(Window in Neumann Shrine, Philadelphia)

Unfortunately, the mechanisms of the Church were not as simple as I would have liked them to be. It was difficult for Church officials in Rome to imagine why a bishop in a prestigious diocese like Philadelphia would want to move to a lesser diocese. Such a move would certainly raise some eyebrows. They were certain that the press would attempt to find a reason for the "demotion"—even if I insisted that I wanted to make such a move. When someone misinterpreted my suggestion as an indication that I wanted to resign from the episcopacy itself, things got really complicated. Resigning from my post never crossed my mind. The Holy Father had asked me to accept the post under obedience, and I never, ever had any intention of resigning from the office due to any difficulties involved! But in a strange turn of events, a rumor surfaced that Rome was inclined to accept my resignation. Suddenly, my proposal to divide the diocese became very complicated. I was simply looking to resolve some of the difficulties associated with operating such a large diocese.

A coadjutor bishop with the right of succession eventually was brought in to help me. Once on board in the diocese as coadjutor, it soon was apparent that he thought he would be moving into my position upon my resignation. Furthermore, he thought I would remain in Philadelphia only long enough for me to transfer all the properties of the diocese from my name to his so that he could take over for me after my resignation. Oh my goodness, my goodness!!! Bishop James Frederick Wood started his post as coadjutor bishop under a false assumption. He was a good man and had many, many talents that I greatly admired. But the fact that I had no intention of resigning was not something he had anticipated when he was appointed coadjutor. I wasn't even 50 years old, so he could have a long wait before he would be able to take my place! Eventually, this misunderstanding about the nature of the situation became more obvious, and it caused some strain between us.

I asked Bishop Wood to assume oversight of the finances of the diocese, and he did a marvelous job. He had worked in finance before entering entered ministry, and was well prepared for the task. Of course, there were times when I overruled his position. Other times he was frustrated with me because he did not feel he had enough authority to do his job. I understood how he felt based on my experience as superior to the Redemptorists, a position that also seemed to lack sufficient authority. I tried not to interfere too often, or at least not in a manner that would embarrass him. Nevertheless, we had our differences of opinion.

My decision to give St. John's Church to the Jesuits was one he disagreed with. When I first arrived in Philadelphia, my greatest support was Father Edward Sourin, the vicar general who also was pastor of St. John's Pro-Cathedral, a prestigious parish of the diocese. There was a building in the parish that originally was intended for use as a parochial school, but a clause in the deed for the church would not allow it to be used that way. What was the parish to do with the building if it could not be used as a school? Father Sourin suggested that it could be used as the site of the new St. Joseph's College. At the time, the Jesuits had a far inferior building at Willing's Alley. The parish building structure on Broad and Juniper streets could be put to good use. And if the Jesuits assumed the $30,000 debt, the parish and the college both would benefit. I thought it was an excellent idea, but I took it even further. This is where the problems arose. Since Father Sourin was leaving his position as pastor to become a Jesuit, I proposed that the parish itself be handed over to the care of the Jesuits. So a contract was drawn up to reflect this arrangement. Some expressed their displeasure, even in the secular press. The timing of this commentary was inopportune—especially given the rumors that I was on my way out, and that Bishop Wood was ready to take over my post. Nevertheless, the move took place in spite of the opposition, and I believed it to be a great step forward for the future of the diocese and the college.

The reason that some of the clergy had problems with giving St. John's to the Jesuits was due to the customary parochial authority and responsibilities that local pastors had at the time. At that time, all the property of the parish was considered the pastor's personal property. It was a situation that could be lucrative for the local pastor. I already had started drafting rules that drew a portion of this income from the local pastor, and that maintained the facilities as part of the parish operations. I felt I had to take this action, but some of the clergy interpreted my actions with regard to St. John's as another loss. Many would have loved to be the pastor of the elite parish.

My motives regarding St. John's, as well as other actions I took to limit a source of revenue for the individual pastor seemed necessary to me. To illustrate, there was one instance in which a pastor was transferred to another parish. When the next pastor arrived to take his place, he discovered that the former pastor refused to surrender the rectory since it was considered his own personal property. As a result, the new pastor had to rent a house. When the former pastor died one year later, the court ruled that the property was the personal property of the former pastor, that it should be sold, and that the proceeds should be given to his heirs. I had to address this situation. In addition, I put a stop to pew rental fees because it prevented some of the poor from attending services. I could not tolerate that either. Still, some of the clergy believed I was interfering with their income. So when "I gave away" St. John's and confronted some of these situations, some in the clergy felt that I was unnecessarily interfering with their futures and the potential plums that could have come into their possession.

The bishop's role had many requirements that demanded difficult decisions. Only a close relationship with the Lord could sustain a bishop! Others would forsake the bishop if things did not go their way. I spoke of this during the vesper service in Cincinnati after Bishop Juncker's ordination to the episcopacy. The Germans in the city had presented him with a chalice as a gift for his service to them. The chalice, which was to hold the blood of the Savior, was exceedingly symbolic for a new bishop. I told the congregation at the vesper service: *You have scarcely any idea how difficult and painful the office of bishop is, especially here in America. Catholics come from all parts of the world, all nationalities mingle with one another and the bishop is supposed to please all, an impossible task. Where are we to get strength? Where will Bishop Juncker receive the strength he needs? From the Blood of Christ, from…the Chalice.*

In May of 1858, I went to the Ninth Provincial Council of Baltimore. We discussed a number of Church issues, and I reintroduced the idea of splitting the diocese. Beyond the reasons I had advanced earlier, I did this because it became apparent to me that Bishop Wood had expected to take over Philadelphia after a short period of transfer. Since I had no canonical reason for resigning, he felt stuck. *I made known...that it seemed opportune to me to request my translation to one or other see that was to be erected... But to give up the episcopal ministry never entered my mind.* So to ease the situation, I proposed again that the diocese be divided and that I take the lesser part. Having done that, all was left in the hands of Rome for its own decision in the matter.

The teachings of the great saints, and the tradition of the Church outlined four duties of a bishop—preaching, conferring sacraments, administration of the diocese in spiritual matters, and administration of the diocese in temporal matters. The clergy were essential in fulfilling these tasks and I called three synods of the diocese in 1853, 1855, and 1857. On each occasion, we addressed the regulations needed to fulfill these duties.

Out of all of the responsibilities of the bishop, I preferred the opportunity to catechize the children, and to spend time in the company of the poor. One time while performing visitations in the diocese, another priest accompanied me to dinner. We had visited a wealthy house, followed by one with a poor family. Reflecting on this, I told him: *yesterday we were treated to a well-filled table, empty forms of politeness and useless conversation, but today we had the charming simplicity of a pious Catholic home.* Whenever I hear myself addressed "Right Reverend Sir" or "Right Reverend Bishop," I imagine behind me some distinguished personage to whom the title belongs.

In 1859, we found some property for our minor seminary. I had wanted to establish one for a long time, but it finally happened in Glen Riddle. In the fall of that year, we opened the preparatory seminary with four professors and twenty-six students. I was delighted and hopeful about the institution and what it would mean for the future of the diocese.

Neumann establishes prep-seminary at Glen Riddle
(Historical Sketch of the Philadelphia Seminary, 1891)

Not as easily established—but of equally great importance to the future of the diocese—was the establishment of the Immaculate Heart of Mary Sisters. In 1845, Mother Theresa Maxis, along with Father Louis Gillet, C.Ss.R., gathered a community of women together in Monroe, Michigan. This community would eventually become the Sisters of the Immaculate Heart of Mary. Mother Theresa was a dynamo and had very definite ideas about the way things should be operated, but she was very compliant with Father Gillet regarding the writing of the rule for the community. But Father Gillet was transferred from Monroe, Michigan before the task was completed, and Mother Theresa wanted a Redemptorist to help finalize the rule of life for the Sisters. Mother Theresa wrote to me, letting me know that the Sisters were available to minister in the diocese.

An opportunity soon presented itself. In 1858, Father John Vincent O'Reilly in Susquehanna County found himself with an empty academy when the Sisters of the Holy Cross withdrew due to their lack of success starting the school. Redemptorists who had given missions in the area suggested that Father O'Reilly contact the Sisters in Monroe to help him with this work. The

Sisters were growing in number, and happened to be looking for a good place to expand the community. In addition, having a Redemptorist bishop was an advantage to these Sisters. When Father O'Reilly asked me what I thought about this arrangement, I gave him a favorable reply. I was always interested in establishing solid educational institutions. Bishop Lefevre of Detroit agreed to the arrangement, and the work began.

But as so often happens, an unplanned and innocent glitch entered the picture. The Sisters were to remain under the jurisdiction of Bishop Lefevre of Detroit since the Sisters' motherhouse would remain in Monroe, Michigan. This is the way Bishop Lefevre

Neumann welcomes the Immaculate Heart of Mary nuns to the East *(Window in Neumann Shrine, Philadelphia)*

and I both envisioned the arrangements, and based on that understanding, I thought he had taken care of the details to make sure everything was in place. But we were mistaken! When the time came for renewal of vows, I delegated Father O'Reilly to represent me for the canonical action of receiving them. By this act, these Sisters were incorporated into the diocese under my jurisdiction. I had no problem with this arrangement since I was under the impression that everything had been worked out. But that was not the case.

In the end, the Sisters had to split into two groups. They became the IHM Sisters of Monroe under Bishop Lefevre in Michigan, and then there were the Sisters who fell under my jurisdiction in Philadelphia. I tried to resolve the issue, but due to the complexity of the situation, that was not possible. I wrote to Bishop LeFevre: *The Very Reverend Provincial of the Redemptorists showed me last Friday a letter addressed to him in which it is stated that you cannot help suspecting me of being the chief instigator or promoter of the schism of the disorder among the Sisters of the Immaculate Heart of Mary.* Indeed, some Redemptorists had suggested that the Sisters leave Monroe and designate Pennsylvania as their only mother-house, but this was not my intent. *In order to remove from Your Lordship's mind any suspicion against me, I beg leave to state before God that the idea of creating or encouraging , even passively, among the Sisters, especially in Your Lordship's diocese any like discontent or schism has never entered my heart or my mind.*

But things had taken their own course. A second house was purchased for an academy in Reading. I did not want the situation to escalate where the Sisters of the Immaculate Heart of Mary were concerned, so I insisted that other orders staff the academy. None were found, so the Sisters of the Immaculate Heart of Mary went there as well. As you can see, the situation continued to escalate even though I had not wanted that to happen. God might have had different plans, or perhaps I did not handle the situation very well.

This was a very difficult situation for me but harder for the community of the Immaculate Heart Sisters. Human actions sometimes bring about events that holy souls should never have to experience, and that was certainly the case in this situation. At the same time, God worked a miracle in providing the Church in America with the Sisters of the Immaculate Heart of Mary. They provided so much ministry to countless souls in this diocese, in spite of the turmoil that existed among the various personalities involved. In the end, God conquered human weakness.

Slow progress on the cathedral was another complicated

issue, but good also came from that situation. On September 14, 1859—the feast of the Exaltation of the Holy Cross—we completed the structure of the building and finally were ready to place the gold cross on the dome of the roof. It was a long time in coming, and much work still needed to be done to complete

Cathedral of SS. Peter and Paul in Philadelphia
(Sketches of the Catholic Church and Philadelphia, 1891)

the project. And while we were only finished with the exterior, it was a marvelous milestone. Six thousand people joined us in Logan Square for the occasion, and watched the eleven-foot cross lifted to the rooftop. I asked Bishop Wood to be the celebrant for the ceremony, and he gladly accepted. I assisted, content enough to have completed this part of the task.

I was in Philadelphia for Christmas in 1859. I heard many confessions and pontificated at the midnight Mass at St. Peter's. It was so wonderful to celebrate the birth of our Lord with such a wonderfully large and devout congregation. I recalled the silence of the stable in Bethlehem when I said my second Christmas Mass in private after walking back home from St. Peter's. I then did the ten o'clock Mass at St. John's Parish, the pro-cathedral. In early January, I had desk work to do, but I would have rather spent time among the people. I was pleasantly surprised when a friend came to visit from Buffalo, and updated me about so many of my former parishioners.

Later, when Father Urban, C.Ss.R., stopped by, he asked how I felt. I must not have looked too well. *I have a strange feeling today. I feel as I never felt before. I have to go out on a little business and the fresh air will do me good. A man must always be ready, for death comes when and where God wills it.* Years before, as a seminarian, I noted to myself: *Your body, oh my soul is mortal; it will be necessary to leave it without knowing the time….You know neither the place nor the time nor whether you will die suddenly nor after a painful sickness. Will you be able to confess your sins and receive your God in Extreme Unction? You know nothing! You will leave the world and all you see here below; neither will you be able to make your parents nor your friends come with you.* In any case, I had to take care of some business that day. I had to go visit a lawyer about a property deed, and I had to check on a chalice that was sent to Father Kopf, but had gotten lost in transit.

On that errand at Vine Street, near Thirteenth, I met my end. I suppose I had prophesied when I was talking to Father Urban. We never know when or where we will die, but I am happy to say that I was ready! I died in the parlor of a Protestant gentleman after collapsing on his stoop. I would have preferred to have been surrounded by my confreres and to exit this world in the midst of the Divine Office. Instead, I died with a simple sigh that committed my soul into the hands of my Savior. I was 49 when I died of apoplexy, left this world, and entered eternal life.

I never seem to be able to quietly enter places, even heaven. When I returned to Prachatitz, it seemed everyone knew I was coming and turned out to welcome me. I have no idea where the people came from on the day of my funeral. Logan Square was packed when they carried my remains from the chapel to St. John's for the first funeral Mass, and then again as we processed to St. Peter's. The police and a brass band led the procession, which included a rifle company, various societies and sodalities, my dear seminarians, half a hundred prelates, hundreds of priests and religious, and our dear faithful. I could not believe how many people came to pay their respects!

You never would have guessed that anyone had ever said a word against me if you would have heard the outpouring at my funeral. In fact, I was beginning to wonder if I would ever be laid to rest in my grave! I had made it known that I wanted to be buried among my confreres. So I was pleased when Father John De Dyker, the provincial, asked to have me buried at St. Peter's. Bishop Wood left the decision to Archbishop Kenrick who gladly consented, and was content that I would at last be able to rest among my confreres. I am now at peace, buried among my confreres in the basement chapel of the parish church.

PART II

Writings and Documents

Neumann's Spirituality

This article was first published in Spicilegium Historicum Congregationis *Sanctissimi Redemptor,* Rome, in November 2010. It considers more directly the spirituality of the saint and is reprinted here in the hope of identifying for the reader the expression of St. John N. Neumann's formation of values that directed his life and were expressed in the zeal exhibited in his ministry.

On the day of St. John Neumann's funeral in early January, 1860, Father William O'Hara, then rector of St. Charles Borromeo Seminary in Philadelphia, reported to Rome concerning the death: "The Church in America has suffered a great loss."[1] The funeral outpouring in Philadelphia demonstrated that he was not alone in that evaluation. Nonetheless, the end of Neumann's life on earth was not the end of his influence on the American Church; from the first days after the funeral obsequies until today, the faithful are inspired by his life and seek his ongoing assistance in their needs.

Pope Paul VI canonized John Nepomucene Neumann on June 19, 1977. In his homily on the occasion, he pointed out that we need to "ask ourselves…what is the meaning of this extraordinary event, the meaning of his canonization. It is the celebration of holiness. And what is holiness? It is human perfection, human love raised up to its highest level in Christ, in God."[2]

Neumann's story usually consists of a series of accomplishments. There is much to admire—the organization of the Catholic

School system in Philadelphia, the institutionalization of the 40 Hours Devotion for the diocese, the founding of a religious order of women religious, the Sisters of the Third Order of St. Francis of Glen Riddle, and the help he provided to other religious communities in their struggles to find a foothold in America. He published catechisms and established institutions of charity to care for the needs of the poor, especially the immigrants who were flooding the shores.

His presence to the faithful wherever they might be found was untiring; his founding of a minor seminary to provide future priests to serve the people of God was notable; the construction of many churches and schools was impressive. The list of activities is lauded and is the usual focus of attention when considering the glory of St. John Neumann.

There is more. "For true activity," Pope Benedict XV declared at the decree proclaiming the heroic virtue of the saint, "does not consist in mere noise, it is not the creature of a day, but it unfolds itself in the present, it is the fruit of the past and should be the good seed of the future."[3]

Neumann's past, the unfolding of the ministry, and the good seed produced are all indications of something deeper, his spirituality. He developed firm convictions and a basic framework for all of the activity that would flow from them from his response to the experiences of his life and of God's presence in these events. To understand his spirituality, it is indeed necessary to be familiar with his curriculum vitae but study is needed to understand Neumann's spirituality.

"Christian spirituality studies the reactions which Christian belief produces in the religious consciousness."[4] The way an individual interprets his or her experience and places it within a context of a philosophy for living, as well as the success or failure of the individual to live according to his or her foundational belief are the context of spirituality. "The experience, reflection and articulation of the assumptions and consequences of religious faith as it is lived in concrete situations"[5] is the definition given by Carolyn Osiek for spirituality and is also the understanding of this study.

Neumann's spirituality is rooted in his European background and is expressed in his missionary career in North America. By the end of his seminary experience, Neumann had embraced a poverty of spirit, often ascribed to him as the virtue of humility, a virtue that, in his theological notes, he ascribed as essential in the Christian life: *Without humility, other virtues could be neither genuine nor permanent.*[6] This foundational virtue made his apostolic zeal, expressed in the ministry, all the more authentic.

Neumann's years can be divided between the time of formation in Europe and of ministry in America. His first twenty-five years of his experience were completely European—Bohemian, to be more precise; the last years, almost of equal number, were those of a minister in the United States. The blending of these experiences in the life of Neumann produced the first American[7] male canonized by the Church in 1977.

We Were Brought Up in the Old-Fashioned School

Neumann writes of his early life in Europe: *We were brought up in the old-fashioned school. Our parents were both deeply Christian. While our father from morning to night supervised the apprentices and workers, of which there were at times five or six in the house, our mother never missed a day hearing Mass. She always took with her one or the other of the children who was not yet in school. She went to Holy Communion often and fasted not only on the fast days of the Church but at other times as well; my father, however, did not approve of this. In my case there was needed at times the promise of a penny or something similar to bring me to Mass, Rosary and Stations of the Cross.*[8]

Philip Neumann, John's father, emigrated from Obernburg, Bavaria to the village of Prachatitz (modern-day Prachatice in the Czech Republic) in Bohemia in 1802 to ply his trade as a stocking maker; Agnes Lebis, a native of the village, became his wife in 1805. There would be six children from the union, John being the third child, born March 28, 1811. The village church was as central to daily life as was the town square. John's birth year had been just a bit more than twenty years after the French Revolution and the spirit of nationalism, even in ecclesiastical circles, was a reality; this, however, was less in the villages than in the larger metropolitan areas. John grew up in the old-fashioned school.

We can further categorize Neumann's family life not only as being of the old-fashioned school but of the Roman Catholic school. Phillip Neumann was known for his justice in his shop and for his charity as the distributor of alms while the prefect of the poor in the town. In his office as prefect, Phillip cared for the indigent and sought to care for their needs from taxes levied for this purpose. This was a lesson John learned and emulated later in his ministry to the immigrant.

Of the children of the family, John would be ordained a priest and eventually profess religious vows as a Redemptorist; his brother Wenzel would profess vows as a Redemptorist Brother and be known as Brother Wenceslaus. Of the girls, the two eldest, Catherine and Veronica married; the fourth eldest child in the family, Joan, entered the Sisters of St. Charles and became known as Sr. Caroline; Louise, the youngest girl, took care of Phillip Neumann until his death and then lived out the remainder of her life with the Sisters of St. Charles. The only grandchild born to John's Parents was Catherine's son, John Berger, who would later go to America and become a Redemptorist priest and the first biographer of John Neumann.

Though John grew up in a traditional Catholic family, he confided that he didn't feel an inclination toward priesthood, even in the midst of the family piety; he was more intrigued with science. He did study Latin with the town catechist, but that was the custom for all students who were interested in pursuing advanced studies. After his time in the village school, in 1823, John with approximately twenty others students from Prachatitz moved on to Budweis (modern-day Cescke Budejuvice in the Czech Republic) for the gymnasium. During these years, he continued the routine of a sincere religious practice: *We went to confession every three months. As far as I can recall, it was always a truly serious matter with me to receive the holy sacraments properly, for the first instruction that I received in my home kept me from the pitfalls in which most of my school companions were trapped.*[9]

At the end of the gymnasium, John entered his two years of philosophy. *During the two years of philosophy, many changes took place in me.*[10] He continued in the revelation of the evolution of his vocation: *In those two years I avidly followed my bent for the natural sciences: botany and biology, geography, physics, geology, astronomy. And I applied myself with the greatest enthusiasm to algebra, geometry, and trigonometry, subjects that formerly were not to my liking. When the time came, at the end of the philosophy course, for me to decide either for theology or law or medicine, I felt more of an attraction for the latter.*[11]

John's father was not disappointed with the inclination toward the study of medicine; his mother, however, persuaded John to apply also for the seminary in Budweis. He protested that he did not feel worthy of the high calling nor did he have testimonials from influential people to help him get accepted. Furthermore, only twenty of the eighty applicants would be accepted and he did not feel that he would be one of them. Nonetheless, he did apply and was accepted. He confessed that he was not disappointed and gave up the thought of medicine. *From that moment on I never gave another thought to medicine and I also practically gave up completely the study of physics and astronomy on which I had preferred to spend time, and this without any great difficulty.*[12] Neumann began his theological studies on the Feast of All Saints, 1831.

The seminary for the Diocese of Budweis was established in 1804 and numbered 140 students in Neumann's day. Neumann was content in the seminary: *I studied* con amore *Old Testament, Hebrew, Church History and so on to my own satisfaction and that of the professors who were diocesan priests and who, with the exception of the professor of Church History and Canon Law who was more of a Josephinist, had a good spirit and with great ease taught us in a short time a great deal of useful material. At the end of the first year of theology I was one of the few who were to receive Tonsure and the four Minor Orders. This actually took place on July 21, 1832.*[13]

The second year of theology continued as smoothly as the first. It was during this year that Neumann made his decision to be a missionary in America: *In the second year of theology we had New Testament in Latin and Greek together with Exegesis and Canon Law. What appealed to me most were the Letters of the Apostle, St. Paul, which the professor knew how to explain very well. About this time I began to read the reports of the Leopoldine Society, especially the letters of Father Baraga and other missionaries among the Germans in North America. This is how there arose in one of my fellow students, Adalbert Schmidt, and in myself on the occasion of a walk along the Moldau River, the determination to devote ourselves to North America as soon as we acquired some experience after ordination.*[14]

The decision to become a missionary effected Neumann's choices from that time onward. It was the determining factor in his decision to transfer from the diocesan seminary in Budweis to the archdiocesan seminary in Prague. He reasoned that learning English and French would be essential elements for his future ministry in America and that the study of these languages could better be done in the larger city of Prague. He applied for one of the two positions made available each year to seminarians from Budweis and was accepted, along with a classmate Anton Laad.

Unfortunately, Neumann's plans to study new languages never materialized: *I had hardly gone to the French classes at the Clementinum for a few [days or weeks] when an order came from the archbishop that no seminarian was to attend these classes. As for English, I could learn even less because that language was not taught at the University then.*[15]

In spite of the restrictions on the study of French and the absence of classes in English, Neumann was able to learn enough to begin recording his thoughts and feelings in his journal which he began while he was a student at Prague and which he continued almost until he entered the Redemptorists in 1840. The journal was not a diary but a means of reflecting upon his own experiences. Neumann was lonely during the years at Prague and he would continue to live a life that was often isolated while serving as a diocesan priest on the frontiers of western New York State. The jottings in the journal gave him a means to externalize some of the deepest streams of his heart. It was found among his personal things at the time of his death; though he had not made an entry in the journal for twenty years, he kept the writing for his own reasons.

The seminary of Prague was radically different from that of Budweis, if for no other reason than that it was part of a large city and large university. As part of the university, it boasted a history of over 450 years, located in the former Jesuit College of the Clementinum which housed the Royal Imperial Library. It is not surprising that many of the theological currents that Neumann would find offensive could be experienced in this setting: *At Prague I was likewise displeased with the professors of Dogmatic and Moral Theology as well as Pastoral Theology. The first was more against the Pope than for him....The second was far too philosophical for a single one of us to understand him. The third was an out and out Josephinist.*[16]

During the Prague years, the seminarian reacted and responded to his environment and many of his principles of life took root in those days, especially his ecclesiology. Some of the divergent streams of Prague were not much to Neumann's liking.

Neumann did not consider his Prague period profitable, neither in 1835 nor, even less so, later. He concludes his criticism in these words: *It took a lot of effort and self-control to bury myself in the study of subjects and ideas whose foolishness I had already come to realize.*[17]

He kept a copy of Peter Canisius' *Summa Doctrinae Christianae* next to his text books and would be chided for his "hyperorthodoxy." His personal study of spiritual writers verifies that this criticism of him, though he found it offensive, was not inaccurate.

"Neumann's diaries spread out before us his interior, spiritual development during his Prague sojourn. They deserve special study with regard to the psychology and piety of the Catholic Restoration. The essential point is that Neumann's piety stands within the renewed classical-baroque tradition of Ignatius of Loyola, Francis Xavier, Peter Canisius, Louis of Granada, Theresa of Avila, Vincent de Paul, Francis de Sales, Joseph of Calasanza, Scupoli, Fenelon, Alphonsus of Liguori, Jean Crasset (1618–1692), Jean Crosset (1656–1738), Bourdeloue, and the Roman Catechism."[18]

In 1814, three years after Neumann's birth year, Pope Pius VI returned from exile to Rome and within the context of this historical moment a new spirit pervaded the institutional body of the Roman Church aimed at bring back into the fold many of the tangents of the Enlightenment. This direction continued in the time of his successor, Pope Pius VII.

"Under Pius VII and his successors the Church undertook a general redefinition of Catholic life. Inspired by the sixteenth-century Catholic Counter-Reformation and the Council of Trent, restoration churchmen expanded the institutional structures and devotional activities that gave form and substance to Catholic communities throughout the West."[19]

By the end of his seminary years, Neumann was well rooted in what came to be known as the Catholic Restoration.

"On one level restoration Catholicism can be seen as a reaction against the Enlightenment (counterpoising universalism to nationalism, supernaturalism to secular rationalism, and authoritarianism to liberalism), but it also attempted to reform Catholicity in all its aspects and to recapture the aggressive vitality of the tridentine Church of the sixteenth century. Once more the Church became a militant and transforming force in Western culture."[20]

In the years of formation, Neumann's convictions concerning the value of the institutional church took deep root in him went with him from Europe to the New World. While a student in Prague, in 1834, Neumann wrote a letter to a friend, John Holba, back in the seminary in Budweis concerning his belief that it made sense to follow the pope when there was doubt. Of course, this was before the declaration of papal infallibility and Neumann did not base his conviction on the doctrine but on a propensity to believe that the universal church needed to be in union with the pope. When there was doubt, the position of the pope could be safely followed.

His pro-Roman bias is demonstrated while still a seminarian in Prague; he was impatient with Josephism and Febronianism and referred often to the Roman catechisms to verify all opinions offered in his theological studies.

In ministry, Neumann's ecclesiology would prove a determining factor in setting the parameters of his ministry. An even more important determinant, however, was a spirituality rooted in humility.

Poverty of Spirit

"To become human means to become 'poor,' to have nothing that one might brag about before God. To become human means to have no support and no power, save the enthusiasm and commitment to one's own heart. Becoming human involves proclaiming the poverty of the human spirit in the face of the total claims of a transcendent God."[21]

From Neumann's journal it is possible to identify the evolution of the basic value that directed so many of his actions—a genuine Poverty of Spirit. Coming to such a profound spirituality did not come easily; at one point his inner sufferings were so profound that he gave passing thought to suicide as a possible escape from the torment: *My God, do not let this despair of mine continue...it could lead me to suicide. This faintheartedness and lack of faith is frightening.*[22] On the other hand, with St. Paul,[23] another avenue opened for Neumann. It was in his weakness that he found his strength.

The Prague years were profoundly lonely years for Neumann; he was removed from the more familiar rural setting, separated from friends and confidants, foiled in the very reasons for venturing the capital. The study of French was forbidden and English was not available in the academic setting. In addition, Neumann had a tender conscience and was, at times, rather ruthless in confronting his sins and imperfections. He often longed for the opportunity to confess his sins and imposed rather severe punishments on himself as restitution for his offences. He was introspective and had a tender conscience and often complained of despondency. In this setting, Neumann was led to spiritual poverty.

"Dear God, everybody is displeased with me. How can I evoke their affections? I am so fainthearted and timid! ...Thinking about my friends today made me feel so disconsolate, especially after supper, that I started to cry! Here I am, with all my carelessness and indifference while my friends in Budweis are surrounded by remarkable people and enjoy wise and holy spiritual direction! They don't even think of me anymore. In my loneliness and grief they have forgotten all about me."[24]

He was not gregarious and he missed the few, deep friendships he enjoyed over the years. After reading St. Theresa, he knew how important a spiritual director could be to his spiritual development, but this relationship was also absent to him. He was obviously a very capable and talented man, but was troubled by his inadequacy. It is not surprising that the exposure that is part of preaching was challenging to him and an incident in homiletic class crystallized all of these realities.

Neumann would never become known as an orator in his ministry; it was not finesse but only the depth of content which sprouted through his dryness that made his words sought by the faithful. In the experience of preaching, Neumann felt all his weakness and even wondered if prayer could help him: *You are aware of my weakness, my inclination to discouragement; my lack of skill in preaching worries me so much. I would readily turn to you in prayer, Lord, but so many of my prayers, marred by my sins, go unheard, that I no longer have the confidence to approach the throne of your mercy.*[25]

His anxiety was justified. He forgot his sermon and had to step down from the pulpit in homiletics class. He chided himself because he not only failed in the delivery but also because he lied by saying he knew the text in Latin but not German.

Enduring the inner feelings that assailed him in these years was most difficult. Time after time, he accused himself of personal weakness. His honesty made him wonder if he had the ability to live the Christian life in the manner he thought proper.

I was worse than lax most of the day, for I often actually took delight in the impure thoughts that occurred to me. I was glad that I had them and maybe even coddled them! I no longer value humility or make an effort to acquire it because of my tepidity, lack of love, wavering faith and my despair of recovering God's grace. Indeed, the condition of my soul is simply astonishing…Right now I would gladly quit this particular path of salvation I have trod for so long![26]

Emptiness went far beyond a guilty conscience for his faults, he was entering into an experience of spiritual poverty, the lack of power or control except in God, the negation of all illusion of self sufficiency. *We really hope when we no longer have anything of our own. Any possession or personal strength tempts us to a vain self-reliance.*[27] The intensity of poverty was all the more difficult because it was coupled with a sense of absence from God.

Jesus, my delight, has fled; alas, I seek for him in vain! I have lost my Beloved. He hearkens not to my sighs, he heeds not my voice. My eyes are blinded by tears, my voice has grown weak from lamenting; but he is not moved. He does not show himself to my poor soul. Jesus, Jesus, where are You?[28]

Neumann continues his lament: *That Love, O my God, which once united me to You has completely disappeared. O my Jesus, I am lost to heaven, I am dead to Thee!*[29] Nonetheless, in the depths of the via negativa, Neumann continued his routine of faith.

I am assaulted by the demon of discouragement and despair; but my soul, hold fast to Jesus. He will have mercy on you!…All my comfort, all my joy must come from him. Worldlings may call me unhappy, but I will rejoice in you alone… O my Jesus, if it be your will that these terrible temptations against faith should again assail me, I beseech you suffer me not to fall! Let me taste their full bitterness, but let me not fall! O my Lord, my God, I cast myself entirely into your hands! Worn out by the struggle, I will rest beneath your cross; I will embrace it; I will kiss it as the symbol of my victory![30]

"Neumann's growth into humility was as it should have been: We dimly begin to realize that we are poor, that our power and strength are derived from the wellsprings of invisible mystery.… Worshipping in 'spirit and truth' (Jn. 4:23), we no longer bear ourselves with the swagger of the executive who knows what is up and has all under control.…In worship we hand over even our poverty and pledge it to this mystery of God's all-encompassing presence.…Surrendering everything, even our poverty, we become truly rich: 'For when I am weak, then I am strong' (2 Cor. 12:10)."[31]

The genius of Neumann's spirituality emerges from experienced nothingness and even more because he was able to allow the absence of God to unfold into an even deeper faith. His poverty of spirit progressed to a surrender into the God who pervaded his life and it continued to deepen in the ministry. There was not a specific moment that can be identified as his "conversion moment"; his ongoing jottings in the journal show that he continued to refine the virtue as his life progressed. He did not record having experienced any kind of ecstatic union, only the ongoing faithfulness to the transcendent God.

When I beg your grace in order to practice virtue, you grant it to me and it does help me accomplish something worthwhile. But then I become conceited and proud. When I ask you to send me misfortune so that I may learn the path of salvation, I then bear it with little resignation. I even ask you to deliver me from it. If you remove it, I get depressed and desolate and I feel miserable. Behold me, dear God at the foot of your throne. Give me whatever you will. Spare me from whatever you will. Let me know your will without a doubt, for that must be my law.[32]

"The richness of a self-awareness that led Neumann into God made it possible for him to give himself completely to the ministry. His zeal flowed not from a perceived personal strength or ability but from an abiding awareness that it was no longer he that lived but Christ lived in him."[33]

At the end of his seminary studies in Prague, Neumann was saddened that ordinations were to be postponed for the Diocese of Budweis. There was a sufficient number of clergy and the bishop was old and sickly. The seminarians, therefore, had to return home and await the announcement of when or if ordinations would take place in the future. Neumann had hoped to be ordained in Bohemia, surrounded by his family, and to celebrate his First Mass before journeying to America as a missionary. It actually took him three weeks time before he had the courage to inform his family of his intention to emigrate to the New World. When he did so, there was some opposition but, in the end, he received the blessings of his family.

Neumann's Transition to North America

Between 1836 and 1860, the American years of Neumann's life, 4,300,000 immigrants arrived in the United States and, of these, 1,493,155 were German-speaking. Like Neumann, most arrived impoverished, had no one to meet them at the docks and didn't really know what they were going to do when they had arrived in the New World. The Catholic Church served as an anchor for many of the immigrants.

One landmark that Catholics recognized on either the urban or rural front was the church. Transplanted from the old country, it was a nostalgic reminder of what had been. In New York, Irish and German parishioners were located within walking distance of one another, but they were as distinct as German beer and Irish whiskey. They reinforced the ethnic differences of the people and enabled a neighborhood to build cultural barriers among themselves. As the center of their religious life, the neighborhood parish exhibited the piety of the people, and the differences in piety proved to be more striking than the similarities of the urban environment.[34]

April 12, 1836, marked the day Neumann sailed from Havre for America. The crossing took forty days, which he considered akin to Jesus' time in the desert before he began his public ministry. He would return to Europe only one time, nineteen years later in 1854 for the solemn declaration of the Immaculate Conception. When he arrived in the United States, he had no indication that he would be accepted for ordination in any diocese. He was a stranger in a strange land. He had completed the seminary curriculum and had many talents; his zeal motivated the journey but he was unable to get the assurance of ordination that he wanted due to a very slow and unreliable postal service.

Neumann set foot in New York City June 2, 1836. After a day of search, he was able to find the bishop: *Fr. Raffeiner brought me at once to the most Rev. Bishop Dubois—a born Frenchman—who in his glad surprise did not know whether he should address me in Latin, French or English. As soon as he had seen my testimonials, he told me at once that he was determined to receive me into the diocese.*[35]

The immigrant found his ministry in the New World; he was ordained a priest in Old St. Patrick's by June 25, 1836. *O my Jesus, how I glory in belonging to you! O Jesus, Searcher of hearts, you know how mine longs to be holy, to be united with you! Your death, O Jesus, made all people my brothers and sisters! Come, then, O Holy Spirit, come upon me that I may show forth to your world the way of eternal salvation! Come upon me, Strength of the weak, that my life and my works may exhibit faith made fruitful by your grace! O Holy Spirit, direct me in all my ways! With the Blessed Virgin, your mother, and with St. Joseph, I kneel at your crib and weep over my sins but ask again your grace. You are my all, my Lord, my God!*[36]

Zeal for Your House Consumes Me *(Psalm 69:9)*

One dictionary defines *zeal* as "Enthusiastic devotion to a cause, ideal, or goal and tireless diligence in its furtherance."[37] Neumann was clear in his basic motivation, his cause: *This will be my thanksgiving: I shall make you known and loved, while for myself I ask of you and the whole court of heaven, the light I need to follow the way of your law.*[38] The "house" for which Neumann had zeal was the Catholic community: *I want to dedicate my every effort to your glory, to spread your Kingdom over the face of this earth which you have loved enough to become the God-Man.*[39]

That Neumann was zealous there is little doubt considering his accomplishments; his "religious faith as it is lived in concrete situations."[40] All the effort which he exerted were directed toward the Church, "the community of men brought together by the profession of the same Christian faith and conjoined in the communion of the same sacraments under the government of the legitimate pastors and especially the one vicar of Christ on earth, the Roman

Pontiff."[41] The ecclesiology encased his spirituality and was in harmony with most of the hierarchy of America. The Church was the *societas perfecta*. There were a set of doctrine to be believed, a sharing in a life of prayer and sacrament in the institutional cult, and obedience to legitimate authority. The distinction between the teacher and the taught, the sanctifying and the sanctified, the governing and the governed was rather clearly understood and accepted by those who wished to be part of the institution. This strong corporate identity served the American Church well, the Ultramontane spirit of the day was embraced and, as the immigration of peoples from many lands with language and custom that were often peculiar to the homeland was encountered, the institutional model served to offer an anchor to the faithful of diverse cultures.

"Restoration churchmen expanded the institutional structures and devotional activities that gave form and substance to Catholic communities…and reforming bishops everywhere undertook elaborate and expensive building programs with the intent of making the parish church a physical presence in every community in which Catholics lived.…Reformers assiduously promoted the formation of a variety of religious societies, confraternities, sodalities, and devotional associations all of which had as their purpose the involvement of Catholic laymen and women in a comprehensive social network centered on the parish church."[42]

I Shall Make You Known and Loved: Neumann's Pastoral Presence

"True, I feel but little devotion; my soul is dry and sluggish; but yet, O Lord Jesus, I believe in you, I hope in you, I love you, and I grieve of having ever offended you! Behold my resolution to live entirely for you, to be patient in sufferings, diligent in the fulfill-ment of my duties, humble before you and my neighbor, and devout in your service. O my God, accept the sacrifice of my lowliness!"[43]

Neumann accepted the call to leadership within the Catholic community; in this, he was never known to be authoritarian, yet he did govern with conviction. In this he followed the opinion of St. Vincent de Paul. *Since the superior takes the place of God, he should after the example of the Redeemer strive to bring to God the souls entrusted to his care. He is not to appear as a superior and master, for nothing is more false than to allege that in order to govern well and to maintain authority, those in authority should make it felt that they are superiors, since Jesus Christ taught the contrary by work and example.*[44]

As a young priest, he confronted a saloon keeper who was going to have a festival which was not to Neumann's liking. The pastor threatened to leave the parish if the event was held. On the day of the festival, the parishioners, thinking their beguine pastor would not carry out his threat, were shocked to see he had packed his wagon to move on. When the innkeeper implored Neumann to allow just this last celebration, Neumann refused, saying they knew he had spoken the ultimatum. The festival was canceled.

While vice-gerent for the Redemptorists in North America, Neumann believed his primary responsibility was to carry out the directives of the Belgian provincial. Fr. Frederick DeHeld, the provincial, had ordered the Redemptorists of North America to retrench, meaning no further communities could be established until more men were recruited from Europe and the astronomi-cal debt was paid down. Many Redemptorists, for very zealous reasons, argued that it was not according to God's will that the American Redemptorists should not continue to expand to serve the needs of the ever growing population of German-speaking

Catholics. In spite of their reasonable objections, Neumann held strong to the directives of the provincial. He believed in authority as being intimately tied to his relationship with God. In a letter to his friend, Blessed Francis Seelos about the religious obedience owed superiors, he explained his rationale:

Our greatest mistake is that we allow ourselves to be deceived by a spirit of worldly shrewdness, the desire for fame and the love of comfort. We ought to fight the temptation to make spiritual things a means of temporal advancement. Thus the things we should and could do, become for many an occasion of sin and unfaithfulness to God. The principles of faith fade out of our hearts in proportion as we allow the principles of the world to come in. We place our confidence not in God but in our own intelligence, experience, and so on. We seek not what is least or most difficult or most despised but what is easiest and what redounds most to our own glory. If we only love God alone and from our whole heart, how easy it would be for our superiors to lead us according to the prescriptions of the rule. God would then urge us on and we would not resist. This, my dear Father, in my opinion, is the cause of all the unhappiness that seems to reign here. I believe that what is most necessary is that we should pray for one another daily with great confidence: Spiritum rectum innova in visceribus meis. Advenat regnum tuum.[45]

While Bishop in Philadelphia, he urged all parishes to establish a school for the children. One of the prominent pastors said it was just impossible for the parish to do so at that time. Neumann, with understanding replied that if it was impossible for the pastor to do as he directed, perhaps another could be found to pastor the parish. The local pastor started a school.

Bishop Neumann called three synods in Philadelphia with his clergy. At them, they deliberated immediate concerns and Neumann listened attentively to the group's wisdom. He commented that he knew *of no better means than these synods to settle things at once.*[46] He executed the decisions of the synods, and the laws promulgated were direct and to the point. They implemented regulations from higher authority both of Rome and of the Plenary and Regional Councils of Baltimore. They dealt both with regulations for liturgical services and prayers as well as regulations that governed the clergy themselves and the establishment of board of consultation.

Neumann is better known for his pastoral presence than as an authority figure. His ministry always encompassed large areas. He began his ministry in western New York State. There he was given charge of the region north of Buffalo, up to the Niagara Falls, roughly 900 square miles of parish. The nearest mission was two hours from his rectory; the most distant was twelve hours by horseback. *Like an old German emperor followed everywhere by his court do I carry with me all needful church articles while visiting my three parishes.*[47] Neumann made it a point to be available to his parishioners and traveled constantly from region to region. As vicegerent of the Redemptorists in America, his frequent visitations to the local communities brought him across vast areas. As bishop, he assumed a diocese that encompassed 35,000 square miles—two thirds of Pennsylvania, all of Delaware and half of New Jersey.

In spite of the areas, Neumann's visitation records show that he was concerned for each member of his flock. He set a goal for himself that he would visit each parish in the city of Philadelphia once each year and every parish in the country districts every two years. While on visitation he not only reviewed the parish books, both financial and sacramental records, but gave the spiritual exercises to the faithful and performed the sacraments. When complaints about his absence from the city of Philadelphia were expressed, he answered that the diocese was too large for one bishop. He even proposed that the diocese be split and he be given the country area. That did not happen.

Neumann's pastoral presence was especially noted in his ministry to the immigrant. While he neither avoided nor refused to serve those who were more established, his experience was that the poor were in greater need. This also flowed from his own spiritual bent which sought only God as the foundation of his life and was careful not to allow lesser vanities take control. He was criticized for this in his role as Bishop of Philadelphia. The sophisticated Catholic society of the city would have boasted of the presence of the bishop at their functions, but Neumann did not attend if it could be avoided, rather he sent the coadjutor bishop. At the time of his death, the Catholic Herald described the bishop as "not solicitous for the shadow of a great name, neither did he seek to be familiarly acquainted with many nor to be particularly loved by men."[48] An anecdote is related by one of Neumann's parish priests about an incident that took place on one of the bishop's visitations: "One day we were obliged to dine at the house of a very rich Catholic. The guests were numerous and the appointments brilliant….The very next day brought us quite a change of circumstances, for we dined in a log-cabin, off simple fare, our only beverage pure water.… When out of the house, he remarked: *What a difference between yesterday and to-day! Yesterday we were treated to a well-filled table, to empty forms of politeness and useless conversation; but today we were surrounded by the charming simplicity of a pious Catholic home.*[49]

Neumann didn't theorize about his inclination to serve the poor but his actions demonstrated his preference. The poor who most received Neumann's attention were the immigrants. Like many missionaries who joined the American Mission, Neumann had intended to work with the native people. It did not take long, however, for him to learn that there was a more pressing need. He was inclined to the adage that *language saved faith*,[50] and he became passionate in trying to care for those who were in such great need. Like his confrere, Father Alexander, C.Ss.R., he became convinced that for every one hundred Indians who were baptized, a thousand German Catholics fell away from the faith.[51]

He tried to recruit classmates from the seminary in Europe to join him on the missions, urging them to join him in the work of the missions.

The need of Catholic priest and the spiritual desolation of the faithful is increasing day by day. Judging from a human standpoint, the disproportion would have lamentable results—only God alone is the support of His Church. When I arrived here in America three years ago, it seemed as if the Germans in America would soon have sufficient priests. But the results taught otherwise. The Most Reverend Bishop Hughes, the coadjutor of this diocese, declared not long ago, that he would receive 7–8 if they were to be had.[52]

Neumann was so convinced of the need that he joined his voice to the possibility of establishing a seminary to train ministers for the American Missions. The purpose of the new seminary was "to provide for those who feel themselves called to the exalted and divine work of devoting their energies to the salvation of souls in distant parts of the world, an opportunity to prepare themselves in every way for this important field of labor."[53] The project came very near to being implemented, but the funds that would have supported the seminary were more urgently needed in the United States and the idea never reached fruition.[54]

Neumann was talented in language and was himself available throughout the years of ministry to serve those who struggled with language. At one point, he studied enough Gaelic to be able to hear the confessions of the Irish immigrants. On one occasion, the penitent, after leaving the confessional, confided to a friend that Philadelphia at last had an Irish Bishop. Neumann would give the Italian immigrants the use of his chapel for services in their language and, a couple months later, purchased a Protestant chapel to establish the first Italian Catholic parish in Philadelphia, St. Mary Magdalen de Pazzi.

In the midst of poverty, social needs pressed upon the Catholic community. Works of charity were necessary to care for the immediate needs of the immigrant. Neumann elicited the care of religious orders in the tasks of teaching and caring of all the faithful but, especially for those most in need, the sick and orphans. The thrust of social ministry was not systemic so much as a response to pressing problems—houses where the sick could find care, schools to instruct the children and orphanages to protect those who lost their parents or whose parents simply could not care for their children in the early days with the wages of the labor. Parishes were established to nourish the faith life of the immigrant in language and cultural familiarity. All of these, Neumann, who was sometimes reputed to be unskilled organizationally, developed. "Like adolescence, with its spurts, the task was to stay alive and to develop correctly."[55]

The Light I Need to Follow the Way of Your Law

Neumann prayed for the light he needed to follow the way of God's law; he also worked tirelessly to spread that light to those he served. Religious experiments were common enough in the New World and most had a philosophy that endorsed, at least in part, the perfectibility of humanity. The many experiments were as individual as were their leaders. "They were, nonetheless, bound together by what they called "the spiritual principle"—a principle which was articulated in three major agreements: an insistence upon divine immanence, a dependence upon intuitive perceptions of truth, and a rejection of all external authority."[56] It is not surprising that Neumann did not embrace the perspective. In an address to the Philopatrian Institute of Philadelphia, a prominent, Catholic literary society, Neumann clearly stated to the audience that all learning should enhance our love of God. If one can't say an Our Father with devotion after the study of some material, he counseled, it was not appropriate for a Catholic scholar. The local paper reported his thoughts:

"He recommended the members of the Institute to study those works of truth on which sound, useful knowledge could be founded. He cautioned them against the admission of the false Philosophies of Germany and France. The writings of the Transcendentalists, and so-called Socialists should find no place in a Catholic library. Such works could mislead, unsettle, and corrupt the mind. The general tendency of novels, too, was injurious; they filled the mind of the reader with frivolous imaginings and too frequently displaced the love of God for an unhallowed love of creatures…All their labors in the pursuit of knowledge should be made subservient to the service of God."[57]

These words did not come from an anti-intellectual but from a man not only of learning but one who called himself a "bibliomaniac."[58] Neumann's zeal was not insular but neither was he in favor of unguarded assimilation at the expense of faith. Neither did he freely embrace the concept of the perfectibility of humanity; for him, the reality was a humanity redeemed.

Neumann's concern was for truth, which for him was synonymous with the teachings of the Catholic Church, and this caused him to beg for good literature and spiritual books from Europe and a relentless quest for the education of his parishioners.

I began yesterday to instruct the children. They are in a sad state. The poor little creatures have had few advantages. They speak both German and English badly, and have little idea of religion. From lack of care and instruction, many weeds have sprung up among them; and yet a school cannot even be thought of. O God, how melancholy is the spectacle in this part of your Kingdom! ...Enlighten me, strengthen me with your powerful grace, that I may snatch from Satan his unfortunate prey, and lead them back to you.[59]

His efforts at instructing the children met with the approval of his parishioners. "As may be imagined, with such a teacher and such rewards, Father Neumann's school was well attended."[60] Every Sunday afternoon Neumann and his students could be found studying catechism.

The catechism was the anchor which prevented the various cultural communities from dividing into separate denominations as so often happened in Protestant sects. It held communities together as a systematic approach to learning the basic tenets of the Catholic faith universally held by all regions. While pastor in Pittsburgh, he published two catechisms, one smaller, the *Kleiner Katechismus,* and one larger, the *Katholischer Katechismus¸* both in the traditional question and answer format. Years later, his *Larger Catechism* would be chosen to be used in by all German-speaking Catholics in the United States and go through thirty-eight editions before it was no longer needed.

"He was an accomplished catechist and a great lover of children. His gentleness, meekness, and perseverance in communication religious instruction to the children often awoke my astonishment, and the salutary impression he made upon even the most faulty and troublesome of our little people was quite remarkable....They often said to me, 'Sister, Father Neumann looked right into my heart.'"[61]

Neumann's most famous contribution to education was the

establishment of the first Catholic school system in America. He wasted no time in this effort after arriving in Philadelphia as bishop. In his mind, Catholic schools were desperately needed both because students were sometimes ridiculed for their faith in the public school and also because he was convinced that all subjects should be imbued with Catholic principles when they were taught.

The school system of the United States is very liberal in theory; but in reality it is most intolerant toward Catholics. Everyone has to contribute to the erection and maintenance of the public schools, in which instruction is restricted to reading, writing and ciphering. As respects religious instruction which is excluded from those schools, parents are free to have their children reared in whatever religion they please. Notwithstanding these liberal concessions, it cannot be doubted that the young mind is influenced by the irreligious dispositions of teachers....Due to the prejudice against the faith that was infused in the public school system as we knew it, the determination that religious instruction needed to be part of the daily curriculum and the conviction that Catholic values need to permeate even secular subjects, we will spare no effort in the establishment of a solid, Catholic school in every parish to guarantee, as best we can, that the gift of the faith continues into future generation.[62]

Behold My Resolution
to Be Devout in Your Service

The worship within the liturgies of the Church was central to Neumann's ministry. In the eulogy delivered by Father Edward Sourin, S.J., who had served as Neumann's vicar-general at the beginning of time in Philadelphia, Neumann was described as a man "who spared himself in nothing." This was most certainly true in the administration of the sacraments and as leader of prayer. Twice he suffered from exhaustion—at the end of his time as a diocesan priest in New York[63] and again at the end of his first term as pastor at St. Philomena's in Pittsburgh.[64] He died at age forty-eight, just shy of his forty-ninth birthday.

Neumann was insistent that the liturgical norms of the Church be honored in all services. At the first Plenary Council of Baltimore, he served on the committee which consolidated the rituals for the celebration of divine worship. With the many customs that were brought to the New World by immigrants from many parts of the world, this was all the more necessary. At a synod within his own diocese, he sought to implement the direction of the Plenary Council in Philadelphia.

Last month I assembled all the priests of the diocese, and gave them the spiritual exercises; then followed a synod: and I have reason to rejoice over the success of both. These synods are especially needed in the United States, in order to secure uniformity in the performance of clerical functions. As missionaries come here from all parts of Christendom, each bringing with him the peculiarities of his own nation, discord may thereby be engendered. I know of no better means than these synods to settle things at once, as is done in the Eternal City.[65]

At the same synod, Neumann introduced his idea for instituting an ongoing 40 Hours Devotion in the diocese. The reaction of the clergy was not positive. Anti-Catholic prejudice was strong in the diocese and a church had recently been burned, all of which led to a fear of sacrilege in such a public display of devotion on the part of those who heard the proposal. Neumann was disappointed and continued to think about the proposal. One evening, working late, he fell asleep at his desk. He had steadied the candle that provided his light on the desk since it had almost been spent and could no longer keep burning in the candlestick. He awoke with alarm and found that the candle had scorched his papers. The writing was still legible. He knelt for a prayer of thanks that he had not burned down the house and he heard a voice: *As the flames are here burning without consuming or even injuring the writing, so shall I pour out my grace in the Blessed Sacrament without prejudice to my honor. Fear not profanation, therefore; hesitate no longer to carry out your designs for my glory.*[66]

Neumann instituted a schedule in the Diocese of Philadelphia for the 40 Hours Devotion so that exposition continued unbroken for adoration of the sacrament and for the reception of a plenary indulgence for those who participated. This practice touched the piety of the age and many bishops followed Neumann's example in their own diocese. Neumann himself proscribed a ritual to be followed and prayers to be said. No sacrilege from anti-Catholic sympathizers ensued.

Various confraternities of prayer were also established and special events urged upon his pastors for lent. He encouraged parish missions. *He that has not given missions or heard confessions during missions cannot know how useful these exercises are. Owing to the manner in which the Bread of the Divine Word is broken, when eternal truths are methodically exposed to the hearers who have assembled in great numbers, it is nearly impossible for them not to be converted.*[67]

From his youth, Neumann exhibited a great love and devotion to the Mother of God. This became even more public when the Church announced that there was to be a solemn declaration concerning Mary's Immaculate Conception. In October 1854, Neumann received an invitation from Pope Pius IX to attend the ceremonies in Rome and to have, at the same time, his *ad limina* visit to report on the diocese. This gave Neumann great joy and provided him his only opportunity to return to Europe and his homeland during his missionary career. The honor given to the Mother of God inspired Neumann, his visit to his homeland was tender. To his people in Philadelphia, he wrote a pastoral letter before the trip and a second pastoral letter on his return, praising Mary and attesting to his deep devotion to her.

Never, Christian brethren, never can we admit that she was for one moment the slave of the devil;—the Virgin who was destined to be the Mother of God, the Spouse of the Holy Spirit, the Ark of the New Covenant, the Mediatrix of Mankind, the Terror of the Powers of Darkness, the Queen of all the Heavenly Hosts.

Purer than heaven's purest angel, brighter than its brightest seraph, Mary, after her Creator, God,—who made and gave her all,—is the most perfect of beings, the masterpiece of Infinite Wisdom, Almighty Power, and Eternal Love.[68]

His pastoral letter of 1855 continued his unbridled praise of Mary in her Immaculate Conception.

To whom, with more reason, propriety, confidence and venera-tion can we turn than to a being whom, from all eternity God has so loved and honored?…At the same time, no more powerful friend have we with God! The humbler of our chief enemy, Satan, she is in a noble sense, the strength of the weak, the Help of Christians.… No day should be allowed to pass without some actual proof of your confidence in her protection, of your perpetual joy and gratitude for her Immaculate Conception and for all the other graces, glory and the power which God has bestowed upon her.[69]

The Religious Life

A special word must be given to Neumann's decision to enter religious life. Becoming a Redemptorist was a very deliberative choice of St. John Neumann and his life as a religious was a vital part of his spirituality. Neumann did, indeed, live a life of poverty and simplicity as a diocesan priest and was chaste and obedient to the laws of God and the Church. It was not a need of reform that inspired him to seek entrance the Redemptorists. Neumann sought community and as a means of experiencing the good example of the confreres and expressing a personal spirituality with them, a brotherhood which would be mutually beneficial to all for eternal salvation.

Neumann had first mentioned the passing thought of joining either the Redemptorists or the Jesuits when he was a student in Prague; this, however, seems to have been ruminations on the choice of his vocation to be a missionary in North America. Both communities had men serving on the mission and being a member offered an opportunity to execute his decision to go to America. After ordination, while a parish priest in New York, Bishop Du-Bois, accompanied by the Redemptorist, Fr. Joseph Prost, C.Ss.R., made a visitation to the parish and, while there, Fr. Prost spoke to Neumann about joining the Redemptorists. Prost's primary motivation in doing so was because he would have liked the bishop to turn over Neumann's parishes and Buffalo to the care of the Redemptorists. Prost did not persuade Neumann.

In 1840, Neumann was exhausted. He confided to Fr. Pax, his friend and neighboring pastor in Buffalo that his health was gone. During his convalescence, Neumann spent some time with the Redemptorists in Rochester.

For four years, I had spared myself no pain to bring the parishes under my care to a fervor similar to that which I had observed at St. Joseph's Parish in Rochester. This, as well as a natural, or rather supernatural, desire to live in a community of priests where I would not have to be exposed alone to the thousand dangers of the world, made me suddenly resolve to request from Father Prost...admittance into the Congregation of the Most Holy Redeemer...and received from him acceptance in a letter of the 16th of September from Baltimore.[70]

After a year of novitiate, on January 16, 1842, John Neumann professed his religious vows as a Redemptorist, the first to do so in North America.

I now belong body and soul to the Congregation of the Most Holy Redeemer. The corporal and spiritual aid mutually given and received, the edification and good example which, in a society of this kind, one has around him till death, wonderfully facilitate the life I am now leading, the vocation to which I have been called. I have every reason to hope that death will be more welcome to me in the holy Congregation than it usually is to seculars.[71]

Neumann continued to live his life as a sincere religious. Even after his ordination to the episcopacy, he continued in the fraternity of the confreres, had a Redemptorist as his confessor and made his monthly day and yearly extended retreat in the community. He often wore his habit when in their midst, disrobing from the more distinguished garb of bishop. It was his will and testament to be buried among his confreres in death and it is for that reason that his shrine is located in St. Peter the Apostle's Parish in Philadelphia. For him, the religious life became a safe place to live his profound spirituality. He directed other religious to live the life he himself embraced. *Your chief study is your rule. If you observe it faithfully and conscientiously, God will bless your work. Our labors are crowned not so much by our own efforts as by God's blessing.*[72]

Conclusion

From all indications, Neumann was a holy man; but proving it to a Roman tribunal investigating the heroicity virtue in the saint was not easy. The judge protested: "The testimony shows the Venerable Servant of God to have been indeed a good and pious man and bishop, remarkably zealous for God's glory and the salvation of souls, but it does not show that he surpassed the bounds of ordinary virtue of the sort that any upright priest, missionary, religious or especially bishop would have."[73]

The postulator returned argument that the judges had conceded to John Neumann a high place in heaven but how could they have come to that conclusion if not on the testimony of the witness presented? It was finally Pope Benedict XV who settled the debate.

"The merits of an active man are measured not so much in the number of deeds performed, as in their thoroughness and stability. For true activity does not consist in mere noise; it is not the creature of a day, but it unfolds itself in the present, it is the fruit of the past and should be the good seed of the future. Are not these very characteristics that mark of the activity of Venerable Neumann. Bearing all this in mind, no one will any longer doubt that the simplicity of the work performed by our Venerable Servant of God did not hinder him from becoming a marvelous example of activity. The very simplicity has forced us...to impress on our children...the proclamation of the heroic virtues of Neumann, since all find in the new hero an example not difficult to imitate."[74]

This decree is footnoted in the Vatican Council's document *Lumen Gentium* and notes that Benedict XV *unraveled the question and taught openly that the one norm for heroic virtue is the faithful perpetual and constant carrying out of the duties and obligations of one's proper state in life.*[75]

In 1860, Fr. O'Hara sent word to Rome that the American Church had lost a hero. He had died and was gone from the earth. In 1977, Pope Paul VI canonized the same man which, in effect, gave him back not as a man living on earth but as a saint and companion who, by the simplicity and the thoroughness of his deeds, gives all an example to imitate. In that regard, he is still with us.

Endnotes

1. Archives of the *Sacred Congregation de Propaganda Fide*, Rome, Italy, Vol. XVIII, January 7, 1860.
2. Paul VI, AAS, 1977.
3. Benedict XV, AAS, 1922.
4. Bouyer, Louis, *A History of Christian Spirituality*, vol.I, trans. by Ryan, Mary Perkins, New York: Desclee, 1963, p. vii.
5. Alexander, Jon, "What Do Recent Writers Mean by Spirituality," *Spirituality Today*, September, 1980, p. 250. Hereafter cited as "Alexander."
6. Curley, Michael J., C.Ss.R., *Venerable John Neumann, C.Ss.R.*, Washington: The Catholic University of America Press, 1952, p. 373. Hereafter cited as "Curley."
7. Neumann's passport showing his American citizenship can be found in the Archives of the Redemptorists of the Baltimore Province, Neumanniana.
8. Rush, Alfred C., C.Ss.R., trans. and ed., *The Autobiography of St. John Neumann, C.Ss.R.*, Boston: St. Paul Books & Media, 1977, p. 17. Hereafter cited as "Rush."
9. Ibid., p. 19.
10. Ibid., p. 20.
11. Ibid.
12. Ibid., p. 21.
13. Ibid., p. 21.
14. Ibid., p. 21–22.
15. Ibid., p. 22.
16. Ibid., p. 22.
17. Huber, August Kurt, trans. Schmandt, Raymond H., "John N. Neumann's Student Years in Prague, 1833–1835" *Records of the American Historical Society of Philadelphia*, 89 (Number 1–4, 1978).
18. Ibid.
19. Light, Dale B., *Rome and the New Republic*, Notre Dame: Notre Dame University, p. 247.
20. Ibid.
21. Metz, Johannes Baptist, trans. Krury, John, *Poverty of Spirit*, New York: Paulist Press, 1998, p. 10. Hereafter cited as "Metz."
22. Neumann, trans Hayden, William, "Spiritual Journal" *Spicilegium Historicum, Congregationis SSmi Redemptoris, 1978–79*, March 4, 1834. Hereafter cited as "Journal."
23. 2 Cor. 12:10.
24. Journal, May 1, 1835.
25. Journal, December 22, 1834.
26. Journal, June 10, 1835.
27. Metz, p. 38.

28. Berger, John A., C.Ss.R., trans. Grimm, Eugene, C.Ss.R., *Life of Right Rev. John N. Neumann*, New York: Benzinger Brothers, 1984, p.212. Hereafter cited as "Berger."

29. Berger, p. 211.

30. Berger, pp. 75–76.

31. Metz, pp. 50–52.

32. Journal, December 12, 1834.

33. Gal. 2:20.

34. Dolan, Jay P., *The Immigrant Church*, Baltimore: The Johns Hopkins University Press, 1975, p. 44. Hereafter cited as "Dolan."

35. Neumann's Letter of June 27, 1836.

36. Edited from Neumann's prayers as recorded in Berger upon his ordination as subdeacon, deacon, and priest, pp. 151 and following.

37. *The American Heritage Dictionary of the English Language*, Fourth Edition, Boston: Houghton Mifflin Company, 2000.

38. Journal, October 1, 1834.

39. Ibid., May 11, 1834.

40. Alexander, p. 250.

41. Dulles, Avery, S.J., *Models of the Church*. Garden City: Doubleday and Company, 1974, p. 2. Hereafter cited as "Dulles."

42. Light, Dale B., *Rome and the New Republic*, University of Notre Dame Press, 1996, p. 254.

43. Berger, p. 70.

44. Neumann's Theological Notes, "*De Statu Religioso*," Redemptorist Archives of the Baltimore Province, Neumanniana.

45. Neumann Letter, January 3, 1850.

46. Berger, p. 372.

47. Neumann Letter, February 5, 1836.

48. *Catholic Herald*, Philadelphia, January 7, 1860.

49. Berger, p. 424.

50. See Gannon, Michael V., ed. Ellis, John Tracy, "Before and After Modernism: The Intellectual Isolation of the American Priest," The Catholic Priest in the United States: Historical Investigations, Collegeville: St. John's University, 1971.

51. Lenhart, J.M., O.Cap. "Projected Missionary Seminary for America," *Social Justice Review*, May 1941, p. 50.

52. Neumann Letter, May 31, 1839.

53. Matthaeser, Willibald, O.S.B., "The Proposed Mission Seminary at Altotting, 1845," *Social Justice Review*, November, 1935, p. 250.).

54. See Boever, Richard A., C.Ss.R., "A Pressing Need of the German Immigrants, Proposed German Seminary to Train Men for Ministry in America," *The North American Historical Bulletin*, 2010.

55. Dolan, p. 8.

56. Hudson, Winthrop S., *Religion in America*, New York: Charles Scribner's Sons, 1965, p. 175.

57. *The Catholic Instructor*, Philadelphia, April 17, 1852.

58. Journal, March 22, 1836.

59. Journal, July 6, 1836.

60. Berger, p. 167.

61. Berger, p. 298.

62. Berger, p. 268.

63. Berger, p. 216. "When Easter of 1840 rolled round, it found Father Neumann completely broken down. He was seized with intermittent fever in its most violent and obstinate form, and for three months he was prey to its weakening attacks, being often obliged to keep to his bed."

64. Berger, p. 281. "At last his brethren believed themselves in duty bound to procure from the Provincial for Father Neumann to submit to medical treatment. A physician was consulted, and, after a thorough examination of the sick man, declared his lungs involved: the worst results were to be feared if remedies were not promptly administered."

65. Berger, p. 372.

66. Berger, p. 374.

67. Curley, Michael J., C.Ss.R., *Venerable John Neumann, C.Ss.R.*, Washington: Catholic University of America, 1952, p. 353.

68. Neumann Pastoral Letter, 1854.

69. Neumann Pastoral Letter, 1855.

70. Rush, p. 39.

71. Neumann Letter, January 16, 1842.

72. Berger, p. 329.

73. *Positio Super Virtutibus, Animadversiones*, p. 30.

74. "*Decretum approbationis virtutem in causa beatificationis et canonizationis Servi Dei joannis Nepomuceni Neumann*," *Acta Apostolic Sedis*, 14, 1922.

75. Rush, Alfred C., C.Ss.R., "The Second Vatican Council, 1962–1965 and Bishop Neumann," Records of the American Catholic Historical Society, vol. 85, (September–December), p. 125.

FUNERAL OBSEQUIES

THE DIOCESE OF PHILADELPHIA was deeply moved by Neumann's death, and many showed their affection for the saint in the funeral rites. These were recorded in a short booklet entitled "Funeral Obsequies" (*Obsequies,* published by Downing & Daly, Philadelphia, 1860) and are reproduced here to demonstrate the affection shown to their beloved bishop. These include the letter of Brother Christopher Froehlich to Fr. Louis Coudehove, C.Ss.R., a friend of Neumann who had returned to Europe after some years on the American Mission; the sermon given on the Sunday before Neumann's funeral by his former vicar general in Philadelphia, Father Edward Sourin; the funeral eulogy of Archbishop Francis Kenrick.

These obsequies demonstrate the affection and high regard those closest to him had for Neumann. Brother Christopher stated the conviction of all concerned: The people "didn't pray for him after his death, but rather prayed to him for help."

Letter of Brother Christopher Froehlich, C.Ss.R., to Father Louis Coudenhove, C.Ss.R.

January 15, 1860

Reverend Father: A very important occasion has moved me to write again to your Reverence, and this occasion is the death of our dearly beloved Chief-Shepherd, the Most Reverend Bishop John Nep. Neumann. It filled us all with great grief and fright, for it came suddenly and unexpectedly and took from us of a loving and good father.

On Christmas, he (Neumann) rendered us the grace by saying the midnight Solemn High Mass. Before it he heard confessions in the evening until eleven o'clock. After the Solemn High Mass, he said a low Mass in the bishop's chapel and 10 o'clock found him offering a low Mass in St. John's Church. The Most Rev. Bishop Neumann scarcely craved for any hours of necessary rest in the night, for he worked indefatigably in spreading the glory and honor of God and the salvation of his faithful in the diocese either at home or on his journeys which he undertook on account of his appointment, and it can be said that he was a sacrifice for the honor of God and for salvation of souls, as his holy death showed.

In the week before Epiphany, Father Urbancik came from Pittsburgh to leave from here with three other priests to conduct missions in New York. On Thursday afternoon, the Rev. Superior said to Father Urbancik, "Will you please visit the Most Rev. Bishop this afternoon." Father Urbancik obeying, left the house around two o'clock. The Most Rev. Bishop was occupied with much work, but since he loved the members of our Congregation, he always knew how to take himself away for a few moments when someone of them came to him. Every member, whether he was Priest or Brother, was received joyfully. Among other things, he said to Father Urbancik, "I feel terrible today as I never felt before in my whole life." They continued talking and a bit later the Bishop remarked, "Let us always be prepared well, so that death may come at whatever time and at whatever place it pleases God."

This conversation took place on the eve of Epiphany at half past three in the afternoon. Towards evening of the same day, the news of the bishop's death was sent around. Definite news reached us later on and made us all sorrowful and frightened us and none of us could keep from shedding tears.

Most Rev. Bishop had gone over to the alderman about a certain matter. Returning from him he was about to cross the street, when he somewhat staggered. Coming across to the other side, he reached the steps of a house in which a protestant minister lived. On the steps he sunk on his knees and fell. Immediately two gentlemen ran to him and picked him up but the poor man took two or three breaths and then died.

These gentlemen, by looking at the cross and the ring, found out he was a Catholic bishop and so they immediately called up the Bishop's residence. After this, they carried him into the nearest house, because he couldn't be taken home until after the coroner saw him. One doctor declared that the deceased was struck with apoplexy. This is still unknown with full certitude. The news of the deceased Bishop spread rapidly and widely, and caused a universal sorrow.

On the feast of Epiphany, the Bishop's body was laid out in the home chapel. On Saturday, because of the great throngs of people he was carried over by men of the St. Vincent de Paul Society into the great chapel. This chapel was built a few years previously because of the scarcity of churches. Besides the above mentioned service, this sorrowful event was announced in all churches and preparations for the funeral were begun.

During his life time, the Bishop often expressed the wish that he would like to be buried amongst his confreres. Since he was a member of our Congregation, and since he expressed the wish that he would like to rest amongst us, we had in a certain way the right to demand his body. Very Rev. Bishop Wood said that it would be settled according to the statement of the most Rev. Archbishop. In the meantime throngs of people, Catholics, Protestants, and

Jews, were coming to the Bishop's residence in order to view the Bishop's body.

On Sunday night, Archbishop Kenrick came. Father Provincial with some priests from Baltimore and also fathers of our congregation in New York also arrived. Besides this, there arrived about 150 members of different Catholic societies from Baltimore. The Most Rev. Archbishop, loving our congregation immensely, decided the burial place in our favor. On Monday morning, about seven o'clock, all the local societies, the Baltimorean societies, and likewise the men of the Archconfraternity of the Holy Family with their badges, all were arranged in order in their respective places. The Society called "Hunters" which was founded some time previous for the celebration of divine service, began the procession with their musicians at the head. This whole procession made its way towards the main church. It seems that God Himself wished to celebrate on this day, for He sent a very clear day. Some days before and after the funeral the heavens were covered with heavy clouds. At the main church were gathered all the Catholic Sodalities from all the churches of the city, all the benevolent and relief societies. The order of the procession was conducted in the manner arranged on Epiphany. Between eight and nine o'clock the procession commenced from the Bishop's residence and went to St. John's church, where they arrived around ten o'clock. Since great throngs of people were running from all sides, such a great pushing began that all who fainted had to be carried away. Later on, the same thing happened at our church.

The procession was held in the following manner: At the head were the musicians, who played a very touching march written especially for this occasion. After them followed a line of officers and a society of "Hunters." The seminarians from St. Charles were next in the line; after them the Christian Brothers and the

Religious Orders; then the Society of St. Vincent de Paul, Catholic benevolent societies and the sodalities from the churches. Immediately after these sodalities, the hearse followed. This was very magnificent and the whole back of it was open. The sides of the hearse were made of glass so that the Bishop could be seen from all sides as he lay in a prepared open coffin, decked out in his episcopal vestments, wearing a mitre and crozier. Behind the hearse, which was drawn by four white horses, the clergy followed consisting of four hundred priests, four bishops and an archbishop and then the rest of the people. In St. John's church after the women's section was well occupied in the morning, the church was closed in order that the clergy and the various societies would be able to get in. The church was veiled in black, the windows were draped with black silk, the pictures covered with a thin black material and the candlesticks were covered with black. On the catafalque and alongside of it were burning large and small candles numbering around forty-two. On the right side a beautiful coffin was placed on whose top was found a silver cross and below it, on a silver plate, was the following inscription,

Joannes Nepomucenus Neumann
Episcopus Quartus Philadelphiensis Obit Non.
Januaranii Anno MDCCCLX.

The body of the Most Rev. Bishop was carried to and from the church by six priests. All the while his facial expression remained the same as during his life. The eulogy pronounced by Archbishop Kenrick as well as the entire funeral service, made a great impression. In the course of his talk the archbishop touched the hearts of many when he said: "Blessed is the servant, whom the Lord finds watching and at his work. Men should not specially prepare for death, but he should be perpetually ready. God did not have to announce to the deceased his approaching end with a long sickness nor any special event. No, for he was entirely prepared. He led a holy life, and he was fulfilling his office when the lord opened the gates and received him with open arms, saying, 'Come my servant, you have done enough, you have become a sacrifice for my glory, enter into the joy of Thy Lord.'"

After the ceremonies in St. John's Church, about one o'clock, the procession made its way to our church. At one o'clock we began to toll the large bell and closed the iron gates before our own church. We had to do this because of the great crowds of people. About three o'clock we rang all our bells. I had the privilege to be in the tower of the church and so I saw the coming procession. The immense throngs of people in the streets, in the windows of every house, on the roofs, the solemn ringing of the bells and the approach of the procession, all this touched me with a kind of amazement. Rev. Father Superior and some of the other fathers came first and at the main gate received the corpse which six priests carried from the hearse into the church. The parish society stood as guard before the church, in order that the priests and societies could get into the church. The church was practically filled with men. On account of the lack of time, we were unable to decorate our church as the St. John's church was; however, we had more space for the priests and the people.

In the evening about seven o'clock, the priests recited the office of the dead. At half past twelve, the church was closed so the people dispersed, we however stood there keeping vigil with six candles burning at the same time. The next day, it seemed as if there was a holiday. The crowds were pushing into the church, and the sidewalks likewise were jammed.

After the early morning Masses Bishop Wood celebrated the

Solemn Requiem Mass. He was assisted by Abbot Wimmer and about fifty priests who had come from all over the diocese. After the Mass, when the ceremonies were finished, the corpse was carried by priests into the lower chapel. The Jesuit Scholastics and the clergy were the only men allowed there. The blinds and the doors were closed and everything was performed with the lights on. If the chapel had not been closed, the throngs would have crushed themselves and the pews would have been destroyed, as had happen to the wagons on the streets upon which the people had climbed. It is good that our garden has a wall around it and not a fence. It used to have a fence. That would collapse. In the chapel, before the high altar, there was prepared a special crypt for the bishops. As the corpse of the Bishop was laid in the grave, there was much weeping especially among the German Fathers. After Bishop Wood gave the blessing, there was a cloth spread over the coffin, which will remain there until a marble tombstone is completed. Our seal and that of the Bishop will be carved out on it.

What must we say about the honor which the people are bestowing upon the deceased? The Bishop in his last will made in 1856 left all his furniture to his successor, provided he gives it to his successor. Therefore his most important things could not be obtained, but the trifling articles which he left behind him were all given out to the people. With great difficulty, I saved his religious habit which had been kept in our house in the Bishop's room. Even this they wanted to cut into pieces. This might still happen. Everything else was taken, even the wax which had melted from the candles standing at the body. The deceased Bishop's apparel was kissed by the people with great devotion; and if they could, the people would have cut it up. And one more thing, a woman filled with much hope begged permission to lay her stiff arm on the deceased Bishop's body. Permission was given and from that time on, as she says, it is somewhat better. Though not cured entirely, yet she has high hopes of a complete recovery. The grave is covered with blossoms and flowers and is constantly visited. Many have come to confession who have not gone for some years. When asked why the change, they answer that the death of the Bishop Neumann had moved them to it.

This Bishop, whose death made such a marvelous impression, was an example to all during his life. Everyone must admit that his life was one of humility and holiness. How humbly and simply he acted as a Bishop over such a large diocese! How many and great things he accomplished in the course of seven or eight years as a Bishop! Yes, God wished to make him known in a special way. Is it surprising? A man so humble and simple walked the streets without being recognized. He lived so unnoticed. Now, after his death, such a grand honor is bestowed upon him, from the noble and simple, from young and old, from poor and rich. Even the Protestants themselves and unbelievers were moved. The city of Philadelphia never witnessed such a sublime Catholic celebration. It is as if God was governing it in a special manner; everyone had to cooperate to overcome any disturbances. One hundred Special Police were sent to see that the procession was not interrupted by people or wagons. Yes, the crowds on the streets and on the roofs were tipping their hats to express their respect. There was not one offensive or disrespectful word either from the crowd or any individual. This is true of the newspapers, something exceptional. Did this all happen by accidents? Certainly not! A Higher Being was present. Even to our Congregation was shown respect and reverence because the deceased Bishop was one of ours.

It is fitting for us to follow his example of virtue, in which he was to us a shining model. We are rejoicing the more, because we have him amongst us. At the same time we are hopeful that he is a saint in heaven. This presumption, as mentioned above, was so prevalent among the people that they didn't pray for him after his death, but rather prayed to him for help.

This joy lessened the great efforts and labor which we sure had to undertake these days. I can say in truth that I was so fatigued I could hardly stand on my feet. It took me 8 days to get back to my regular daily routine of work. But all this, I willingly did and yet I would have done much more.

Now, however, I must end. It is about time and the paper is scarce. What's happening in Vienna? There is talk here that Europe is in for hard times. May God be with us and may the most Blessed Virgin Mary protect us. If you will be persecuted, come to us. We can stand many men here in America; we shall receive you with open arms. With sincere greetings in the Sacred Heart of Jesus and Mary, I am your most worthy servant and confrere.

Sermon delivered in St. John's Pro-Cathedral by Rev. E. J. Sourin at the Sunday Liturgy, the day before St. John's Neumann's funeral

It is not for me to anticipate what will be said in this Church tomorrow. Nevertheless, this is the Bishop's Congregation. We only serve you in trust at the particular request of the Bishop. Hence, I deem it well to remind you that one of the last acts of this truly learned, devoted, and saintly Bishop was to invoke a plenary blessing upon you all. For my part, I am sure that the hand of death was on him then. It has been my duty for a long time past to call on the Bishop, to consult with him about facts, which he knew better than I, and also to borrow from him valuable books, which I could not obtain from any other source. The last time I visited him, I noticed that he was very unwell. I begged him to let me go and call in the assistance of his physicians. But he answered with a smile, and said, "I will be well enough tomorrow." Tomorrow he went on one of his usual missions; in other words, he went to toil and suffer for the benefit of God's creatures, and did not again return. Having been closely associated with the Bishop for some time past, I can testify that upon many occasions, he was unable, on retiring at midnight, to utter a word to any one, so exhausted was he with the arduous labors of the day.

I do not intend to give you any special instruction upon this subject, but I will read the first words of the Epistle of St. Paul to the Romans, commencing with the 12th chapter, and will call your attention to the circumstance of how the Bishop has verified in his life the Apostle's recommendation.

"I beseech you, therefore, brethren, by the mercy of God that you present your bodies a living sacrifice, holy, pleasing to God, your reasonable service." What is the pith of the Apostle's exhortation to the Romans? Why does he say, I beseech you for the mercy of God, that you present your bodies...? It is that the Christian may recall from time to time, that God requires of him that he should offer himself, not as a dead victim, as the victims of the ancient law, but as a living sacrifice unto God. Our existence on this earth should be a living sacrifice for the honor and the glory of God. It should be a perpetual sacrifice—such as that which our venerated Bishop led from his early youth to the moment of death—a life devoted to God's service and the promotion of His will alone.

It has been observed, that it was strange he died so suddenly, so strong and robust did he always appear. And indeed he appeared to have an iron constitution. Yet such labors as he underwent, would, sooner or later, weigh down the strongest constitution. It has been eight years since the Bishop came among us. From that first day to the moment of his demise, the period has been, as he knew, one of labor and suffering. He knew, very well, my dear brethren, that when he came to this proud city, there were many, not only among those who differ from us in religion, but hundreds of our own faith, who have wished, as an occupant for the Episcopate of this Diocese, a man more according to the judgment and the tastes of the world; he, therefore, tried to avoid the cross laid upon him, and to shun the dignity. It was only when he had reason to believe that it was the will of God, that he should accept that mitre and that crozier, that he consented to do so. It was with the same spirit of self sacrifice that he has dwelt amongst us. He has labored through every part of the Diocese, and has, undoubtedly, done more for its better organization, and for the spread of piety throughout the various Congregations, than might have been otherwise done in even ten or twenty years by another individual. In one word, he spared himself in nothing. He has received the noblest, highest recompense that a priest or bishop can desire—to fall laboring in his Master's service. He was called away in the midst of his toils, his duties and his sufferings.

There was not in the United States, a Priest or Bishop his superior. He spoke some ten or twelve languages. Besides these literary acquirements, he was a profound theologian. When any of us were in doubt respecting any subject in theology, we could go to him for advice, and he could at once make plain the explanation we desired. He also possessed a thorough acquaintance with scientific subjects. I might here mention a circumstance which will tend to show the extensive learning and memory with which our beloved Bishop was gifted. On one occasion he visited Eden Hall, an Academy of education, with which you are all, perhaps, more or less acquainted. During his visit, the ladies of the seminary were examining a flower lately plucked, and found themselves at a loss to state, to what class of flowers this certain one belonged. True, they had their text books, and their works on Botany, but with all, they were unable to come to a conclusion respecting it. The Bishop was consulted. He told them it belonged to such a species of plant, such a class of flowers. This, you know, is a peculiar kind of knowledge—a kind which many persons would suppose a clergyman would not possess. So with regard to Astronomy and other departments of scientific knowledge, he was singularly at home.

Let us, according to the beautiful teachings of our religion, pray for him. Remember him when assisting at the sacrifice of the Mass; when repeating those prayers to which indulgences are attached, that God may give him a place of refreshment, life and peace, if he has not already attained to it.

Funeral Sermon of Archbishop Kenrick
for St. John Neumann,
Delivered at St. John's Pro-Cathedral on January 9, 1860

The text was taken from Luke 12:40–44

"Be you then always ready; for at what hour you think not, the Son of Man will come. And Peter said to him: Lord, dost thou speak this parable to us or likewise to all? And the Lord said: Who is the faithful and wise steward, whom his Lord sets over his family, to give them their measure of wheat in due season. Blessed is that servant, whom when his Lord shall come he shall find so doing. Verily I say to you he will set him over all that he possesses."

You perceive, my Christian brethren, that in the text selected for this occasion, the Apostle tells us, that we should be always ready for the messenger of death. He tells us, that neither he nor any human creature can know upon what day, or in what hour the Son of Man comes. Snatched away from our midst by the ruthless hand of death, as the deceased suddenly was, we are warned by his end to be prepared to meet the summons whenever it shall be given us. That the deceased servant of God was prepared for death might confidently be believed. He had lived in the performance of his duty, and death had found him doing the work which his Master had given him to do. Important spiritual interests had been entrusted to his charge, and in the performance of those duties he had been overtaken by death. Your beloved Bishop has been taken from your midst, and you are warned by the solemn dispensation, to be yourselves always ready; sudden as has been the stroke by which he has been deprived of life, we may hope, confidently hope, that this Prelate of the Church of God, this servant of the Lord has been rewarded with the crown in store for those who are always found doing the will of their Maker.

For myself, I have no hesitation in saying, that, at the moment of his death, he was found most acceptable to God, and that his soul found mercy from his Heavenly Father. Although human frailty is found even in perfection, though even the saints themselves are not free from the impurities of earthly life, and although the just and holy have something to expiate before their admittance into the Kingdom of God, yet we may hope that for him God has reserved the reward which only saints obtain.

To this end, let us hope that the prayers of his clergy, of his successor in office, of the flock whom he loved, and of the very many Christians beyond his own Diocese, may be efficacious in procuring his speedy entrance into the paradise of his risen Lord.

My dear brethren, although our chief duty is to pray for our departed Bishop, yet for your edification something may be said, without fear of contradiction, without fear of incurring the censure of any one, that he has been glorified beyond measure. What then shall I say of my departed brother?—one who was a faithful, prudent, and pure servant of his Master. He was a man, in great measure, unlike other men. Of his youth I know very little, but I know that he graduated in the University of his own country with the highest honors. He was a proficient in the sciences, in polite learning, and in all that is calculated to adorn the mind. Providence directed his course to this country, where he received from the hands of the venerable Bishop of New York ordination to the priesthood. He accepted the Episcopate in order that he might consecrate himself more entirely to the service of God and lead in the ways of salvation those who have wandered from virtue. He was, for a long time, a humble but energetic missionary in the western part of New York. He labored amidst dangers and troubles. His desire was to attain to the perfection of the saints. He embraced the Order of the Redemptorists, founded by the learned St. Alphonsus. That Order had little to attract him at that time, there being embraced in it comparatively few men, and these separated from each other by considerable portions of space. He, however, assumed the labors, which his new station entailed, until, at last, he became a Superior of the Order itself. He exercised his functions, as Superior, in Pittsburgh, Baltimore, and other places. He soon won the affections of his flock. His exhortations were earnest, his instructions replete with learning, and, although he made no display of his abilities, it was impossible that they could be concealed. He practiced a life of virtue and lived in the world a pattern of Christian purity.

It was these labors, and these virtues, that attracted the notice of the Prelate, the bishop of Pittsburgh, under whom he labored for several years, and it was on his commendation, I do not say recommendation, that he was promoted to the See which he has so lately filled. It was in reply to inquiries made of him that the bishop of Pittsburgh testified to the exalted character, the labors, learning, and prudence of Father Neumann. His name was accordingly placed second on the list of those who were candidates to supply the vacant See. The Holy Father judged proper to call him to the high office. Father Neumann would have shrunk from it, but the Pontiff enjoined it by a positive command. He bowed in submission to the Divine will. He loved retirement, he loved the society of his brethren, he loved the Church to which lie was attached, yet he forsook all to become the Bishop of Philadelphia. He did not rely upon his own abilities, or his own strength, but relying on the Almighty, prayed earnestly that He might furnish him with all the means necessary to discharge the duties of the Episcopate with fidelity and success.

My brethren, nearly eight years have passed away since your late Bishop was consecrated. It was on Passion Sunday, in the

Church of St. Alphonsus, in Baltimore. When he was only forty-one years of age, having accepted this office, I may appeal to you to testify how, since that time, he has discharged it—with what fidelity, with what devotedness he has labored for the salvation of his brethren. His Diocese was one of the most extensive and most important in the Union. It embraces a vast population, and, at the time he took it in care, numberless institutions were rising within its limits. He sought, by every means his power, to advance the interests of his Diocese, and to promote piety in it. He established the Devotion of the Forty Hours. His example, in this respect, has undoubtedly been influential in extending this Devotion to other Dioceses. He labored for the instruction of his people, it being his deep conviction, that on their Catholic education depends their perseverance in faith, and their adherence to the principles of piety. He maintained the institutions which he found established in the Diocese, and added to their number. He found himself, at the moment when he was called away, the father of a number of institutions that looked to him for their support and their direction. His people appreciated his zeal and learning, yet he possessed accomplishments of which the world knew not, and virtues of which Heaven alone took comprehensive cognizance. He multiplied the number of his clergy and treated all with a kind indulgence. He was a father to the poor, the humble and lowly. He shrunk, as it were, from contact with the rich. His years passed rapidly in doing good, and going round his Diocese instructing, admonishing, entreating, and laboring for the benefit of all, if he has been suddenly called away, what matter is it? He was prepared for the sudden stroke of death. The lesson given to us who survive, is, that we should be always ready. We are warned never to remain in a state of sin—never falter in the performance of our religious duties. It is an admonition to us ever to be mindful that we, too, may thus receive a hasty summons, and that our lives should be so passed as to he prepared at any time to meet it. To your late Bishop death could bring no terror. He was a man of prayer, daily communing with his God, in the contemplation of His high perfection.

We have reason to believe, my brethren, that after those few sighs and groans that caused those around him to think that life was about to cease, his spirit soared on high, to mingle with the saints of God, and with the holy Prelates of the Church.

Let us, then, brethren, give thanks to God, for having given to us so faithful, and so devoted a Prelate. Let us remember the example of his unexpected death. Let us cherish his memory, and try to imitate him in our humble spheres. Let us hope that he will plead for us before the throne of God, and that, through him, abundant blessings may be showered upon us.

Be careful, brethren, to correspond to each grace bestowed upon you. Be careful to fulfill all the duties of your station in life. Live as strangers and as pilgrims, abstaining from those carnal desires that war against the soul. Remember that heaven is your home. Be mindful of the uncertainty of life, and live with the consciousness that every day may be your last. When you go out in the morning to your affairs, understand well that you may not return alive to your home. When you lay down to rest at night, be fully sensible that the morning may find you a corpse. Commend your souls to God, and ask of him to forgive you your manifold faults and transgressions. Ask of him to guard you against the many dangers that beset you. Ask of Him to bestow His grace more abundantly upon you, that at the close of life you may be received into that kingdom, into which nothing defiled shall enter, but into which all the servants of our Lord and Master shall be promoted, there to enjoy with the saints the blessings of his presence forever and ever."

MEMORIAL OF PRACHATITZ
TO BISHOP NEUMANN

WHEN BISHOP NEUMANN traveled home to Prachatitz while on his European visit for the declaration of the Immaculate Conception of the Blessed Virgin Mary, one of the gifts given to him by the people of his hometown was a poem written by the people honoring him. It touched him deeply because he knew the affection it carried for him. Father John Berger, C.Ss.R., Neumann's nephew and first biographer and included the poem in the book (pp. 404–406), which was published in English by Benziger Brothers in 1884.

**To His Lordship, The Right Reverend
Bishop JOHN NEPOMUCENE NEUMANN,
Bishop of Philadelphia**

The best of sons, the pride and honor of his native place, this memorial is respectfully dedicated, as a slight token of esteem, by the representatives of the city in commemoration of his happy return to the home of his infancy, and in memory of his departure thence.

> *PRACHATITZ, the year of our Lord, 1855.*
> *God hath not given thee in vain*
> *A noble soul, a spirit choice.*
> *Regardless of all toil and pain,*
> *Go forth, obedient to His voice!*

For thou hast heard the call divine
Unto a life of toil and care;
But, fired with love, that soul of thine
Shrinks not to labor everywhere.
Like to the fishermen of old,
Obedient to the Master's call,
With hearts sincere, with spirits bold,
Who left their nets, who gave their all,
Thou, too, hast gladly cast aside
The glittering fetters of the heart
And all that flatters human pride,
To choose the nobler, 'better part.'
Led on by God's protecting hand,
Across Atlantic's billows far,
Unto a strange, benighted land,
The holy cross, thy guiding star,
That standard of our saving faith,
In triumph there thou didst display,
Thou'lt grasp it faithful unto death,
Loyal and true thou'lt own its sway.
Thy God watched o'er thee when alone
On arid plain, in forest dim,
Where thou the seed of faith hath sown,
And nourished well for love of Him,
Who well repaid thy toil and pain,
Since thou didst labor for thy God;
Lo! it sprang up as golden grain.
And idols sank beneath the sod.
Because a faithful servant thou
In lesser things hath been, thy Lord
Hath set thee over greater now,

And glorious shall be thy reward.
Hail, faithful shepherd, to thy fame
Thy Lord hath added honors new,
Far, far beyond all earthly claim,
Rich guerdon of the 'chosen few.'
Off in the West, where thy flock feeds,
The Lord of Hosts bestowed on thee,
For noble acts, heroic deeds,
In Holy Church high dignity.
Thee hath the Lord most kindly led
To view once more thy childhood's home,
To greet loved friends, whose hearts oft sped
In anxious thought where thou didst roam.
O'er prairies vast, through forests grand
That teem with Nature's riches rare,
Yes, in that strange and distant land
Our spirit traced thee everywhere.
Permit us, then, most honored guest,
Our welcomes at thy feet to lay,
By which the joy that swells our breast
In trembling accents we would say.
Accept the heart-felt salutation,
Feeble though the tribute be,
Accept the love and veneration
Thy native city brings to thee!
And, noblest of her sons and best,
Whose virtues magnify her fame,
List graciously to our request:
When'er thy glance rests on these names,
Think kindly of thy home of yore.
May God be with thee evermore!

NEUMANN'S LETTERS
FROM AMERICA
to *Family and Friends*
in Bohemia

THESE LETTERS can be found among a collection called the Rodler Papers, which include twenty-four letters written by Neumann to family and to friends in the clergy in Bohemia. While in America, St. John Neumann wrote home to his family almost every year.

The Rodler Papers were selected for inclusion because they were primarily correspondence between Neumann and the people he loved. And they are less concerned with business than with communication between friends and family. Only letters from America are included in this grouping—letters that he wrote home from other places in Europe were not included. The letters help demonstrate the inner heart of St. John Neumann.

New York
June 27, 1836

Reverend Sir Dean (Endres),

If I omitted to give you information immediately after my arrival in America, I only did so in order to be able to write more good and pleasant news at once.

All things considered my journey passed off very well, only somewhat slowly. Still I will keep a more particular description of it for a letter to my dear parents, which I intend to write soon.

Already on the vigil of Trinity-Sunday we sighted America through a fine mist. On Sunday evening we anchored at Quarantine about one hour from Staten Island. It is indescribable how good it is for human eyes when one sees land again after wandering about for 40 days. In spite of the heavy rain we all stood on deck as long as anything could be seen and took delight in the beautiful green of the shore, in the light-red houses and in the landed estates which could not be painted more beautifully. All who could only stand on their feet a little came and as if by magic lost all sickness and weakness. There was no end to the rejoicing and singing. What happiness may not the just man feel, when on his deathbed he sees the end of his misery approach and the land of his yearning lie before him:

But the rejoicing soon had an end. The Captain announced that the wind was unfavorable and as we had some sick aboard we would have to remain some days yet, perhaps a week even at sea, which was all the more unpleasant as the water was stinking already for 14 days and full of worms, and the provisions had disappeared to a great extent. Besides that there was a strong contrary wind and entering the harbor was dangerous. So we waited some days. There was no improvement, therefore, with the Captain's permission I crossed over to Staten Island in a row-boat, and from there I rode with the steamer 'Hercules' to New York, which was about three hours distant from the boat.

It was the feast of Corpus Christi, about 11 o'clock, when I landed in America. You can well imagine how I felt. My first care now was to find a Catholic church, because as I had not brought along any address, I could not hope to find out a priest by asking in an entirely strange land. In spite of a constant downpour,

I walked along the mile-long streets of the city until evening. I found a large number of churches, chapels etc., but no Catholic Church wanted to show itself. I had to put all my philological knowledge together to explain to myself from the inscriptions of these buildings, often decorated with ideal beauty, whether and in which Christ they believed. Often there was nothing on the top of the church-roof, often a weather-cock, sometimes a cross indeed, but over the cross, a weather-cock. The devil, I thought to myself, may present himself ever so beautifully, still he must let his cloven foot be seen a little. All these houses and chapels were closed, only from one Wesleyan chapel I saw some men come out, with their hats on their heads and cigars in their mouths. For this day my search was fruitless and I was forced to take lodging for the night with a Swiss inn-keeper. He told me then also on the following morning, in which direction of the city, which in extent yields nothing to Paris, I could find the nearest Catholic church. At last I recognized it by the simple cross, and when I afterwards made inquiries about it in the neighborhood, I found out that it was English Catholic. In the school adjoining it, I then got the address of the Most Rev. Bishop and of the German pastor who lived with him. In an hour I was then at the Cathedral, beside the episcopal residence. At my ringing a short copper-red servant came, who led me first to Rev. Raffeiner, for whom Rev. Cannon Rass in Strassburg had given me some books to take along. He was greatly delighted at my arrival and told me that the former had written on my account to the Most Rev. Bishop and already three weeks ago a letter had been sent to Europe, informing him of my reception into the diocese of New York....

Father Raffeiner brought me at once to the Most Rev. Bishop Dubois—a born Frenchman—who in his glad surprise did not know whether he should address me in Latin, French or English.

As soon as he had seen my testimonials, he told me at once, that he was determined to receive me into his diocese; he had expected several others, who were to have come with me and was sorry that it could not have been. He was just in greatest need for a German priest, and was on the point of asking the Bishop of Philadelphia for one. At the same time he said that he was compelled to ordain me at once. When I represented to him, that it could not be done, as I had no written dimissorials from his Excellency, even if I left with his knowledge and consent and that I wished to be able to prepare myself for some months for the reception of the Holy Orders, he answered that he could and must ordain me as soon as he returned from the visitation already scheduled, which in spite of his age of 80 years he conducts every year without interruption.

As there is here no Religious Fund nor Benefices, I was ordained Subdeacon on the 19th of this month, Deacon on the 24th, and priest on tile 25th of the title of the American Mission. Yesterday, being the feast of the holy Martyrs John and Paul, I celebrated my First Holy Mass in the German Church of St. Nicolas; it was as solemn as it could possibly be here. After the Gospel, Father Raffeiner preached the sermon before a crowded assembly of people, whom the feast, unheard of here, had attracted. 0h, how I wished to know that all my dear ones were here in body! From my whole heart I prayed to God for all of you, and called down His blessing on you. At the end, I gave 30 children their First Holy Communion, for which I had prepared them since my arrival.

A special pleasure was prepared for me after the First Holy Mass. My little communicants came with their parents, thanked me for the trouble I had with them, and according to their means, brought me so much, that it was clear to me, how I would be able to reach my distant mission-station. My present Most Rev. Bishop, namely, has assigned to me the region between the Lakes Ontario and Erie, near Niagara Falls, where there are several German congregations, which I am to unite into one congregation from Buffalo.

Father Raffeiner furnished me with new clothes instead of mine, worn out in stage-coaches and on the ship. The Most Rev. Bishop loaned me, in view of possible repayment, the supplement for my necessary travelling money, and so I will set out tomorrow morning with bag and baggage by steamer for Albany, then via Utica to Rochester and from there to Buffalo, which is about 500 American miles distant from New York.

According to the direction of the Most Rev. Bishop, I shall stay for some time in Rochester, because the numerous German congregations there has been missing almost all the blessings of our holy religion already for years.

Buffalo is situated on the same Lake as Detroit, from there I shall be able to forward easily and surer the church furnishings destined from the church made up of converted Indians, existing there. My Mass-vestments, given to me as a present as well as myself are entirely intact. As often as I see and use them, I shall remember the donors. Pictures and rosaries soon turned out here to be too few, I ask, therefore, that your Reverence and all the benefactors of the poor American Catholics to remember us soon with a plentiful supply of pictures, rosaries etc. If anyone should, as I expect, soon present himself, who wishes to go to America I ask to send me by all means pictures and crucifixes for the decoration of the church, because in the churches here everything looks as if the enemy had been in them.

In conclusion I ask you, my Reverend Dean, to remember me before our Good God; to your prayers and to those of the other priests of Prachatitz and of the other pious benefactors I recommend the Germans of North America, who are languishing not only in bodily, but still more in spiritual want. Their misery is greater, than you are able to imagine; they persecute their priests, accuse their Bishops. There is an almost total lack of Christian pious books and prayer-books. How can this lack be best met, at least to some extent? What a great reward awaits him, who gives not only a drink of cold water to those who ask, but who allays their spiritual hunger, when they ask for it; who almost forces them to receive worthily the real food of heaven! Oh, pray as much as you can!

Your obediently beholden parishioner,
Johann, Nep. Neumann

P.S. I ask your Reverence to write to me very soon, if you do not do it yourself, then by another and have the letter sent to me through Rev. Father Dichtl.

Erie County, Cayuga
June 4, 1837

Reverend Sir, (Father Hermann Dichtl)

You can easily imagine how much I yearned for news from my dear fatherland, as in spite of the five letters, which I have written since my departure from Bohemia, I have not received a syllable. I have not received your first letter, without doubt, on account of a defect in the address. Not till today, when I returned from a mission in the vicinity of Niagara Falls to Williamsville, I learned that there was a letter for me in the post-office. From the address I recognized at once, the hand of the sub-prior of Strassburg, to whom I had just sent a letter.

Your silence has often inspired the thought that matters in Bohemia were miscarrying, something which seemed all the more probable, when I thought of my own situation in similar circumstances. But God be praised, these obstacles promise a good outcome. There will be a few difficulties to meet here in America, if God, as I firmly trust, will help us. We will be able to reap fruit with determination and resignation to all the dispositions of Providence. You certainly desire to know how I find myself justified for these fond hopes and what I consider beneficial from known situations.

When in Munich I learned from a priest of the Cincinnati diocese that I could promise myself little in Philadelphia, I was at once determined to go among the Indians. God in the meantime arranged otherwise and I became a missionary in the diocese of New York, and was sent among the Germans between Lakes Erie and Ontario, by which I seemed for the time to be forced to banish the idea of working with the Indians, if not forever, at least for a long time. But now I realize that that was the best way to bring me nearer to my goal. I interested myself in learning the ideas and views of the bishops in the United States. For the western Indians in the United States much has been done, because according to a decision of the Roman See, the missions of this immense district have been entrusted to the Jesuits; this I learned from a Jesuit of the St. Louis diocese. However others are by no means excluded, but this resolution seems rather to direct the attention of this Holy Order to this part of pagan America.

But now, as I am scarcely a half-day's journey distant from Canada, I have often made inquiries, especially from the Canadian French who come here to make their Easter-duty, about the condition of the Catholic religion there. Naturally it is sad enough. There is indeed already for a long time a well equipped seminary in Montreal, but the activity of the Most Rev. Bishops confines itself, almost exclusively to the French and the Irish who live on the northern shore of the St. Lawrence River five to six miles further north, as well as along Lakes Huron and Superior. There are immense stretches, mostly of forests, which are inhabited only by Indians, and are seldom visited by European fur-traders, no more than every couple years. Therefore there is enough work there, and what is to be especially noted, the English government, which has the civilization of the Indians more at heart than that of the United States, often supports with money and provisions the undertaking of the missionaries without distinction of religion.

For a long time already I resolved to visit the Most Rev. Bishop of Kingston on Lake Ontario, and learn from him how the project might best be undertaken and promoted for the Indians, but until now this was entirely impossible—I have three churches, on which building is going on all the time and, in a few weeks, I shall again begin a new one. The extensive pastoral care, the schools, all that prevented me from going to Kingston. But now I have found a way to be absent for four weeks.

Although I continue to live in extreme want, I can nevertheless assure you, that my mission district might support 2 or 3 priests as well as me alone. Only poor priests can thrive among the Germans here. The reason is, because one can little think of a fixed dwelling-place and the priest is forced to be travelling all the time because only a few good Catholics settle in the villages. Decent Catholics look for some stretch of woods, build in the midst of it a block-house in 2 or 3 days, then begin with burning and felling of trees, prepare fields for potatoes and oats, in 6–7 years also for wheat. All the Germans live at a distance of 2-10-12 miles from the church, often 2–4 miles from each other in the midst of the woods. Then the heart of the pastor can have pleasure in nothing else than the salvation of the souls of his children. If he loves comfort, honor or even money, he loses in a moment patience and with it all confidence; his effectiveness is at an end. For the rest, the character of the German Catholic gives the priest much work. A foolish love of freedom has brought a large part of them to this country. Now they are free here, in a certain way their own masters, yet in reality nothing but deceived slaves of their ambition. He would like so much to imitate his temporal rights in spiritual matters, choose for himself a God, or at least a way of honoring Him which suits his inclination. The example of the Americans surrounding him, partly through ignorance, partly through depravity, makes an impression on him. As these are usually wealthy, and he tries above all to become so too, he believes that he must imitate them also in their unbelief. Oh, to how many evils has this mania for imitation already given the occasion of sin to the German!

Here, moreover, everyone is called upon to contribute to the support of the church, the school, the pastor and teacher; and be his contribution ever so small, he believes that by it he has bought the right to speak like a dictator in everything. Here the views differ widely. Everyone wants the unessential customs of his country, of his diocese, or even of his parish introduced and obeyed exactly. Here patience is the most prudent thing. As soon as they notice unyielding character, the congregations generally divide into two parts and only after a long time, reunite when they are tired of obstinacy and resistance.

A priest must love poverty also because his parishioners are, as a rule, avaricious. In order to maintain his necessary independence, it is allowable for him only seldom and to a small amount to make any claims on their possessions; otherwise they get angry. Only the disinterestedness of the priest can secure for him all the necessaries. These are the observations made by Father Raffeiner in New York and Father Pax in Buffalo. They receive confirmation every day.

If at times whole congregations write to a bishop in Germany for a priest, or without further ado apply to a priest directly and plead for God's sake with the most touching sentiments for the bread of life and if everything turns out as he wished it, then the moment of arrival is indeed sweet and very consoling; but among the Germans it does not last long; the applicants think indeed of the great grace which will fall to their lot, but soon the reality becomes unbearable.

Should any of the confreres in Bohemia make up their minds to devote themselves to the missions of the northern Indians, we could find no better preparation for that than in the temporary ministry among the Germans. The body becomes hardened by fasting, travelling and frequent exertions; one gradually becomes acquainted with the country, its customs and in many sections also with the Indians, because many of them are constantly roaming around.

Should any be able to leave at once, I should advise to travel via Havre, because conditions are bad on the ships from Bremen. American ships are the best. Nevertheless I shall write again about this matter, as soon as I can spare a few minutes.

English I have learned very easily from an American to whom I taught astronomy. Through frequent intercourse with the French I have also learned their language, so that I understand everything perfectly and can also converse with them without much trouble.

I shall speak with my Most Rev. Bishop Dubois about the project of my dear Schmidt in regard to mathematics. The bishop will visit this section in two or three weeks to confer the Sacrament of Confirmation, and I hope for very much from this.

As I am in the constant necessity of travelling through the forests, I have endeavored to renew my botanical acquirements by the collection of many flowers and plants, entirely unknown in our forests and regions. Should I find any occasion to forward them to Bohemia, I believe that I should do it, all the more, as I met many very strange things. You gave me also very great pleasure by informing me in regard to the state of health of my dear parents and sisters and brother. The resolution of my sister has given me altogether new strength; if only the merciful God would enkindle in me more and more the fire of Christian Love of my neighbor. As soon as possible I will send to my parents and to my brother especially a letter, begun already long ago.

For the admirers of Bolzano I should wish that they might dispute for some time with the superstitious Americans; this is the best means to quiet all doubts. As soon as one separates one-self from Holy Church and her teaching only in a single thought, one becomes unreasonable, falls into contradictions, doubts and stubborn heresy.

It gives me great pleasure that Rev. Dr. Koch remembers me and I ask him as well as all my fellow-students in Budweis and Prague for their prayers. I ask you to inform our pious country-women in Lorraine that I am ever mindful of my promise to pray for them, that they also do it for me, I expect from their compassion.

How is the Institute for the Blind getting along? I recall often and with pleasure the hours which I spent there. Here in America a much larger one would be necessary for the poor blinded, for unbelievers. May God some time finally have mercy on this country, bring it to its sense by want and misery.

Give my respects also to the family of Reinhold, Lampl, etc. as also to all my benefactors, who by their generosity have furthered my undertaking until now. If you have collected any money, I ask you to send it either to Augsburg or Strassburg (Rev. Fr. Fischer, Schmid, Brug, Rass) for German books. "The Confessions of St. Theresa; Katherine Emmerich; -Goffine" as also for the works of the Mechitarist Fathers, of St. Alphonsus Liguori etc. these cannot be obtained here at all and yet they are so necessary. I ask you to send them direct.

Should you make any regulations in regard to any proposed Society of Missionaries, I give my approval to everything in advance.

Remember in your prayers
Your Most obedient,
Joh. Nep. Franz Neumann, Missionary

Erie County, North Bush
September 5, 1837

Dear Parents,

Although I had determined to await your answer to my letters before informing you of my present condition, the thought of a long uncertainty that you would constantly have regarding me induces me not to delay to gladden you with a new letter. You will doubtless remember my promise to describe to you my present circumstances. I can do that now more easily as I have no fear that the description will make you die either of joy or of sorrow.

By order of the Most Rev. Bishop of New York, I am now living for the most part here in a place called North Bush because a congregation can more easily be formed around the Church of St. John the Baptist in this place. Like an old German emperor with his court, I travel about with my church utensils to my three old congregations of Williamsville, North Bush and Cayagua Creek. To these will be added two more churches as I have received two acres of land from an American gentleman as a site for a church; and as the rather large number of French and Irish in the vicinity of Niagara Falls makes a church or at least a chapel there a necessity.

You would never have imagine, much less I, when looking at the engraving of Niagara Falls that one day it would lie within my parish. During favorable weather, especially in the morning and evening, I can hear the rush of the waters in my house just like a heavy hailstorm. However, I have not yet seen the falls; in a fortnight I shall be there.

Here in North Bush I am living with a native of Lorraine who looks for payment only in the next world. He also furnishes me with board and has placed at my disposal a room which is very similar to yours and to the little one I had at home. Moreover, the house is not of brick or stone but of maple and oak. My furniture consists of four chairs which I bought recently out of my savings, two leather trunks from Budweis and books. For your consolation, I must also inform you that the lumber for my future rectory is already cut and that my people are looking forward with joy to the time when they will be able to fill it with potatoes, grain and bacon. Here I have not yet suffered hunger and as soon as any of my garments is somewhat worn out, it is soon replaced by another, even if I do not know where it comes from. The linen which you gave me is likewise still in fairly good condition. You see, then, that everything is according to my desire. Were it otherwise, that is, had I greater domestic cares and conveniences my necessary and constant traveling would soon be too difficult for me. This way I live free and can look upon every house as my home. As is usual in virgin forests, the roads from one settlement to another are swampy. Where the roads are made of hard trunks of trees, they look just like the road from Pfefferschlag between Kubinbers and Schwarzberg.

The surrounding country is very monotonous, very level and the view restricted on account of the nearby thick forest. Where, after years of exertion, the forests have been cleared, they first plant grass. This dies out completely in two or three years and must be sown again. Then comes potatoes, which are much larger than in Bohemia. Finally in seven or eight years, wheat and peas can also be planted.

The state of New York is far less cultivated than New England or Pennsylvania. The fields and meadows have quite the same appearance as our field in Reuth except that everything is level.

Since spring, food here is six times more expensive than in past years, a bushel of potatoes costs in New York two piasters. The famine is due partly to the excess of immigration, partly to the usurers who find no hindrance to their greedy speculations. Very few silver coins have been seen here since April; and the hundred kinds of banknotes are on account of the daily bankruptcies continually decreasing in value. What once had happened in Austria on account of the Financepatent happens here almost every month on account of the avarice of several merchants. Thousands of Germans who entered into business partnerships with Americans will this year be reduced to beggary. This year's crops are good but the scarcity of money still continues and therefore all industry is at a standstill.

In the forests there are to be found trees that are for the most part different from those in our own country; at least they are very distinct. Sugar maples, beech, oaks, linden trees are most common. In our section of the country, there are also many peach trees. Enclosed you will find a few sugar maple leaves; even these leaves seem to have a flavor about them. The trees are tapped in the spring and ordinarily a tree will give about a bucket of sugar water in a day. This is then boiled down to a thirtieth part, producing a species of honey-sweet sugar syrup, here called molasses. Boil this to half the amount and we have brown sugar which can be refined. The taste of sugar, thus produced, combines the sweetness of honey with the sweetness of the white sugar which is made from sugar cane in the southern states. Apple, pear and cherry trees are doing well but they are still very young as the land has been cultivated only a few years. But plum trees do not thrive at all here. They dry up and are unfruitful. They are entirely unknown to the Americans. It is remarkable that among apples and pears you find no wormy ones. This may be due to the fact that there are scarcely any cocoons at all and very few colored butterflies. Besides that, the fruit is not so sweet as in Europe. Equally rare are snails and eyeworms. But a class of gnats, called mosquitoes, is very numerous, especially in the forests. Their sting will almost always cause inflammation and they are the greatest trouble for men and animals. As I often preach I must constantly drive them off with my handkerchief. In the beginning, this fighting of mosquitoes and the hefty slaps re sounding from the cheeks of the congregation disturbs me in preaching and the congregation in listening. At night it is necessary to start a great smoke fire around the house and the stables if one wants to sleep for their continuous buzzing defies all thought of rest. But smoke drives them away.

Plants and flowers are varied and very beautiful. Lilies grow wild in the forest, likewise currants, gooseberries, blackberries and raspberries. Black strawberries are not found here but red are. Among the fruitful forest plants we find most commonly thorn apples (crabapples) birdcherries, hickory nuts, butternuts, etc. Among birds, I found crows and night owl. But the birds are far more beautiful here; however they are rarely heard to sing. Beautiful yellow canaries with black wings, colibri (humming birds), the smallest of the birds, and several species of parrots are found the most pleasing. Bears and wolves were found until lately; but now, it seems, they have been entirely destroyed by the Indians who constantly roam through the forests. Deer are also frequently met; so too, skunks whose odor is so abominable that in comparison with it a rotten carcass is perfume. Rabbits are smaller, very rare, and in winter they are white as snow. Poisonous rattle snakes are frequently met;

but against their bite the Indians have shown the immigrant various herbs. Among the many poisonous herbs, there are especially two kinds that are so harmful that they cause some a swelling of the members without being touched. The farmer with whom I live brushed against one of these with bare feet and for months had to suffer the most excruciating pain in both feet. Some people, however, can meddle with it without danger. They are called *rhus taxicodendron* and radicans. Both grow in the swamp.

The weather here is very unsettled. Seldom does rain or fair weather, heat or cold last more than a few days. The heat often reaches a temperature of 97 degrees and many are overcome by it. The majority of the immigrants who settle in the lowlands catch the putrid fever, of whom two or three in the same family, especially the children, may die of it.

The place from which I am writing to you lies between Lake Erie and Lake Ontario and is somewhat healthier on account of the most steady winds. These two lakes, like the others in North America, contain the purest drinking water but as the water is not so heavy as the salty sea water, it is far more dangerous for ships on account of frequent and violent storms. The great advantage of the inhabitants, these lakes are rich in fish.

I am entirely satisfied with my resolution and will probably have no time to walk about idle as John thought. As much as I should like to spend a few days with him, relating all to him myself and answering all the questions he would like to put to me, still I must check this longing and await more favorable days. I have promised to pay him a visit after a few years, and if it be the will of God, I will surely keep my promise. The ocean voyage agreed with me very much and if it were necessary, I could easily make up my mind to take it again. In the meantime, let the will of God be done in this and in all things. The reverend Dichtl in Prague, as well as the Reverend

Schmid in Vienna have written that the pain of my separation from my former pastor, though it has not ceased entirely, has diminished. The pastor wishes to be good to us in the future as he has been in the past. I have often wished to be able to be two persons so as to do the necessary work of a priest here and at the same time to be with you. But I am consoled and strengthened at the thought of divine reward after the labor is endured and of that life in which the beloved ones are not separated by any ocean. I am constantly thinking of you, of my brother and sisters and of all my friends. For all these I daily offer the Most Holy Sacrifice of the Mass and all my joys and sorrows. All the good which God wishes to do through me here will redound to your welfare as well as mine for, after God, I owe it chiefly to you that I am a priest.

What a joy it would be to you to see the love with which my parishioners meet me and to see our holy religion, through the help of divine grace, planted and nourished in the midst of these dark forests. If only the parents of my comrades knew how necessary priests are here; could they see the tears shed by those work, like the children of Israel in the Babylonian captivity, and for years were deprived of all divine service; could they see how many innocent children thirsting after knowledge grow up in ignorance and un-belief; how many are battling with death and pass away without having anyone to offer them the consolations of our regions! Could they imagine this and many other things, they would willingly do without temporal consolations and sacrifice many joys to be able to procure spiritual consolation for Catholic foreigners in North America. On the day of retribution, God would surely not let it pass without reward. From Lorraine and Alsace, there come so few priests because there, as a rule those who only study theology, are well-to-do, who from childhood have accustomed themselves to many comforts of life which they would have to forego in America.

I have not been sick one moment since I left with the exception of a few days of sea-sickness. How does it fare with brother and sisters, with Catherine and Veronica and my brothers-in-law. I would greatly rejoice if Charles and Philip would become a pair of American missionaries. I suppose Mary is studying diligently. Sister Johanna has chosen the better part. May God strengthen her in her pious intention. Will she write me soon? Did Aloisia pray for me at Marie-Zell? Wenzel also has a strong desire for deceptive happiness and he is sighing so much to come to the sugar land of America. He surely has not yet forgotten German. I could very well use him here if you could spare him. Do write to me all things as they seem at home—how it fares with our relatives, especially the Windisch and Faber families in Prachatitz, Dano Gruenai and Lennikau, where Jacob, for whom I was sponsor in Confirmation, and Felix are staying for the present.

I have distributed all the pictures and rosaries except the silver one. I'll make a present of that one to my Indian chief. At the first opportunity, send me another good supply, perhaps even through Rev Schmid. The holy oil stock and sick call pyx from my deceased grandmother are put to good use. As I have neither ciborium or monstrance, the pyx has to take the place of both. Equally of good service is the burse which I received from R P. Guenter. The Mass vestments, a remembrance of Prachatitz and its friends of missionaries, are beginning to wear out for they are packed and unpacked many times every week. I would long to have written to the Rev. Dean for another but I doubt whether he is still alive for otherwise he would surely have answered my letter. Of the Holy Masses which R.P. Danish gave me, I celebrated four in Rochester and the rest in Buffalo. If you or the Rev. Dean write to me, I beg you to send me some information of him as well as of the rest of the clergy. I greet you all, especially you my dear parents, then my brother and sisters, all my friends and relatives and companions and the whole of Prachatitz. I beg all you to pray for me that the Lord may grant me pardon of my sins and give strength and success to my words. I recommend you all to the loving Hearts of Jesus and the Virgin Mary. I remain,

Your obedient and grateful son,
John Nep. Neumann,
Missionary

Town of Tonawanda
October 7, 1838

Meine lieben Eltern und Geschwister:

Every day for a year I was waiting and believed that I could greet my brother Wenzel here in America. But now, as the equinoxes and fall-storms make ocean-travel dangerous, I have given up the hope of seeing him this year.

I received the last information about him through Rev. Rass in Strassburg, but I did not learn more than that he was in Paris. Should you, as I do not doubt, know his place of abode and address, I ask you to write to him, that he may leave for New York as soon as possible. I have deposited there with the Rev. German priest, Stephen Raffeiner, twenty-two Spanish dollars for him, that he may have the means to be able to travel to me with the steamboat on the Hudson from New York to Albany, and from Albany to Buffalo on the great Erie Canal, immediately after his arrival in New York.

He will learn at once at Father Raffeiner's in New York, or in Buffalo from Father Pax, where I am staying, something which I do not know for certain at this moment, as I am travelling about almost constantly and visiting my parish. But should he be in need of the necessary travelling-money in Havre de Grace, the last city in France, then he should write under what address I should send him that money to Paris, Rauen or Havre. Once he has landed in America, I will provide that we find one another soon. For the rest I should like it very much, if he came very soon, because I need him very much partly to take care of my house during my frequent absences, partly also on account of the school.

Your need have no further worry on account of our well-being, as we are in the hands of the Almighty God here as well as everywhere else. My labors are increasing daily; now I have five Catholic parishes to attend, of which the nearest is two hours, the farthest twelve hours distant from here. The Catholic parish in Rochester also, which at present has no priest, asks that I visit it, or even reside with it. I am waiting daily for instructions from the Most Reverend Bishop of New York.

The past year was very sad in many respects. Most likely you have read in the papers about the general bankruptcies; the effect on the people was very depressing. One saw almost no silver and the countless kinds of bank-notes, which today were good and tomorrow had no value, deprived many of their means of subsistence. On account of this shortage of money, there was also a general stagnation of trade and agriculture. Since the month of May there is indeed more money in circulation, but the uninterrupted heat and drought have done much injury to fruit.

During this summer the heat was greater than during the last thirty years; in the state of New York, it reached 98–100 degrees Fahrenheit several times. The western section of this state is generally flat, and the shortage of water can be explained easily from the fact that since spring it never soaked in three inches. This year potatoes will not yield one quarter of other years; a bushel, that otherwise cost about 20 silver francs, now already costs two florins C.M.

In the section, where I generally stay, namely on the bank of Niagara River, then along the great Erie Canal, very pernicious fevers broke out, so that 3–4 persons were sick in most houses. Still few only died in proportion. It was unheard of that several dropped dead suddenly from sunstroke. Thanks be to God, that at the time of the equinoxes the very cool winds from the upper lakes cooled the air and brought some rain.

To judge from the letter of Rev. P. Schmid in Verona, Father Dichtl is no longer in Prague, something that seems certain to me from the silence of the latter to my letter of the month of May. I ask you to forward to him the enclosed note from Rev. Schmid. I should have liked it very much if I could have seen him in America, as he promised me; he believes that he can come here in 2 or 3 years.

In the diocese of New York, there would be enough work for five German priests; the Rev. Vicar General of the diocese of Cincinnati assures me of the same fact for the state of Ohio. In his last letter, Father Dichtl gives much very gratifying news about my sister Johanna. God be praised that He has inspired her with the praiseworthy resolution of devoting herself entirely to works of charity and has also strengthened her to carry out this holy resolve under the most unfavorable circumstances. I greet her from my heart, and ask her for her prayers for the poor and scattered churches in America.

Through the charity of several friends of the Missions, I have a case of books in Prague, (because I have not yet received them) should this case still be in Prague, I ask Father Dichtl to send the same, if possible, to Strassburg, from Strassburg Rev. Rass would have the kindness to send it by the Roulage acceleree to my brother Wenzl, best to Havre, and he could then bring it along in spring. Another way would be to send it from Prague to the Austrian consul in Hamburg, through him to the Austrian consul in New York, but in this case I would first have to be informed.

No day or night passes that I do not think often and long of you and our friends and relations. I can repay you for the benefits which you have conferred on me with nothing, except that I offer all my joys and sorrows, above all our Lord in the Holy Sacrifice of the Mass for you. I have also offered many holy Masses for my deceased grandparents and relations, as well as for my sponsors at Baptisms and Confirmation and for all our benefactors, and will continue to do so in future, if God gives me the grace for that.

I should like very much to see all of you in Prachatitz again; many remarkable things could be told about my trip and the New World; for the present this is not possible, but in two years, if not sooner, I have sure hope of being able to visit you, if God so wills. Write to me, I beseech you, dearest parents, very soon, how you are getting along, whether there has been any change in our family or in those of our sisters; how the Miko families in Prachatitz and Krumau are getting along.

I greet all of you and send my compliments to the Rev. Dean, the School Director, and the Rev. Chaplains; to the Rev. Pastor, Ant. Dichtl, as well as to my benefactors. As soon as I shall have received a letter from you, I will at once write a much longer one. I ask R.P. Zdiarsky to write first how our never-to-be-forgotten fellow-students are getting along and if each single one of them has already done much good for the glory of God; then he may rest assured that I will at once write the promised letter.

I commend you all to the protection of God, of the Most Blessed Virgin Mary and remain,

Your most beholden son,
Joh. Neumann, Miss.

Tonawanda
May 31, 1839

Reverend Sir (Father Hermann Dichtl),

The second step in fulfillment of our agreement has, with God's help been taken. Herewith I am sending in writing the authorization of Bishop Dubois, which assures two or three priests or finished theologians the reception into the Diocese of New York. Nothing is wanting now, except that God the Holy Ghost inspire some of his faithful to devote themselves to the service of our Holy Church in North America.

The need of Catholic priests and the spiritual desolation of the faithful are increasing day by day. Judging from a human standpoint, the disproportion would have lamentable results,—only God alone is the support of His Church.

When I arrived here three years ago, it seemed as if the Germans in America would soon have sufficient priests, offers came from everywhere sometimes from excellent priests in Germany. But the results taught otherwise. The return to their country of several missionaries partly also the description of the conditions awaiting them made them think otherwise. Some unworthy priests have brought great scandals. They came here in order to force upon the people also their blasphemous heresies in the confusion of so many others, or they wished to continue their disorderly life. However, the strict vigilance of the Most Reverend Bishops over doctrine and morals of the priests bring them into greater discredit here than in Europe, and they, therefore, return before they have learned to speak a word in English. Other pious and learned priests return on account of old age and bad health, some also because the corruption of morals seems too great, nay even beyond cure. The latter condition is often enough not without foundation in the case of emigrants and French Canadians, also alas of the Germans.

However, among the Germans the causes are manifold; because as a rule, only adventurers and restless liberty enthusiasts come here or such as wish to escape the threatening hand of Justice, etc. But with the cool and sincere Catholics of character, all the attacks of heresy, which here are very fanatical, are mostly fruitless. Apostasy from the Faith is very rare here, in spite of many and strong inducements, and is more than compensated by the number of those who return to the bosom of the only saving mother. If, humanly speaking, any danger threatens the Church here, it is to be feared above all from the total lack or insufficiency of Christian Education. The education of growing youth takes up much of the missionary's time; but God's help shows itself here in an almost wonderful way. The desire for knowledge and the ardor of our young Catholics is often astonishing.

When I was preparing the children at Williamsville for First Communion last year for three months, many came daily five and six miles, even in the worst weather to attend the instruction, and in this short time not only the main chapters of Christian doctrine and morals had been sufficiently learned but greater progress had also been made in reading and writing, than according to my experience, is made often in several years only with hard work. As the Catholic Church needs nothing except respect and love, than that men should learn to know her well, but here in so many parishes, the opportunity is wanting an account of the need of priests, your Reverence can easily realize why the Most Rev. Bishops of North America long for good priests. They have often been deceived, and unawares have sent scandal into their parishes.

At every yearly Visitation, they are convinced of the increasing number of German Catholics. The favorable moment has, therefore, arrived, when I should like to remind my dear confreres of the words of Christ: "Go into the whole world and teach all nations." The Germans have little to expect from the seminaries in America now in existence. They are incomplete and studying is expensive. Most Rev. Bishop Hughes, the coadjutor of Bishop Dubois, wrote through Father Raffeiner that several others can come next year. The most Rev. Bishop of Boston in Massachusetts also wants a German priest for his diocese. Another large field for German missionaries is opening up in the new republic of Texas, northwest of the Gulf of Mexico, because many Germans from the United States are preparing to go there, nay, as one reads, have already formed settlements there.

Not to forget the hardships of the missionary, I must say, that they are many and considerable, but just for that reason, this calling will be welcome to those, who like myself, seek an occasion to propitiate the Divine Justice for sins committed. The violence, which the missionary must do to himself, is for him a consoling pledge of heaven. The mission-work among the immigrant Germans, French and Irish has, indeed, not the attraction, I might almost say, the adventure of that among the Indians, but it is also not so laborious and the thought that one is taking care of the members of the body of Christ and attending, according to the will of our Divine Master, to the lost sheep of the house of Israel, necessarily teaches humility and love of God and His Holy Church.

It generally happens, that those congregations are the most ungrateful who before begged most earnestly for a pastor. In this difficult case, the missionary must reckon it an honor that he can follow a long and eagerly expected Messiah, who also was badly received, in patient resignation. Everyone, who leaves his fatherland to serve our Holy Church in this country, must be determined to sell his life as dearly as possible; his motto must be: "*Auto patria auto more.*"

It is gratifying and very consoling for every Catholic in America to learn, that only his Faith alone is the same everywhere and with all nations. My Germans, as also the Irish, have often told me, that they now felt themselves more strengthened in their Faith, since they, especially the former, see the most perfect unity of Faith with all Catholics, whether they come from Italy, Germany, Ireland, France or America, and amid the indescribable confusion of the Protestants. Here we find the unity of our Church demonstrated to eyes and minds, so that belief in it loses almost all merit.

The number of Catholics is almost beyond number, people are beginning to notice them, and in some places they predominate. In Buffalo, at the mouth of Niagara River into Lake Erie, a German Catholic Church is now being erected of brick, which is 180 ft. long and 80 ft. wide. It will be under roof this year yet, and the largest church in the State of New York, if not the United States. Father Pax, a missionary from the Diocese of Metz, lets one hope from his tireless zeal, that he will soon have completed this undertaking of his. The poor Germans in Buffalo and in this vicinity are exerting all their strength, to promote the undertaking. The Irish also, who have had a priest for some years, who formerly was a Methodist preacher, will also begin a church of their own this summer, as the future one for the Germans, will be too small even for them.

Six miles from Buffalo is the church of St. John the Baptist, built from untrimmed tree-stumps. Here I generally stay and here is the mission-house. Eleven miles north of Buffalo is the church of Sts. Peter and Paul, and still seven miles further the small unfinished church which perhaps, this summer yet, will be dedicated to St. John Nepomuk (Transit). Ten miles east of Buffalo is the church of the holy Archangel Michael, on Cayuga Creek. Thirty miles south of Buffalo is the church at Sheldon which may like-wise be finished this summer. Its patroness is the Blessed Virgin Mary.

These five churches and the congregations belonging to them are entrusted to my care. Moreover, I visit the congregations in Rochester, seventy miles; in Batavia, forty miles; and one on the big Canal, Pendleton, twelve miles from here.

At most of these churches a building is in course of erection for the priest and for school. Father Merz, an eighty-year old missionary, takes care of the congregations south of Buffalo—Eden, Collins, and Hamburg—and at present is engaged in building an orphan asylum, which he will soon have completed with the aid of pious benefactors from northern Germany. He will entrust the direction of the same to the Sisters. From all this you, Reverend Sir, can conclude that much can be done here, and still more could be accomplished, if there were more priests here. The 500 mile stretch along the Erie Canal and the Hudson River, frequently settled by Germans, is almost entirely unprovided for, because the older Germans hardly learn enough English to wish you "Good Day"; they feel the rod of God: "I will speak to this people in other languages and tongues." God only grant that their prayer for a German priest may soon be heard. For in spite of their petitions, I can scarcely ever visit them, as I am hardly equal to my so extensive circuit.

In regard to the Mission-House, I have by no means given up the idea, because its utility and indispensable necessity is the same and becomes more apparent. To carry out the idea, I should advise, but without presuming to dictate, to begin on a small scale. Even should the moment not yet have arrived, when an institution can be erected in our Fatherland. The temporary promise of voluntary poverty and of entire obedience to the respective Bishops with which some are willing to devote themselves to the American Mission, assures us of the realization of a congregation of Missionary priests. If only two or three can come, they would have to take over a station like Rochester, Albany, Syracuse or Lancaster.

In case of sickness, or if more come than can be used at once, this house would furnish a quiet place to prepare for the beginning or continuation of apostolic labors. I have provided the means for a bare existence; perhaps, in case of need, our Most Reverend Bishops could ask the Leopoldinen-Foundation for a little help. Therefore, I beg my dear confreres, who have made the resolution to come to America, to come in God's name, and to support the arms of our militant and praying Church. If Father Sartori in Vienna, Father Schmidt in Verona, Father Peter Michel, Schneider, etc., still find themselves willing, I urgently invite them. Should any others report, I beg you to look especially into this: whether their principles agree with the teachings of the Roman Catholic Church exactly, for otherwise they would have to take along double travelling expenses for a journey home. Should my request and invitation, as I hope, receive a hearing, I ask you, Reverend Sir, and also in the contrary case, to let me know kindly at once, and mention not only the names but also the time, when they will begin their journey. Without much luggage, the way over Paris and Havre is the best. I ask you also to inform the Dean of the Cathedral in Augsburg of the possible resolution of budding missionaries, for Father Raffeiner, will most likely visit him in the course of this summer, and from him they could ask for further instructions. They should also provide themselves with the necessary altar linens and church vestments, missals can be bought here. I also advise that they provide themselves well with clothing, because those made here are very expensive but nevertheless of poor quality.

Should anything at times be collected for me by my benefactors, I ask you to hold it until enough is collected to be able to send us a beautiful monstrance. I have heard nothing whatever from my parents, brother, Rev. Schmidt etc., but I daily expect my brother—he should have been in Paris a year ago. I am anxious to learn how my sister Johanna likes it in Prague, and whether she is constantly making progress in holy love.

In conclusion, I heartily greet you, Reverend Sir, and all who rejoice at our plans. Assure my dear parents, brothers, sisters and friends in and around Prachatitz, that I offer the first Mass every Sunday to God for them. I likewise greet the Reverend Dean and his assistants, also our friends in Budweis and Prague, my fellow students and I humbly recommend myself to their prayers. Should any benefit be derived for America also from the Institute of Father Rosmini, I ask you to let me know. Greet also my friends in Linz, Munich, Augsburg etc.

Praised be Jesus Christ forever!

Joh. Nep. Neumann.

Village of the Falls of Niagara
July 20, 1839

Praised be Jesus Christ!
Reverend Sir (Anthony Rost, President of Seminary, Prague),

I am using the time of my short stay at Niagara Falls, to ask you to pardon my silence until now, because, as Father Dichtl has most likely given you news of my whereabouts and condition, I should have been able to write nothing new with my otherwise unchanged situation.

What induces me especially to write to you, Reverend Sir, is that I believe that Father Dichtl has left Prague, and that he has not received my last letter with the episcopal faculties because I have not yet received an answer to it.

Not long ago the Most Reverend Bishop Dubois, from New York, also wrote to me, that a letter had come to him from Prague, inquiring, whether I received the money collected for me in the

Archdiocese of Prague and the Diocese of Budweis. I have not yet received a report of it.

Now if you know anything of this matter, as I do not doubt, I ask you, Reverend Sir, to let me know, from whom in New York or Buffalo I should make inquiries, and heartily to thank in my name the benefactors otherwise unknown to me. I can do nothing else than pray to God the Lord for them for blessing and grace, and with His holy grace, I will also do this diligently.

I have sent to Father Dichtl the authorization of the Bishop to accept several priests or theologians, who have completed their studies for the Diocese of New York; should you, Reverend Sir, find among our confreres in the never-to-be-forgotten Seminary of Prague one or several, who in childlike faith and obedience to our Holy Church wish to devote themselves to the somewhat arduous life of a missionary in N. America, I ask you to greatly encourage them, and when Father Dichtl has the full number, to let me know, that I may be able to send them the necessary reception from New York. Most Rev. Bishop Hughes, the coadjutor of this diocese, declared not long ago, that he would receive 7–8 if they were to be had. It is not necessary that they speak English and French, because they can learn both more easily here. Other qualifications of a priest for America would be health and a strong constitution on account of the frequent journeys, fasting and preaching; still the lack of these ought not to frighten anyone; because where human powers fail, the heavenly ones come to one's aid.

As far as I am concerned, I am very well pleased with my present sphere of action, because I came here to atone for my many sins, and I do not believe that there is a better opportunity. May God only grant that I may administer my office more worthily than I have done hitherto.

The Catholic religion is increasing here more and more, not so much through conversions as through immigration; but the former also are not very rare. Many Catholics live in extreme poverty, especially the Irish. They live in very low cottages of boards, often without windows, chairs or beds. Their burial outfits are their ordinary clothes, in which they lie on a little straw or moss. When I visit them to prepare them for the reception of the Holy Sacraments and to hear their Confession, I sit down on the floor beside them. Children and adults make the holy sign of the cross at the entrance of the priest, and their greeting: "Welcome, Father" sounds more consoling from believing heart than the stereotyped compliments of vain Frenchmen. Even if various national vices are blamed on the Irish, this comes from the bad treatment, which they received in their fatherland.

The agreement of Catholics in Faith and Morals is nowhere more striking than in N. Am., for they come here from almost all parts of the world. As regards Protestantism, I was somewhat disappointed at first in my expectations. I thought that the numberless kinds and varieties of the same would have to bring forth complete coldness; but I found the opposite. As in politics, so the Americans are more fanatical in religion. The most noisy preaching in the public streets and bridges, the importunity of the bible-distributors, their terrible prophecies about the last day, etc., etc., make Catholic wonder. If one attends a Methodist meeting, one imagines himself carried back to the times of Elias and the priests of Baal. Everyone prays aloud, one howls, the other weeps, several sing, until finally one or several sink down as dead and become deathly pale, foam at the mouth, groan, roll about convulsively, and so revive the Holy Ghost, as they claim sacrilegiously.

I should wish that all those super-wise ones attended a jumper-meeting; without doubt they would learn to believe in the devil, if there is still a spark of grace in them. Our Catholics are greatly strengthened by this in their faith as here they can perceive with their eyes and ears what they heard at home, namely, that only the Catholic Church is one, holy, catholic and apostolic.

In conclusion, I ask you, Reverend Sir, to be mindful of me during the holy sacrifice of the Mass, that God may grant me true contrition and a good hour of death. For the same favor I ask my dear confreres and fellow students, whom I greet heartily. Should you know my dear sister Johanna, who is with the Sisters of Charity, I ask her to inform my dear parents of my good health. I should also be pleased, if I could receive news from Prachatitz, from Father Dichtl, and Rev. Schmid in Verona and from Budweis from Rev. Schawel. I commend myself also most respectfully to my most Reverend Rector and the Rev. Spiritual Director.

May the grace of our Lord Jesus Christ through your intercession, Reverend Sir, be with

Your most beholden servant,
Joh. Nep. Neumann

North Busch
October 4, 1839

Dearest parents,

I am extraordinarily glad to be able to let know at length the arrival of my dear brother Wenzel, who took me by surprise two days before his Names-day. I had already almost given up the hope to see him here, all the more as it was the time of the equinoxes when ocean-travel, although not very dangerous, is very troublesome and inconvenient on account of the prevailing storms.

As I had received no news or letter at all from you since my departure from Prachatitz, I was in almost complete ignorance of your circumstances; his stories, greetings, descriptions transplanted me to our native city, which I cannot forget. I thank God that

He has strengthened you for such great sacrifices, that forgetting earthly consolations you give up all claim to that which children otherwise owe to their parents; that it affords you pleasure to serve the Lord in domestic solitude and parental poverty.

There has been no change in my circumstances since my last letter. The past summer was very good, only a little too hot. Our section suffered great loss on account of the indescribable hordes of grasshoppers, which suddenly devoured everything green, so that the cattle had no pasture. In my garden in front of the house also little remains of the cabbage, beans and peas. But these are not the kind of grasshoppers of the East Morgenland but they are all together like those in Bohemia. All attempts to destroy and lessen them were fruitless. They were so numerous that the ground, as if covered, was filled with them, even in the living rooms and in church they were numerous. All told, the evil is lessened by the fact that everything was spared in other places, often very near.

The great heat during the day and cold at night, combined with the circumstance that the stretch of land along the Niagara lies very low and is swampy, have caused very much sickness during this year. Most prevalent is gastric fever and, with the children, whooping-cough. There are very few families in this region into which the former has not entered, in most, old and young are in bed, and where one remains spared and can do the necessary domestic work, it is envied. Scarcely a day passes when I am not called to one or several sick. As painful and lingering as this sickness is, hardly one in twenty dies from it. As far as I am concerned, so far I have always been blessed with perfect health.

Conditions are always improving with our holy religion; it is always spreading more, and the fervor of Catholics is increasing considerably. Twelve years ago there were scarcely 2–3 Catholic families in Buffalo, now the parish already numbers 1,500 communicants. Rev. Pax, who attends this mission, began as you may perhaps have already learned, built a church during the summer of last year which is 180 feet long and 80 feet wide, and therefore should be the largest church in the state of New York. By next summer, if otherwise it is God's will, it will be finished so far that divine services can be held in the same.

Many have already acknowledged that it was for the welfare of their souls that they came to America because in Europe, where churches and all that belongs to divine service exist and are supported as it were by themselves, they had little love for either. Here, on the contrary, if moved by God and their conscience they work during long days and weeks at the construction of a church and the furnishing of the same, God's goodness reveals itself to them; the thought of the church, which they can now really call their own, is very' consoling to them; they do not wish to have labored in vain and are not so easily absent from divine service. Moreover, besides God's Grace, their circumstance, especially those in the country, makes them poor as a church-mouse as the saying goes, and it is beneficial. When they have toiled and moiled for a long time and have found that their hearts, which long for happiness, is not satisfied in the life of the world, in work and sweat, they surrender to the Lord in their poverty, and with this now voluntary poverty contentment, faith and child-like love of God now enter their hearts. Thus, forced like Simon the Cyrene, they carry the cross after our Lord and are overwhelmed with hitherto unknown graces.

Finally those have a great share in this revival of our holy religion who not only pray to God for its welfare but who also prove their love and attachment to the same by pious gifts. The interest and support, which the American mission finds in our fatherland, is a sufficient proof that Bohemia does not wish to bury the pledge entrusted to it by Sts. Cyril and Methodius, but grateful to God and full of charity, the distant fellow-Christian has determined to repay blessing with blessing. God's glory will be their reward. Nevertheless I also owe special thanks to my dear countrymen in Prachatitz and Budweis, to the fraternal charity and paternal care of our Rev. and Most Rev. Clergy. The many and very costly presents will always spur me on more to honor their confidence and charity for me, poor missionary. I make a conscientious use of them, and that I pray for them as often as I see and use them. That is all that I can do, and as long as I live, I will not forget to do so. I ask you especially, dear parents, to make known my heartfelt greetings and thanks to the parish of Wallern. I wish it God's blessing here and in eternity for their many favors.

Your most beholden son,

Johan Nep. Neumann

October 12, 1842

My Dearest Parents,

Since last year when my brother Wenzel wrote you, many things have happened which I should have liked to write to you at once, because it would have brought you much consolation. Nothing but the uncertainty whether you receive our letters or not has kept me from it since these eight years we have not been able to receive a line from you.

Shortly after the last letter last summer had been sent off, I made a rather long missionary tour through the states of New York, Ohio and Maryland. After I had traveled 3,000 American miles, I reached Baltimore again safely, with God's help, at the beginning of December. On the feast of the Most Holy Heart of Jesus, I professed my vows as they are made in the Congregation of the Most Holy Redeemer. To it, I now belong body and soul. The mutual physical and spiritual help, the edification, and the good example which one has around him till his death in such a spiritual society, makes my life and my office a great deal easier for me. I also hope confidently that death in this holy society will not be as unwelcome to me as is generally the case with people of the world.

From here I often make trips into the neighboring states of Virginia and Pennsylvania where our German Catholics are living scattered everywhere. The German Catholic parish in Baltimore numbers about 4,000 souls, for whom there are now only two priests.

The Archbishop of the United States is also here, and besides our Church, there are six other churches mostly of English Catholics. The Catholic Church does not only increase through immigration but also through the frequent conversion of protestants and unbelievers. Hardly a Sunday passes but that one or several adults make the Catholic profession of faith in our church or are baptized. In fact we have again about twenty who will be Catholics in 3–4 weeks. These conversions would increase much more if our church were large enough to be able to receive all who would gladly attend divine services. As it is, however, scarcely one-third of the German Catholics find room. Before a Catholic church in America is finished, it is already too small. Our Rev. Superior, P. Alexander Czwitkowicz, who will also take this letter across the ocean, has begun to build since last fall a large and beautiful church for the German Catholic congregation of this city. The astonishment of the Americans at this church, which now is finished already to the roof and is built entirely after the European style, is just as great as the joy of Catholics. It is only a pity that the means to finish it quickly are not in hand. Our German Catholics are mostly immigrants who have spent most of their money on passage across and are unfamiliar with the language, the business and the work here. They fall into the most dire need with their families, as they are without wages for months.

As Baltimore is in the same latitude as Spain, it often gets very hot here in summer and it frequently storms. Sea breezes do not cool off the air and fevers prevail especially among recent immigrants who are not yet accustomed to the air and different foods.

Recently, Brother Wenzel was also invested in our Congregation and is now more contented and more calm than he ever was. Not long ago, he was sent by the Reverend Superior to Norwalk in the State of Ohio, 12 miles south of Lake Erie, where we also have a church and a house. His work, as a lay brother consists in taking care of the kitchen, garden, etc. for the Fathers there. Now his health is much better than it was until now, namely he is almost entirely free of his toothache. From all this, dear parents, you can easily learn that both of us are well cared for. We also wish you from our whole heart that you are prospering in body but especially in soul, and we will never cease to recommend all of you to the Lord, that according to His infinite goodness, He may reward you a thousand-fold for all that you have done for us in body and soul. That God has protected us in dangers and blessed our work is something which we most likely owe most to your prayers and to those of all our friends and benefactors of the American missions. The world is converted more by fervent, persevering prayer than by all other labors; therefore, we ask you and all our friends and relatives in Prachatitz and the neighborhood, often to offer their prayers, holy Masses and other good works to the Lord of the world that He may never abandon us, but perhaps graciously bless all our work.

Our cousins are not in Gettysburg, in the state of Pennsylvania, at present but in York because they have leased their property in

Gettysburg, but will return to it next spring. They have written to me several times and invited me to visit them. On next Wednesday I shall go to Pennsylvania to celebrate in several parishes of German Catholics the jubilee which His Holiness the Pope has proclaimed for the Kingdom of Spain. On the 23, 24, 25 of this month, I shall be with the German Catholics of York, and get to know our dear relations personally. Cousin Hartlaub has also invited me to baptize his little daughter who was born recently, something that will also be done. You will, most likely, more easily learn of our meeting, conversations etc. from Aschaffenburg than from here.

In Baltimore, most of the Bavarians are from the region, of Wurtzburg, Aschaffenburg, Stockstadt, Great and Little Waldstadt and of Obernburg and Eisenbach. I have often also met some from Bohemia here but they scarcely are any credit to our country. In Richmond, the capitol of Virginia, I met a month ago a musician from Petschau who was also known in Prachatitz. His name is Oppel and he is a music teacher.

How are you faring in Prachatitz, who is still alive, who has already gone into eternity, and how are all getting along? I have not been able to learn anything at all since my brother Wenzel arrived here. I believe, indeed, that the wide separation and that the uncertainty on account of us has caused you much disquiet.

As I have already written, I have given up hope of seeing a letter from you here in America. The present journey of our Rev. Superior to Europe, lets us hope again in receiving a very long letter and many from you. During his trip, he will go to Vienna also and take along to America in the spring the letters for me that he finds there. If you know where Father Dichtl or Father Schmidt is, I ask you to give them my hearty greetings with the request to send me news through the Rev. Redemptorists Fathers at Maria Steigen in Vienna.

We commend ourselves also to the Reverend clergy of Prachatitz, especially to those who we know and we assure all who several years ago made us presents of so many and such valuable church furnishings, that I remember them gratefully when I make use of them Everything that the Rev. Canon Salbacher should have brought for me from Vienna to America was confiscated in London. I ask you to address everything that you wish to send to me in America as to: Rev. Alexander Czwitkowitz, at Maria Steigen, Vienna.

We heartily greet you all, parents, sisters, brothers-in-law, cousins, relations and friends, especially those who have taken such an interest in our welfare until now. Recommending all of you to the protection of Almighty God and to the intercession of our Holy Mother Mary and asking you to serve them most faithfully and with perseverance, I remain, dearest parents, your most beholden son,

Joh. Nep. Neumann
Priest of the Congregation of the Most Holy Redeemer

Baltimore
September 26, 1847

My dearest parents and sisters,

As a favorable opportunity presented itself of sending you a few lines, I am availing myself to it all the more eagerly as it is already a long time since last I wrote. The reason for my long silence is none other than that there has been nothing new happening either with me nor Brother Wenzel. At present he is in Pittsburgh, where I built a large gothic church, 175 feet long, 66 ft. wide, with ten stone pillars in the interior. This church was solemnly blessed, Oct. 4, 1846, and then I was transferred to Baltimore, where I now generally keep to myself.

The German Catholic parish, which we attend, is greatly increasing. When I was here before my departure for Pittsburgh, we two priests had less to do than seven priests have now. The number of baptisms since January 1, 1847 till today is 552. Besides we have three schools to attend. Since my last letter, both of us were generally well, as we are now accustomed to the climate of America. We are likewise entirely satisfied, and should be pleased to hear that all of you at home are just as satisfied.

There are always Protestants who ask to be received into the Catholic Church; many who become Catholic here were not baptized before, but show their gratitude to God by leading such a fervent Christian life as one can scarcely find in Europe. Last year, 36 adults became Catholic in our church, among them one-third Negroes, who are frequently becoming converts.

Of the war with Mexico (pronounced Mechico) we see as little as you do in Europe, and know the news also only from the newspapers or from the reports of crippled soldiers who return. Still, our army loses more from yellow fever than by battles, in which until now the Americans have always been victorious. Nevertheless both sides are tired of war and we daily await the news that peace has been concluded.

Here in Baltimore also, especially during the summer heat which often rises to 104 degrees (Fahrenheit) many are sick from dysentery and the ship-fever, but these prevail usually among the immigrants; otherwise the climate is hot, it is true but yet not unhealthy.

It will give me great pleasure to hear something once again from Prachatitz or from my school-companions. From time to time I receive presents of money and books from the Leopoldine-Verein, but I do not know who the benefactors are. Otherwise I have received no information from Prachatitz since the arrival of my brother Wenzel, although I wrote 3 or 4 times, except one bit of news through a priest of our Congregation who travelled through Prachatitz to Budweis, and he brought me no information.

Among other things, Bohemian is often spoken in our Mission-house. Besides myself, there is here a priest from Prague (P. Stelzig) and one from Moravia (P. Krutil), both of whom recall to my mind everything that I have forgotten about the Bohemian language.

I have heard the confessions of several exiled Poles in their language, which is closely allied to Bohemian; French and English are almost as easy and fluent for me as German, because for years already on my mission-trips I had to use them almost daily.

As we now have a house and church also in New Orleans, in the state of Louisiana, I have already begun to learn Spanish which is spoken in the southern states by Spaniards, Mexicans and by West Indies. At the age of 36 I shall be a child again! Still, this is the least.

In conclusion, I recommend you all to the protection of Almighty God and His Blessed Mother, and remain, my dearest parents, sisters and relatives,

Your most beloved son and friend,
P. Jon. Nep. Neumann, C.Ss.R.

Baltimore
June 10, 1851

Dearest Father—Dearest sisters,

Both of us here, Bro. Wenzel and myself, had given up hope ever to receive a letter from our dear home and from you, when suddenly both the letter of our dear relative Mr. John P Zahn made us glad and now also lately the letter of Mr. Felix Spinka and the first one from sister Caroline arrive safely.

At once I composed the writing in which both of us renounce forever in favor of our dear father all claims on the share of inheritance after the death of our not-to-be-forgotten mother. I am having this writing made legal according to all the usual laws here and hope that it will he legal also in Austria. I have not received this writing back from Detroit, where I had to send it so that Brother Wenzel could also sign it. His enclosed letter was on the way before it arrived here, still I hope that the writing will reach here in the course of the week, on which occasion, I will write something more. Here we have never yet received a letter from you. I cannot imagine what the reason may be. The surest way will be to address the letter for us to our cousin Mr. Joh. Zahn in Munich who will have the goodness of forwarding it to us here. It would please me to know the day of death of our deceased mother, of sister Veronica, and of all our deceased friends and relations that we may keep their anniversaries better.

Since I entered the Congregation of the Most Holy Redeemer in October, 1840, I got around in America quite considerably, especially in the first years when there were only a few of us. For the last five years, I have been in Baltimore, in the state of Maryland, and by the shortest road, about 570 American miles from Br. Wenzel. Our Superiors are very well pleased with him, and we both thank God the Lord that he has called us to this holy Congregation. With a few exceptions, I have been well all the time, and in spite of all the frequent travelling on the lakes, rivers, railroads and on horseback, I did not meet with a single accident, something which I must ascribe especially to your persevering prayer for me. Although no day passes that I do not imagine myself with some longing to be in my father's home and in the midst of my dear relations and friends, still I have never regretted that I devoted myself to the Mission in America. I have considered it my vocation from God to labor here for his glory, and for the spread and preservation of the Holy Faith among the poor German Catholics of North America.

The labors of all my confreres here enjoy the manifest blessing of God and so I hope, yes I certainly expect, that God will not fail to keep all of you and each one singly in His holy Grace, and let you have that blessing a hundredfold in this life and after death, with which the pleasures and advantages cannot be compared which we would perhaps have enjoyed had we remained at home together.

In the United States we have entire peace and all possible security. To be sure, there is a lack of it here and there, and especially in the sea-ports cities, excesses sometimes take place, but order is soon restored. We thought for a while that the mischief-makers would begin their activities also here. They did really try it here and there, but it stopped with some boastful speeches for which they were only ridiculed. They soon get tired of them as no one pays attention to them. They need five years before they can become citizens, and generally work and trouble have given them other ideas long before this time. Many of these unfortunates die in the hospitals of New York, Philadelphia and New Orleans unknown and unmourned.

I am sending herewith a dollar of California gold as a curiosity. The written acknowledgement has just come from Detroit; now I must have it signed by the Austrian ambassador or consul and then, most likely, I shall be able to forward it next week.

In conclusion I greet all of you and all our dear relations and acquaintances. I recommend myself to the prayers of the Rev. Dean Ruzika and the other Rev. Clergy of Prachatitz, of Rev. Dichtl, Schmidt and Zdiarsky and all my fellow-students or benefactors and remain,

> Your most devoted son and brother,
> Joh. N. Neumann, C.Ss.R.

September 10, 1851

Dearest Father and dear sisters,

The execution of this enclosed declaration has required a great more time than I expected at first. Both the considerable distance of Br. Wenzel and also the absence of the Royal, Imperial Austrian charge d'affaires from Washington are the reason for the delay. The latter was away for months and as there seemed to be no end of waiting, I sent the writing to New York to have it certified there by the Austrian consul. He too was away and so it is signed by the manager of the office there and is, as I believe, entirely in order and valid before the law.

Since my last letter, there has been no change in our condition here. The labors here are very numerous because very much still remains to be arranged until Church and school are in proper order. Our Catholic Germans in Baltimore live for the most part near the limits of the city, where the dwellings are cheapest, and as our church of St. Alphonsus is pretty near the northern boundary of the city, the care of souls is, at times, especially during the hot summer, very arduous, but, I hope, also meritorious.

God has always yet blessed the labors of the Congregation of the Most Holy Redeemer and so with great hardships we also have great consolations. Divine service here on Sunday is pretty much the same as everywhere. Holy Masses begin at 5:30. At 7 o'clock there is Holy Mass with exposition of the Bl. Sacrament, and after it, Benediction. At 9:30 the rosary is recited and after it follows High Mass with the sermon. In the afternoon at 2 o'clock there is Christian Doctrine, at 3 there is Vespers and afterwards Confraternity devotion and Benediction. In the evening at 7 o'clock there is devotion to the Holy Heart of Mary with a short sermon in honor of the Blessed Virgin and the prayers for the conversion of sinners.

The two churches which we have here now are packed on Sundays, especially the High Mass and the evening service, although many of the Germans still go to English churches; as soon as the third German church is finished, in 4–6 weeks, it will, without doubt, also be packed every Sunday. The entire Divine service except, of course, High Mass and Vespers, is in German. During the Holy Mass at 7 o'clock on Sunday, as also during the 8 o'clock Holy Mass on weekdays, the school children sing German hymns of which most are sung by us: Grosser Gott wir loben dich, Gnadenquelle, Lass mich Deine Leiden singen, Wir werfen uns darnieder, Hier liegt vor Deiner Majestat, Deinem Heiland, deinem Lehrer. The congregational singing, as well as the beautiful decoration of the altar, and the divine service which we conduct as solemnly as possible, makes visiting the church very attractive. The holy Sacraments of Penance and Holy Communion are received diligently by young and old. In the two churches, 300–400 go to Holy Communion every week, on feast-days many more. The different confraternities which have been introduced for men and women, then for the unmarried of both sexes, produce much fervor; they have their conferences and devotions.

All of this keeps us busy continually, all the more as we must attend several places in the state of Maryland and Pennsylvania where there are small congregations of German Catholics. Since Easter, we have no archbishop here as no news has yet come from Rome as to who will replace the lately deceased. Most likely, one of the older bishops will be transferred here as archbishop; in the meanwhile, prayers are offered every day throughout the archdiocese for an early and successful nomination of the archiepiscopal see.

I ask, in the name of both of us, to extend friendly greetings to our cousin, Mr. Spinka. Also to our little nephew, John Berger. It would give me great pleasure if the Lord God would give him a vocation for America. The best preparation for that would be that he were very obedient and diligent, receive the holy Sacraments diligently and not omit to recommend himself ever day to the most Blessed Virgin. The enclosed picture belongs to him.

In conclusion, I ask that you recommend me to the prayers of the Rev. Clergy of the city and to my fellow students. I remain

Your most beholden son and brother,

Joh. Nep. Neumann, C.Ss.R.

Philadelphia
April 21, 1852

Dearest Father and Dear Sisters,

I do not doubt that you have already received my last letter with the declaratory act. As much as I, as well as Br. Wenzel, wished to receive an answer, none came so far, the cause of which is the great distance in which we live apart from one another.

Since my last letter, a very great change has taken place in my regard, as you have perhaps already learned.

On April 22 of last year the Most Rev. Archbishop of Baltimore died, and the Holy See appointed the Most Rev. Bishop of Philadelphia as his successor. For this diocese of Philadelphia, vacated in this way, I was proposed to the Holy See by the Bishops in this country, without my knowing the least thing about it. When I heard what I had to expect, I could do little more, for already on Feb. 1, my appointment was settled in Rome. The news reached Baltimore already on March 1 of this year, and that in a private letter to the Most Rev. Archbishop. He came at once to the house of the Congregation of the Most Holy Redeemer, and as I was absent, he laid his own archiepiscopal cross and ring on my desk and left without saying a word to anyone. I knew indeed well what that meant, and when I visited him the next day, he let me read the letter. The papal bull of my appointment was made out in Rome on Feb. 13, and reached Baltimore on St. Joseph's day. As His Holiness has commanded me to accept the diocese and to have myself consecrated at once, the Most Rev. Archbishop fixed Passion-Sunday, which by a special dispensation of Divine Providence is the date of my birth and baptism.

At once, I made the necessary arrangements, and after I had made the spiritual exercises for 8 days, I was consecrated Bishop of Philadelphia by the Most Rev. Archbishop of Baltimore, Dr. Francis Patrick Kenrick, who now is also Deligate of the Apostolic See, amid the indescribable crowding of the people and the greatest solemnity in the main church of the German Catholics in Baltimore, in honor of St. Alphonsus. You can read a more detailed description of this solemnity in the enclosed clipping, which I cut out of a Catholic paper in Cincinnati, Ohio. On Tuesday morning at 9 o'clock I left Baltimore with not a little anxiety. Both the separation from my confreres of the Congregation of the Most Holy Redeemer and, according to human calculations, I also could not expect a warm welcome in Philadelphia.

I arrived here on the same day at 3:00 P.M., accompanied by the Very Rev. Provincial of the Congregation of the Host Holy Redeemer and several priests and took possession of this episcopal see. Now since then, I have received from all sides the most friendly and kind reception, both from the Rev. clergy as from the people. Nevertheless, I have such an amount of work and business, that I am bringing this letter to an end only after twenty interruptions.

This diocese is one of the oldest and largest, it numbers about 170,000 Catholics and has about 100 churches and as many priests. Moreover, here every bishop must attend to all his work himself and with his own hand. The city of Philadelphia is one of the largest in the world. According to the latest census of 1850, it has 409,353 inhabitants, but of whom only ¼ are Catholic. In 1840, the number of inhabitants was 258,037, from this you can see how America is increasing in population. The number of houses, among which there are very few of wood, the most of brick or stone, many even of marble, is now about 60,000. All the streets of the city are straight, one about two hours long, and 80–150 feet wide, and planted on both sides with trees. I will sometime send a plan of the city, when there is a good opportunity.

As most bishops of America according to the law go to Rome every ten years, I how have hope on such an occasion of seeing my old, not-to-be-forgotten home, relatives and friends. Nevertheless I shall not be able to undertake this journey this year because the building of the Cathedral, which was begun by my predecessor, as also the necessary visitation of the diocese and the like require my presence.

The need of German priests is very great in this diocese, and is the cause of great spiritual misery. In a short time I will send to Father Dichtl proper authorization to receive young priests or theologians in my name. The Leopoldinen-Verein will then most likely offer them the necessary travelling expenses.

Our relations, who are now living in my diocese, I have not seen for years, but I will visit them on the occasion of the visitation. In conclusion I ask that you greet all our friends and relatives, and that you recommend me to prayers of all, especially of the Rev. Clergy of Prachatitz and vicinity, who were my fellow students that they may pray to God the Lord and to His Blessed Mother for me.

I remain, with love and friendship,

> Your most obedient son and brother,
> + Jon. N. Neumann, Bishop of Philadelphia
> in the State of Pennsylvania

Philadelphia
November 18, 1852

Dear Sister Johanna Caroline,

I received your last letter with the enclosed note of our good father and of my personally not yet known nephew, John Berger, on the feast day of St. Charles Borromeo when I was just occupied with the visitation of the northeastern part of my diocese.

I sent everything to our brother Wenzel, who will laugh not a little that people let him die several times during his life time, as some great lord! He is well all the time and in the house of the Redemptorists in Detroit, in the state of Michigan, contented and beloved by his confreres. I have asked him to write himself to our father; and I hope to receive a letter from him in a few days to send it out. I will also write to our father myself and send him at the next reliable occasion a present that he can use to help our little nephew along more easily.

The offer of your Reverend Superior will, with God's help, not remain without result. I intend as soon as possible to erect an institution for infants who until now have been lost to the Church by the hundreds.

I also hope that a hospital for German immigrants will shortly be a reality. As soon as things are clear, I will not fail to knock at your door. This thought came to me on St. Charles' Day when I read your letter, and the work will be able to be carried out all the more easily because the different Sisterhoods in the United States have a lack of members.

I remember very well the friendly face of Counselor Reinhold, and ask that you give him, with my greetings, the enclosed picture. I am introducing into the diocese the different Confraternities of the Scapular and had pictures like this one made here to sew them on the same. Most Blessed Virgin will obtain for him great graces by her prayers at the hour of his death if he continues to ask her for them. I trust that he will not forget me in his prayers.

As we have now found a reliable way for our correspondence, I ask you to forward your letters in the future as you did the last one. I ask you to greet your Rev. Mother Euphemia for me. I saw her before her departure for Nancy when she lay sick in the hospital in front of the Vienna gateway and the Rev. Krbeczek read for her from the Passion of Christ of Catherine Emmerich. When I travelled through Nancy, she was in Thionville.

I ask the Blessed Mother of God to bless all of you with her holy Child and with devotion I remain,

Your faithful brother,
Joh. N. Neumann, Bishop of Philadelphia

Philadelphia
January 16, 1857

Most esteemed Father,

Only a few days ago, I received the letter of our dear John Berger, which conveyed the news of your good health, even after the so dangerous fire, which gives me so much reason to thank God the Almighty for the so evident protection with which He preserves your house.

Since my last letter there has been no change as yet in my condition. When the Bishops of the province of Maryland held their last Council in May 1855, I proposed to ask the Holy Father for a division of this diocese and volunteered to take over anyone of the new dioceses to be erected. But the answer has not yet come from Rome.

During the spring of last year, I visited all the larger parishes as also most of the small settlements in the northern half of the diocese. During the last years, this can be done much more quickly an account of the ever increasing railroad facilities. Also, accidents on the same occur very rarely any more except through the carelessness of the travelers.

In regard to our John, I can only repeat that if he feels himself called to work as a missionary in America, he will be welcome here any time. Since September I have a Boys' Seminary in which he can prepare himself easily and perfectly for his theological studies. In a few months, I hope to be able to lay something aside to make a trip possible for him. But he must not forget that in America as everywhere else strenuous effort is necessary to get ahead.

The shortness of the time does not allow me to write more. I ask God to bless you all and to keep you under His powerful protection and remain.

With due respect and gratitude,
Your most obedient son.
+J.N., Bishop of Phila.

Philadelphia
June 29, 1857

Dearest Father,

The arrival of my dear nephew, John Berger, gave me a very agreeable surprise as I thought that he would hardly come before fall. Still it is better so because he has two months free to look around some and satisfy his first curiosity before he goes to his studies.

He will make the same with the Benedictine Fathers near Youngstown, where they have one of the best colleges. Both the Rev. Fathers as well as the students, are mostly Germans and the institution has a very healthy site and on the whole is a place in America where his body and soul would be exposed to the least danger. I recommended him very strongly to the Rev. Abbot, who passed through here a few days ago on account of business. He will most likely stay with the Benedictine Fathers until he can be received into the theological Seminary of Philadelphia.

Although it seems that the immigration has decreased somewhat over the past 2–3 years, still the number of faithful in the diocese is ever increasing. For many who on account of a lack of religious instruction in their youth or a senseless pursuit of the goods of this World have neglected every practice of true piety are coming back in large numbers and cheer us by their redoubled fervor.

For the rest, everything is now quiet in the United States and according to all appearances we have to expect some peaceful years. Would to God, that we do not abuse this time of peace as happens so easily from spiritual sloth, and lose during the time of perhaps only short rest much of that which has been acquired under many hardships.

Brother Wenzel has at last written again after years of long silence. His manner of life, as lay-brother in the Congregation of the Host Holy Redeemer, is however so unvaried that even in the course of several years there is hardly enough matter to be found to write an interesting letter.

I myself have not seen him for 8–9 years, but I hear from time to time that he is well and finds himself very happy in his position. In the month of August I shall have to make a journey to Canada, and on the return-trip, I will make a detour via Detroit, and see him once again.

It gave me great pleasure that John brought your well made portrait safely to America. I ask God the Lord to bless you and all my dear relations and friends and remain with filial devotion,

Your most beholden son,

Joh. N. Neumann

P.S. I will write to Sister Caroline in 8–14 days

Philadelphia
March 15, 1858

Most esteemed, dear Sister,

I received your letter of Nov. 12, 1857 as also the two from Prachatitz the day before yesterday in the post from New York. I will communicate both to Br. Wenzel and my nephew John Berger. With the former everything is as usual; he is using the good opportunity which God is giving him, as far as I know, conscientiously. I saw the latter about two months ago in the Benedictine College, where he is studying. He complained of frequent headaches, which hinder him in his studies, and seemed to prefer to study in Philadelphia. However, I told him that this was impossible, because we have not a Boys' Seminary here, and all told, the threat of the constant unrest and the great dangers of such a populous city as Philadelphia would be a bad place for him because he is just too boyish, and will need some time yet before his character is solid enough to be somewhat more independent and he is able to live in the world without being led astray or infected. Otherwise his conduct is very good, and from his last two letters, I see with pleasure that his health is good again and that he is making good progress in his studies.

The Rev. Krasny was here in Philadelphia immediately after his arrival in America. Just then I had no place in which I could use him as he wished and so he went to New York where he was stationed at a church in December to take care of the Bohemians in New York. I will make inquiries in New York and as soon as I receive definite information about him, I will let you know at once. When I was in New York in December and inquired about him, I heard him praised very highly, but on account of my brief stay and the very bad weather I could not visit him.

The immigrants from Bohemia, as a rule, make a very bad

showing where the faith is concerned. An unfortunate priest from Bohemia (I could not learn his name) was trying just then to organize an independent Catholic congregation for Bohemians a La Ronge, and the archbishop of New York had appointed Father Krasny to preserve the Bohemians in the faith.

Since my last letter, there has been no change in my condition. The many bankruptcies in America have reduced many of our countrymen also, who have lost work and wages, to dire poverty. But the last winter was very mild and we could get along without heat until the last two weeks. Provisions also were much cheaper, because they could not be exported on account of the stagnation of trade. So God regarded the need of the poor, and even if the income of the churches and charitable institutions was less, still we always had enough.

Spiritual exercises and missions are held here every year for priests, Sisters and whole congregations and always bring very abundant fruits. It is a pity that there are not more Regulars here to conduct them, as not half of the missionaries who ask for these exercises for their churches can obtain them and then only after a long waiting.

The Rev. Provincial of the Jesuits gave the spiritual exercises in the neighboring church of St. Patrick last week; 10–12 priests heard all the confessions, and 3,000–4,000 received Holy Communion, most of them men. In the next church of St. Paul, the 40 Hours devotion was held Sunday, Monday and Tuesday. The church was always crowded, 14 priests heard confessions and about 3,000 received Holy Communion. Had there been twice as many priests there, twice as many also would have received Holy Communion. And so it goes the whole year almost without interruption.

The consolation which this piety of the faithful affords us, is only consolation on earth. Everything else is continual hardship, tear and work. I ask you to recommend me to the Rev. Superioress, to Sisters Hildegard, Charitas, whatever the others are called. I ask God to bless all of you, and remain,

Most devotedly in J. Ch.
Joh. N. Neumann,
Bish. of Philada.

I remember our god parents, brother and sisters, and old friends in every holy Mass.

NEUMANN'S PASTORAL LETTERS
to the People and
the Clergy of Philadelphia

DURING NEUMANN'S YEARS as Bishop of Philadelphia, he wrote four pastoral letters that are included here. The first, which was written in 1852, was his self introduction to the Diocese of Philadelphia, asking all concerned to continue in their dedicated zeal for the kingdom of God. Neumann also lists immediate concerns of the diocese, including the construction of the cathedral which was already begun under the former bishop and parochial schools. He warns against false philosophies and reminds the people of the plenary indulgence given by the apostolic see to those who fulfill the conditions.

The 1854 and 1855 letters center on the occasion of the solemn declaration of the doctrine of the Immaculate Conception of the Blessed Virgin, who was preserved from sin from the moment of her conception. Certainly, he reminds his people, this is a time for increased devotion to the Mother of God and indulgences are granted for the faithful.

The fourth letter of 1859 was concerned with promoting the preparatory seminary at Glen Riddle. The future of the priestly ministry in the diocese rested on the solid foundation of training worthy priests for the future and the establishment of the preparatory seminary was a great blessing that would reap great reward.

JOHN NEPOMUCEN NEUMANN
By the grace of God and favor of the APOSTOLIC SEE,
BISHOP OF PHILADELPHIA

Easter, 1852

Venerable Brethren of the clergy and dearly beloved children of
the laity:

When it was first announced to us that our Holy Father, Pius
IX, had appointed us to the pastoral care and government of this
important portion of the flock of Christ, we must confess that the
heavy charge filled our heart with great anxiety. To leave those
from whom we had experienced, for many years, the most cordial
affection, to enter upon an entirely new sphere of duty, to assume
the government of so vast a number of souls, who would look to
us to lead them on to our heavenly home, all this urged us to im-
plore the Lord to remove this chalice from us. We have, however,
been compelled to bow in obedience to the successor of St. Peter,
knowing that whatsoever he binds on earth shall be bound also
in heaven; and submitting to the will of God, we humbly hope
that He who has commenced in us what the Apostle St. Paul calls
"a good work," will graciously grant us that sufficiency which is
required to bring it to perfection. This, our trust in God, has been
much strengthened by the kind encouragement we have received
from him (Bishop Kenrick) who, through so many years of untiring
labor, has endeared himself to you all. He has repeatedly assured us
of the zeal and attachment he had experienced on the part of your
Reverend Pastors. Often has he spoken, in terms of praise, of the
piety by which you had consoled him in the midst of his toils—of
your liberality, which had called into existence and supported so
many charitable institutions, and erected edifices to the glory of
the living God, which will bear testimony to future generations

of your lively faith, prompt generosity, and practical charity, when you will be enjoying in His presence the eternal rewards He has in store for those who love Him.

Since we have occupied our Episcopal See, we have daily received unequivocal marks of attachment and obedience. The former administrator of the diocese, the Very Rev. Edward J. Sourin, has accepted the office of our Vicar General, much to our satisfaction. The cordial welcome we have met in the different religious houses and congregations we have visited, has confirmed our happiest anticipations as to the faith, piety, and zeal of the flock committed to our care by the Divine Pastor and Bishop of our souls. For all His mercies we return thanks to Him, "the Holy One and the True, who hath the key of David, who hath given before us a door opened, which, we trust in God, no man can shut."

Venerable Brethren, we beseech you most earnestly to assist us always in your prayers for us, that we may finish our course and the ministry of the word, which we have received from Jesus Christ; that we may take heed to ourselves and to all the flock over which the Holy Ghost has placed us, a Bishop, to rule the Church of God, which He has purchased "with His own precious blood" and that we may use without fear or wavering that power, which the Lord hath given us to the edification of his Church. On our part, we will not cease to entreat the Good Shepherd to increase his grace in your hearts, that as men of God you "may fly all worldly desires and pursue justice, piety, faith, charity, patience, meekness; that you may keep the commandment without spot, blameless unto the coming of our Lord Jesus Christ."

And those amongst you, Beloved Children, who, listening to the invitation of the Most Holy, have left father, mother, brethren and sisters, to dedicate yourselves to the service of Jesus Christ in poverty, chastity, and obedience, truly have ye chosen the better part. Strive, therefore, fervently, to render yourselves evermore pleasing to your Divine Spouse, for your life is hidden with Christ in God. "Put ye on, therefore, as the elect of God, holy and beloved, mercy, benignity, humility, modesty, patience; bearing with one another, and forgiving one another, if any have a complaint against another. But above all these things, have charity, which is the bond of perfection. And when Christ shall appear, who is your life, then shall you also appear with him in glory."

Beloved Children of the Laity, my joy and my crown, if you be faithful in those things which ye have both learned and received, we exhort you with the great Apostle that you "may be blameless and sincere children of God, without reproof in the midst of this world; hating that which is evil, cleaving to that which is good: loving one another with the charity of brotherhood; in spirit fervent, serving the Lord; to no man rendering evil for evil. Providing good things, not only in the sight of God, but also in the sight of all men. And whosoever shall follow this rule, may peace be upon them and mercy: and may my God supply all your wants, according to His riches, in glory, in Christ Jesus."

On your zeal and charity, next to the good pleasure of the Almighty, we must continue to rely for the completion of several important works, commenced by our most reverend predecessor. Among them, not only on account of the grandeur of the work, but even more in consequence of the heavy expense we must incur while it remains in its present unfinished state, I especially commend to your attention, the Cathedral of SS. Peter and Paul. We are not unmindful, beloved brethren, of your many sacrifices for the sake of your religion. We cannot be insensible how greatly your generous devotion has contributed to the diffusion of truth and virtue, and to the relief of suffering humanity. But whilst the gradual increase of wealth on every side,—the accumulation of all the comforts and luxuries of life, attest the prosperity to which this favored country has already attained, in which prosperity many of you participate, let us beware lest the reproaches of the prophet should prove well founded in our regard. "This people saith—the time is not yet come to build the house of the Lord. And the word of the Lord came by the hand of Aggeus, the prophet, saying: Is it time for you to dwell in ceiled houses and this house be desolate? And now, thus saith the Lord of hosts: set your hearts to consider your ways. You have sowed much and brought in little: you have looked for more and behold it became less: and you brought it home, and I blowed it away: why? saith the Lord of hosts: because my house is desolate and you make haste, every man to his own house." To these complaints of the Holy Spirit what answer did Israel give? With zealous emulation, they went in and did the work of the Lord of hosts, their God. And the temple was not yet finished, when they heard—"From this day I will bless you: take courage, all ye people of the land and perform: fear not, for I am with you—and my spirit in the midst of you, saith the Lord of hosts."

Though circumstances do not now allow us to dwell at length on the subject, we avail ourselves of this earliest opportunity to express our approbation of the efforts which have lately been made, in several congregations, to organize parochial schools. We exhort the pastors, and all who have at heart the best interests of youth, to spare no efforts to ensure success. Whatever difficulties may at first attend, and even obstruct this most desirable undertaking, will be gradually overcome by mutual good will and co-operation.

It is with grateful joy we make known to you that our Holy Father has again offered to the faithful throughout the world, a Plenary Indulgence in the form of a Jubilee; the most salutary effects, both for the Church and society having resulted from that proclaimed within the last few years. Amid the many trials and profound sorrows which have marked his pontificate, he has been consoled by the accounts which have reached him from every part of Christendom of the multitudes who with humble and contrite hearts, have thronged our churches to hear the word of God—to purify their souls in the sacrament of reconciliation and receive the Holy Eucharist; performing meanwhile with humble and devout obedience the other spiritual exercises, which, as the Vicar of Jesus Christ, he had enjoined upon them. Thousands in every country, who had been for years astray from the way of truth and salvation, have been enlightened by the grace of God, to forsake the shadows of death, and to commence a truly Christian life.

Notwithstanding this happy result, our chief Pastor is not without apprehension for the future welfare of the Church and society. He beholds the dangers which threaten both; the designs of men who, deceived by a vain philosophy and their false ideas of liberty, despise lawful authority, whether civil or ecclesiastical; pervert the minds of inexperienced youth and expose to contempt the most sacred rites and institutions of religion. Aware that from no quarter can they expect more determined and constant opposition than from the Apostolic See, it is therefore against this venerable authority that they direct their most violent attacks. In these dangers, what other course remains for the friends of order, justice, and virtue, than to recur to the Almighty, who is our hope and our salvation; and to pray without ceasing that He would deign to look down upon the nations, to enlighten their erring minds, to purify their hearts and subdue that rebellious will which now leads them to revolt against Him and His Church, "that being delivered from the hand of our enemies, we may serve Him without fear, in holiness and justice, all the days of our life."

To secure the divine blessings he has in view, viz: the peace and welfare of the Universal Church, the promotion of virtue, order, and true Christian piety, in all ranks of society, His Holiness grants a Plenary Indulgence to the faithful of both sexes who will comply with the following conditions.

1. During the Jubilee, which will continue for one month, from the first of May to the first of June, all who are of the proper age will worthily approach the sacraments of Penance and the Holy Eucharist.

2. They will visit three churches once, (for the city, St. John's, St. Mary's, and St. Augustine's,) or one church three times, as circumstances may dictate; offering up, at each visit, some prayers for the intention of our Holy Father, Pius IX.

3. They who are of age will fast on one day, in the course of the month.

4 It is also required that, besides the usual alms to the poor, a special alms be given to that admirable association, The Society for the Propagation of the Faith, to whose truly Catholic liberality the Church in the United States, as well as all the most remote parts of the world, is deeply indebted.

In behalf of those who, from one cause or another, may not be able to comply with the above conditions, all confessors approved by the Ordinary, are empowered to substitute one good work for another; to dispense from the reception of the Holy Eucharist children who have not yet made their first communion; to absolve from excommunication such Catholics as have been married before a Protestant minister; also, during the continuance of the Jubilee, they have the power to absolve, (*in foro conscientiae,*) from excommunication, suspension, interdict, and other ecclesiastical censures, with the exception of those cases mentioned in the Constitution of Benedict XIV, which begins, "Sacramentum Poenitentiae."

You are probably aware, Beloved Brethren, that the first National Council will soon be held in Baltimore; its opening being fixed for the fourth Sunday after Easter. Every faithful member of the Church in the United States will regard it as an imperative duty to invoke the Holy Spirit—the Spirit of truth, wisdom, and piety, to preside over its deliberations, that all its proceedings and enactments may tend to the glory of Jesus Christ, and the more perfect establishment of his kingdom in all hearts. To this end, we direct that the collect, De Spiritu Sancto, be added in the Mass, whenever the rubrics allow it; the religious communities will recite daily the Litany of the Blessed Virgin; and the same or other prayers for this object, we exhort the faithful of our diocese to offer to God until the close of the Council.

And now, Brethren, commending you to God and to the word of His grace, our daily prayer for you is, "that your charity may more and more abound in knowledge and in all understanding that you may approve the better things: that you may be sincere and without offence unto the day of Christ, replenished with the fruit of justice, through Jesus Christ, unto the glory and praise of God." May the Divine Mother and her Son bless you all. Amen.

Given at our residence in PHILADELPHIA, Easter Week, in the year of our Lord, MDCCCLII.

+ JOHN NEPOMUCENE,
Bishop of Philadelphia

November 4th, A.D. 1854

Venerable Brothers of the Clergy, and Beloved Brethren of the Laity,

With that solicitude to promote the glory of God—the veneration due to the ever blessed and Immaculate Mother of His only begotten Son, our Lord and Savior Jesus Christ, and thereby to establish more happily His kingdom among men, which has, from the earliest ages of Christianity, distinguished the successors of St. Peter in the See of Rome, our present and illustrious chief pastor, Pius IX, has proclaimed a universal Jubilee, inviting the faithful in every part of the world, to unite their supplications before the throne of God; by prayer, fasting, alms, deeds and other good works to obtain from Him who is rich in mercy those temporal and heavenly succors of which the Church was seldom, if ever, more in need.

Come, let us adore, and fall down before our God: and weep before the Lord who made us; He says to all who will receive His word, but especially to those who rejoice in the "divine light of Catholic freedom." Calling to mind the former days of trials that are past, "Let us praise the Lord with joy, let us joyfully sing to God our Savior; let us come before His presence with thanksgiving, for He is the Lord our God and we are His People." (Ps. 94)

On the other hand contemplating the calamities of every kind that afflict His Church, the Vicar of Jesus Christ, partaking in the sufferings of his beloved Master, as he is also of His power, calls upon us to arise—to behold the evils which, as the waves of the sea, on every side, beset the Church—the humiliation of her children, the growing strength and exaltation of her enemies. And since our arms are not those of flesh and blood, nay since experience proves that they who trust in such things, are not of the race of those men by whom salvation is brought to Israel, he exhorts, he entreats us to turn now at length to the Lord our God, and be once more His people, to remember the mighty works, the gracious sign of His Divine Presence and protection which in our own times has not been withheld from his Church, to renew the vows of fidelity, love and obedience which we all made when we were adopted into His family. Most earnestly does he admonish us to shake off the torpor of spiritual sloth and religious indifference which like a cancer still eats its way into the heart of Society, "to cast aside the works of darkness and put on the armor of light, to walk honestly as in the day; not in rioting and drunkenness; not in chambering and impurities, not in contention and envy but put ye on the Lord Jesus Christ, and make not provision for the flesh in its concupiscence." (Rom. 13:12, 14)

Shall we not listen to the voice of our supreme Pastor, venerable not less for his profound sorrow; a pastor whose illustrious name and noble deeds, only a few years since, were from hour to hour on the lips of a treacherous world? Shall we not obey a ruler of the universal Church of God who would indeed have made Rome, in a political, as it has long since been in a sublime sense, a light to enlighten the nations, a joy to the whole earth, had not treachery and ingratitude combined to defeat the work; and this, where such return of hate for love, of basest selfishness for generous confidence were least expected? Well may we be patient with our staunchest adversaries when we must bear witness to the deeds of such enemies within our own ranks.

"With thee I was wounded in the house of them that loved me" (Zach. 13:6), said the prophet, mourning in God's name, over the obduracy of His most favored people. And how truthfully may the Sovereign Pontiff be, who next to Jesus Christ, is the chief bishop and shepherd of our souls, repeat this day the same mournful words. At such a spectacle so humiliating in every true Catholic, faith may waver, and hope grow faint, did we not recall the Apostle's warning—"Dearly Beloved, think not strange the burning heat which is to try you as if some new thing had happened to you—for the time is that judgment should begin at the house of God; and if, first at us, what shall be the end of them, who believe not the gospel of God?" (1 Peter 4:12, 17).

In thus speaking openly of the afflictions of the Church, of which indeed the Encyclical Letter (February 2, 1849) made no secret, we forget not, Christian Brethren, the many motives for thankfulness and hope which certainly exist. Never before, it has been truly observed, has the area of Catholicity been more widely extended. Never before has been there such unanimity on the one grand and only question of a religious character which at present so widely interests the Catholic mind.

The empires of antiquity, at the several epochs of their greatest renown, would now hardly form a third part of that vast dominion, within which the symbol and the altars of our Faith are everywhere to be found, or of that Christian people, composed of every tribe and nation from whose hearts the expression of faith and attachment to the See of Peter, is as ready to break forth as it was in the days of Augustine, '*Roma locuta est, causa finita est*'. Rome has spoken; the controversy is at an end.

Seldom, if ever, have there been more glorious examples of conversion to the faith than within the last half-century. Examples too, of heroic charity have not been wanting: How many have accepted the sweet imitation of Jesus Christ; "if thou wilt be perfect, go, sell what thou hast and give to the poor; and thou shalt have treasure in heaven: and come, follow Me." (Mark 10:21).

Wealth, talent, genius, youth full of joy and hope; and venerable age, the noble in heart and intellect as well as the noble by birth and rank, have heard these words and obeyed. With the apostle have they cheerfully said—"The things that were gain to me the same I have counted loss for Jesus Christ. Furthermore, I count all things to be but loss, for the excellent knowledge of Jesus Christ my Lord." (Phil. 3:7–8)

The testimony thus given to the presence of the Holy Spirit's ever abiding with the Church has produced a world-wide and profound expression. It has been "an odor of life unto life for man; unto others it has been an odour of death unto death." (2 Cor. 2:16) And it must in great part account for the renewed activity with which the foes of our holy religion everywhere combine against it. Even in these our evil days, as in the first age of Christianity, apostolic men have preached the Gospel and planted the Cross of Jesus Christ, in the remotest regions of the world. Martyrs have rejoicingly shed their blood; consecrated virgins have offered their lives to be one perpetual sacrifice in the same holy cause. Their labors have not been in vain. The success of Catholic Missions, not only in distant heathen lands, but in the heart of Europe in old and populous cities where it was justly feared heresy and infidelity had long since destroyed every germ of faith has been confessed by those who, unmindful of our Savior's promises and trained from childhood to hate the Church of their fathers, long for the day when the name of Israel will be remembered no more.

For these, our brethren, it is one of your sacred duties to pray. The more ardent their misguided zeal against us, the more fervent and humble should be our supplications in their behalf. They were all present to the mind of our and their Redeemer, when, on the last evening of His life, and in the midst of a people who were, the next day, to reject and deny and put Him to death—even the death of the Cross—He poured forth this divine prayer as well for them as for his beloved disciples:

"I Pray not that Thou wouldst take them out of the world, but that Thou wouldst keep them from evil. And not for them only do I pray but for them also who through their word, shall believe in Me; that they all may be one, as Thou, Father, in Me, and I in Thee: that they all may be one in Us that the world may believe that Thou hast sent Me. And the glory which Thou has given to Me, I have given to them, that they may be made perfect in one; and the world may know that Thou hast sent Me, and hast loved them, as Thou hast also loved Me." (John 17:15, 20, 23)

In behalf of these especially was the "Prayer Association" proposed to you by the Bishops of the United States in the last National Council (First Plenary Council of Baltimore, 1852), and approved by receipt from Rome, dated September 5th, 1852. It is again recommended to your attention. The conditions for gaining the indulgence attached to the Jubilee, are as follows, and nearly in the words of the Holy Father:

First: To confess our sins with humility and with a sincere detestation of the same.

Second: Having been purified by sacramental absolution, to receive reverently the sacrament of the Holy Eucharist.

Third: To visit devoutly three churches designated by the bishop, or one of them at three different times.

Fourth: To pray therein with devotion for some time, according to the intentions of His Holiness, for the exaltation and prosperity of our holy mother, the Church, and of the Apostolic See, for the extirpation of heresies, for peace and concord among Christian princes, for the peace and unity of the whole Christian people.

Fifth: To fast once and give alms to the poor as your piety may dictate.

The above conditions must all be fulfilled within the period of three months during which the Jubilee will continue, beginning from this day. The churches designated are, for the Catholics living south of Vine Street, in the Consolidated City of Philadelphia, the churches of St. John, the Evangelist, St. Joseph and St. Theresa: for those living north of Vine Street, the churches of St. Peter, the Prince of the Apostles, the Assumption of the Blessed Virgin Mary, and St. Malachy. The more distant Congregations, viz., of Port Richmond, Frankford, Manayunk, etc., will follow the advice of their Pastors with regard to the three visits to the churches.

To the Pastors and Congregations in the Consolidated City of Philadelphia, it is recommended, that the exercises of the Jubilee be made as far as possible, between the present date, November 5th and the Feast of the Immaculate Conception, December 8th, inclusively.

To the many Congregations throughout the Diocese, the same invitation is extended, that "the prayers of many being heard at one time in the sight of the glory of the Most High God" (Tobit 3:24), we may more faithfully comply with the intentions of our beloved Pontiff, Pius IX. Should God so will it, it may come to pass, that like the devout Sarah and Tobias who have left us their example we also, with our Chief Pastor at our head, may be able to say, "Blessed is Thy Name, O God of our fathers! Because after a storm Thou makest a calm; and after tears and weeping Thou pourest in joyfulness. Be Thy Name, O God of Israel, blessed forever." (Tobias 3:13, 22–23)

On which day the fast is to be kept is left for each one to determine for himself. But if we would not lose the spiritual blessings of this season, it must be a fast in reality, at least, according to the present mitigated discipline of the Church.

The alms to be acceptable in the sight of God, should be given from a motive of real charity; and according to our means, not such alms as imply no sacrifice or self-denial. As is the practice usual on these occasions whenever there is only one church, in any town, city or district, a visit to it, three times, will be sufficient to gain the indulgence. In all cases, wherein any of the conditions become impracticable or very inconvenient, we authorize the parish priest or the confessor to commute them provided that the Sacrament of Penance and the Eucharist be received by all who are capable of them; and that prayers be offered up in conformity with the intentions of the Holy Father.

May we not joyfully hope that if the great body of the faithful, with a good heart and willing mind, comply with these conditions, our prayers will be answered? And since, one of the principal intentions of the reigning pontiff in proclaiming the Jubilee, has been by means of your united suffrages, to obtain the grace of the Holy Spirit in giving a decision on the subject of the Immaculate Conception of the ever-venerable Virgin Mother of Jesus Christ, shall we not confidently believe that abundant light will be imparted to him and to the Prelates now convened around his throne in the Eternal City? As the long wished for day approaches, let us pray still more fervently, attentive to the invitation of the Church we so often hear "Sursum Corda" Let us lift up our hearts in frequent earnest prayer that the decision may be such as will redound to the praise of the adorable Trinity, the salvation of man, and to the honor of her, who, next to God is indeed the '*Aeterni Coeli Gloria, Beata Spes Mortalium*' (The Eternal joy and glory of the heavens; the ever blessed hope of fallen man).

If such be the will of God and your piety deserves it, before the close of the year we may hear again the voice of Peter as when the days of the Pentecost were accomplished, making known by the lips of Pius IX, to the assembled representatives of every nation under heaven that from henceforth and forever, all generations of true believers shall invoke Mary, Mother of God, as the Ever Immaculate Virgin, conceived without the stain of Original Sin.

Such appears to be the expectation of the whole Catholic world. The looking forward for the "coming of the Messiah," her Divine Son, Christ Jesus, was not more general in the times before His advent, than is this universal expectation that the Vicegerent of this same Divine Son, our Holy Father, will decide that the Blessed Virgin was never stained by Original Sin,—that by a special privilege, which the Almighty could certainly grant, Mary was always exempt from that law to which all the children of Adam are subject—that from the first moment of her existence Mary was perfect purity itself in the sight of God. And, that therefore the words of Holy Writ and of Christian antiquity are to be understood in their literal sense, when it is said "Thou art all beautiful, O Virgin Mary! And there is not a spot in thee. In thee no spot of sin either is, or ever was, or ever will be." "*Tota pulchra es, Virgo Maria! et macula non est in Te; macula peccati non est in Te, neque unquam fuit nec erit.*"

Although the Church has not yet declared the Immaculate Conception to be an article of faith, nevertheless it is evident she cherishes this most just and pious belief with a loving constancy, second only to that infallible certainty with which she maintains the truth of all those doctrines the acceptance of which is necessary for salvation. With a zeal probably never surpassed in former ages, the subject has been investigated by many of the most gifted and holy men now living; and with such a magnificent outlay of ancient and modern learning, of profound argument, and soul stirring eloquence have they treated it, as to leave not only the more devout clients of Mary, but every unbiased mind, convinced beyond the possibility of doubting, that if there be anything certainly true, next to the defined doctrine of faith, it is this apostolic, and therefore ancient and beautiful belief.

Hence, it is not surprising, that wherever the most enlightened piety exists, there also, hardly a moment's hesitation on this subject will be entertained. *"Caro Jesu Caro Maria!"* "The flesh of Jesus is the flesh of Mary!" They will at once exclaim with the great St. Augustine. How can it be that the God of all purity, to whom even the least shadow of sin is an object of eternal abhorrence, would have suffered His Virgin Mother to be, even for an instant, such an object in His sight! From her He received that flesh and blood, that human nature in which, made one with the Divinity, he redeemed the world, and can we believe that the same in Mary's person, in any possible degree was ever sullied by the demon's breath; dishonored by the taint of guilt? Or again, with St. Cyril, the pious Catholic will ask, "Who hath ever heard that an architect built a glorious dwelling for himself, and at once gave it over to be possessed by his most cruel and hated enemy?"

If there were no other words of Holy Writ on this topic but one "Mary, of whom was born Jesus who is called Christ" (Matt. 1:16), they would be amply sufficient. Behold the divine fact that overthrows every difficulty; the inspired oracle that sweeps away every objection.

Never, Christian Brethren, never can we admit that she was for one moment the slave of the devil; the Virgin, who was destined to be the Mother of God, the Spouse of the Holy Spirit, the Ark of the New Covenant, the Mediatrix of Mankind, the Terror of the Powers of Darkness, the Queen of all the heavenly hosts.

Purer than heaven's purest angel; brighter than its brightest Seraph; Mary, after her Creator, God, who made her and gave her all, is the most perfect of beings, the masterpiece of Infinite Wisdom, Almighty Power and Eternal Love.

To such a being we cannot reasonably suppose that a perfection was denied her which had been already, gratuitously bestowed on inferior creatures: on the Angelic spirits, for example, some of whom afterwards fell away from God and are lost forever. And again the first man and the first woman were created sinless; pure as the virgin world on which the Almighty had just looked down with infinite delight and declared it to be *"valde bona,"* exceeding good. How just and natural, therefore, and may we not add how unavoidable is the conclusion, that this divine privilege was not withheld from Mary, set apart, as she was, from all eternity, for office and honors in the kingdom of God, to which no other created being ever will or can be exalted. The more so, since profound divines do not hesitate to assert, that rather than be without the grace conferred upon her in her Immaculate Conception, and thus, though only for an instant an object of God's displeasure, Mary would have preferred to forfeit forever the infinite dignity of being the Mother of Jesus Christ.

Gladly would we dwell more at length on the subject, but you observe yourselves the occasion does not allow it. The few thoughts we have uttered are but the echo of Christian antiquity; of the faith, the filial love, the confidence in Mary, when apostles and evangelists were still on earth and revered her name.

How profound should be our gratitude, in being able to say that name which we also reverence; their confidence in Mary we cherish; their filial love we share; their faith is ours. Could the Martyrs and Virgins, the heroic confessors of the faith, the renowned Fathers and Doctors of the Church, "beloved of God and men, and whose memory is in benediction" (Eccles. 45:1). Could these arise and unite their voices to those of their successors, now around the Chair of Peter, what would be their testimony? They would point to their immortal writings, and in the language of St.

Augustine, so worthy a representative of the genius, wisdom and piety of the primitive Church, they would remind us, that when they speak of the law by which all the children of Adam are born children of wrath, "they speak not of Mary", with regard to whom, on account of the honor due to our Lord, when they discourse of sin, they wish to raise no question whatever. (*Liber de Natura et Gratia,* 36:42). Nay, with an Amen, loud like the thunder of Heaven, they would respond to the following declaration of the Council of Trent, Sess. V. "This holy Synod declares that it is not its intention to include in this decree, where original sin is spoken of, the Blessed and Immaculate Mother of God."

May the day soon dawn upon the world, whether it be in our unhappy times or not, when with one mind and one heart, Christendom will acknowledge and proclaim this her most honorable privilege. Meanwhile submitting every thought, word and wish to the judgment of the Church, we will continue to confess her power; regarding Mary as that "great sign" which St. John saw in heaven; a woman so resplendent with light, grace and divinity, that he describes her as "A woman clothed with the sun; with the moon beneath her feet; and on her head a crown of twelve stars, whose Son shall rule the nations with an iron rod and her Son was taken up to God, and to His throne." (Apoc. 12:1, 5).

And should the Dragon of Impiety, spoken of in the same mysterious vision, whose power to seduce the nations is but too evident, still continue to make war on God and His Church: should the fearful days of widespread unbelief, foretold by the Apostles, prove to be our own, when man "will no longer endure sound doctrine, but according to their own desires, will heap up to themselves, teachers, having lying lips; turning away their hearing from the truth to give heed to fables; speaking proud words of vain philosophy; despising government and all majesty, audacious, self-willed-fearing not to bring in sects; promising their followers liberty, whereas they themselves are the slaves of corruption; days of calamity, in which the same inspired teachers warn us, men will blaspheme whatever things they know not; that is, the unsearchable ways of God and mysteries of religion, and what things soever they naturally do know, in these they will be corrupted; mockers, murmurers, full of complaints, inventors of evil things, disobedient to parents, without affection, without fidelity, walking according to their own desires in ungodliness, filled with avarice and envy, counting for a pleasure the delights of a day; sporting themselves to excess; rioting in their feasts with you, having their eyes full of adultery and never ceasing sin"; alluring unstable souls who have lost their faith, and leaving the right way, will, in the end discover that they have been following "wandering stars to whom the storm of darkness is reserve forever." (See Jude 1:13, 16, 18; 2 Peter 2:10–15; Rom. 1:30–31; 2 Tim. 4:3–4; et aliter.)

Christian brethren, if these be times in store for the already afflicted Church of Jesus Christ, in the midst of which, with fear and trembling, we, her children, are to work out our salvation, to whom can we turn with more confidence, than to His 'divine' mother whom the Church has never invoked in vain.

Hail, Holy Queen, Mother of Mercy! Guard the kingdom of the Christ-loving Pius, our Chief Bishop. Pray for the people. Intercede for the clergy. Protect the consecrated Virgins. Unto us all give strength against our enemies and thine: courage to the fearful; joy to those who mourn, peace to the contrite of heart; perseverance to the just. Let all experience thy protection, Virgin and Mother, through whom the nations are brought to penitence, the demons are put to flight and they that sat in darkness and the shadow of death are filled with the knowledge and the love of thy Only-begotten Son.

But what will prayer, almsgiving, fasting, even the life-giving Sacraments avail, if we listen not to the warning of our Savior; if we do not avoid the occasions of sin? "He that loves the danger, shall perish in it" (Eccles. 3:27), is a maxim of our Redeemer which no change of fashion can affect; a gracious admonition which should never be absent from our thoughts; above all in times and circumstances like the present. Fly, therefore, from all evil company. "For as the lion always lieth in wait for prey, so do the sins for them that work iniquities." (Eccles. 27:3). Beware of secret societies. Trust not their agents; too often only false brethren in disguise. Trust in God and His Law; and "you will put to silence the ignorance of foolish men," and many a prejudice against the Catholic Church will disappear. Let your ambition be, not to amass riches, but to owe no man anything; not to secure "office", but to live soberly, justly and piously in the world.

Frequent the church and not the taverns. Banish from your homes dangerous books, the bane of purity in every age, the scourge of modern society. Watch over the children whom God hath confided to you, if you would not set the seal to your own condemnation. For Christ's sake who said—"Suffer the little children to come unto Me, and forbid them not, for of such is the Kingdom of God (Mark 10:14)—bring them to Him by your good life and holy conversation. Allow them not to grow up in ignorance and vice. Teach them to pray: to pray for all men; benefactors, friends and enemies; to love their homes, their native land, and never to be ashamed of their Religion; rather to be always ready to reply in the spirit of the noble St. Hilary to the Emperor Constantius, "I am a Catholic, I am a Christian; I will not be a Heretic."

And since the Church in the United States, has solemnly chosen the Mother of our Lord as its special Patroness and Protector; setting apart the Feast of her Immaculate Conception to be our national festival. Oh, first devoutly learn, and then teach your children from their earliest years, to cultivate true, filial piety towards her, letting no day pass without respecting the Archangel's salutation. Encourage them to the sweet task, the salutary practice with the words of St. Bernard, and may we all remember them: "Heaven smiles, the Angels rejoice; the world exults, when we say, Ave Maria, Hail Mary."

For the rest, Brethren, trust perfectly in the grace which is offered to you, "who by the power of God are kept by faith unto salvation, ready to be revealed in the last time wherein you will greatly rejoice, if now you must be, for a little time, made sorrowful in diverse temptations that the trial of your faith—much more precious than gold which is tried by the fire—may be found unto praise and glory and honor at the appearing of Jesus Christ; whom having not seen, you love; in whom also now, though you see Him not, you believe and believing, shall rejoice with joy unspeakable and glorified, receiving the end of your faith, even the salvation of your souls." (1 Peter 1:5–9).

Given under our hand, at our residence in Philadelphia, on the Feast of St. Charles Borromeo in the year of our Lord, eighteen hundred and fifty-four.

+ John Nepomucen Bishop of Philadelphia

May 1st, A.D. 1855

Venerable Brethren, Brethren of the Clergy, and Beloved Brethren of the Laity:

Blessed be the God and Father of our Lord Jesus Christ, the Father of Mercies, and the God of all Consolation, who among other favors bestowed upon His Church in an age so full of trials, has vouchsafed through His Vicar on earth, to speak the word which so many generations of Christians have longed to hear; to proclaim the Immaculate Conception of Mary, the Virgin Mother of the Savior of all. In every age, and in every part of the Catholic Church, and her dominion extends from the rising of the sun, to the going down of the same, and therefore can never be destroyed, illustrious members of the household of the faith, Pontiffs and Confessors, Virgins and Martyrs, and apostolic missionaries have fervently prayed that they might not see death before this last homage of veneration was offered to Almighty God and to her, whom above all creatures He has most delighted to honor. Like the venerable Simeon, one of the first to adore Jesus Christ and to acknowledge the pre-eminent dignity of the mother that bore Him, while he indeed prophesied of the Son's Sufferings, and the mother's sorrow, and the strange ingratitude of mankind, these devout clients of Mary were willing to depart from this world, could they only behold the day, when the holy Apostolic See, ever guided by the light of the Holy Spirit, would define the important question of the Immaculate Conception; being quite confident that such an act would be the harbinger of multiplied graces and blessings, which Mary would obtain for Rome and for the entire Church whose Patroness and Advocate she always is. Rejoicing, as we know they are, with God, their prayers united to those of the faithful on earth, have obtained for our age this signal blessing.

The Letters Apostolic of His Holiness Pius IX, have by this time reached the most distant churches in communion with the See of Rome. Everywhere they have been received with joy and thanksgiving. The unanimity of the venerable assembly of Prelates, Bishops, Archbishops, Cardinals and other representatives of the multitude of believers spread throughout the world, was only the precursor of that joyful accord with which the faithful in every land have hailed the promulgation of the dogma of the Immaculate Conception, as a doctrine revealed by God, always implicitly held in the Church, though not expressly declared, and as such handed down from age to age by those whom the Christian world of the present day, has received together with the Scriptures all the divine truths it now possesses.

Though we do not require such motives to confirm our faith, built as it is on the foundation of the Apostles and Prophets. Jesus Christ Himself, being the chief cornerstone, nevertheless, when we consider who are the principal advisors of the Holy See, in all such matters, and with what consummate prudence, they conduct these proceedings, seeking aid and light from heaven, by those means which have never failed; when we reflect that they are, for the most part, men venerable for their years, their virtues, experience and wisdom; for their eminent talents and acquirements, their profound acquaintance with all learning, civil and ecclesiastical, and others renowned even to the ends of the earth, for their labors in the cause of literature, science and religion, we have even humanly speaking the strongest guarantee imaginable for the most sure truth of any and every decree issued in the name and by the authority of him who is our Chief Pastor—who is ever watchful as being to render an account of your souls.

But when in addition to all this, we have the promise of Jesus Christ that He will guide its deliberations and teach it all truth according to these divine words spoken on the last night of His life: "The Paraclete, the Holy Ghost, whom the Father will send in My name, He will teach you all things, and bring all things, to your mind whatsoever I shall have said to you", we feel a gratitude, a confidence which none but the true children of the Church can experience or even conceive.

What was before the dictate of piety becomes the conviction of faith. What may have always appeared to us as one of the clearest deductions of reason, stands out in the purer light of revelation. And the belief which we have hitherto held in the company of many thousands of the redeemed who have gone before, leaving their doctrine and example as a path of light for us to follow, that same belief we now hold in union with that multitude of the blest which no man can number, the spirits of the just made perfect, who have safely come to Mount Sinai, and to the city of the living God, the heavenly Jerusalem.

For you know full well, Christian Brethren, that the Church of God is one. His elect, whether in heaven or earth, or in the intermediate state of temporary suffering and purification, are all one people, one kingdom of God. His Spirit, the Spirit of truth, wisdom and holiness, animates, protects and governs the Church; and as long as we remain her faithful children, we will no more err from the right way, than the word of God can fail or the throne of His everlasting dominion crumble into dust. It is this firm reliance on His word; this immovable trust in His promises for His own sake and because of His trust which constitutes that divine faith which is the foundation of all Christian virtues. For by faith the just man liveth and without faith it is impossible to please God.

From this faith springs that obedience to God in His Church and the merit accruing to your souls, for which you can never be sufficiently thankful. This filial obedience to which the apostle exhorts us, "Let us serve, pleasing God with fear and reverence", our Redeemer Himself has made the crowning proof of all His true disciples; the sure bond of membership with His mystical body, the Church; the witness of union with Him who is our Head, our life, our salvation. For He has said—and are there any words of the Holy Writ more worthy of being written in letters of gold, or which should be more familiar to Christians?—"If you love Me, keep My commandments. He that hath My commandments and keepeth them, he it is that loveth Me. And he that loveth Me shall be loved by My Father, and I will love him, and will manifest Myself to him. If any man love Me, he will keep My words and My Father will love him, and We will come to him, and will make an abode with him. He that loveth Me not, keepeth not My words. If you keep my commandments, you will remain in my love; as I also have kept my Father's commandments, and do remain in His love. You are My friends, if you do the things I command you." (John 14:15–24; 15:10–14)

Such was the language, such were the thoughts of Jesus Christ on that last evening, when as the God-Man turning once more to His heavenly Father with the words, "that the world may know that I love the Father, and as the Father hath given Me commandment, so I do: arise, let Me go hence" He bent His steps to the garden of Gethsemane, there to pour forth His prayers, His tears, His blood; and the next day to die on the cross of Calvary. Oh! How profitably may man draw near and with all the powers of his soul attend and learn obedience from an Incarnate God who for our example is obedient unto death, even the death of the cross.

As we stand around that throne of infinite wisdom and eternal life, how should the parting words, never to be forgotten, sink into our souls, which we now hear from lips that on the judgment day ill be compelled to condemn so many for their pride and disobedience. "Greater love than this no man hath, that a man lay down his life for his friends; you are My friends, if you do the things I command you." (John 15:13–14) And, what is, Christian Brethren, one of His most solemn commandments? Is it not that, so often and in so many forms substantially repeated throughout the sacred writings? "Hear the Church: If a man will not hear the Church, let him be to thee as the heathen and the publican" (Matt. 18:17); that is, as those who have no part in the inheritance of salvation. To whom but to the very same pastors whom St. Paul had in his mind, when he admonishes us, "Remember your prelates, who have spoken to you the word of God" (Heb. 13:7) did our Redeemer say: "He that heareth you, heareth Me, and he that despiseth you, despiseth Me, and he that despiseth Me, despiseth Him that sent Me." (Luke 10:16)

Again, what a fountain of joy and strength to all the faithful— "for you are the children of God by faith in Christ Jesus" do we possess in that last, most sacred declaration of our Redeemer before His Ascension, whereby He teaches all that would be benefited by His most precious Blood that it is the Faith in His Word which begets obedience to His Church that saves mankind. We give the words as recorded by St. Matthew and St. Mark: "Go ye into the whole world and preach the gospel to every creature: Go ye therefore, teach all nations": i,e., make them your disciples, even as youth are assembled and taught the principles of any salutary knowledge, do you teach mankind the science of salvation: "baptizing them in the name of the Father, and of the Son, and of the Holy Ghost: he that believeth and is baptized, shall be saved, he that believeth not, shall be condemned": that is, he whose faith is followed by obedience, shall be saved; but faith without obedience will save no one from destruction: "teaching them to observe all things whatsoever I have commanded you, and behold, I am with you, all days, even to the consummation of the world." (Matthew 28; Mark 16)

In proportion to the greatness of the commitment is the virtue and merit of obedience to it. The more sacred the law, the more pleasing to God is our reverence for it, and greater is the reward for its faithful observance. Hence, among other views taken of the recent decree on the Immaculate Conception, we should regard it as an opportunity given to the faithful of these later times, to exercise toward Jesus Christ and His Vicar that filial obedience which the members of the Church in earlier ages were happy to manifest on every proper occasion.

In the voice of Pius IX, we recognize the voice of St. Peter. In the person of St. Peter we recognize the authority of the Redeemer who appointed him to be our Chief Bishop; whose pastoral counsel as though he were this day in the midst of us, and witnessed the trials to which our religion is subjected, we hear him in these words; words truly becoming his office and the representative of the Divine Master, who had committed to him the care of His whole flock. "As children of obedience, knowing that you were not redeemed with corruptible gold or silver but with the Precious Blood of Christ, as of a lamb unspotted and undefiled, have your conversation good among the Gentiles, that whereas they speak against you as evil doers, considering you by your good works, they may glorify God in the day of visitation. For so is the will of God, that by doing well you may silence the ignorance of foolish men, being always ready to satisfy everyone that asketh you a reason for that hope which is in you. As free and not as making liberty a cloak of malice, but as the servants of God: for this is thankworthy, if for conscience toward God, a man endures sorrows, suffering wrongfully. For what glory is it, if sinning and being buffeted you suffer it! But if doing well, you suffer patiently, this is thankworthy before God.

For unto this you have been called: because Christ also suffered for us, leaving you an example that you should follow His steps: who did no sin, neither was guile found in His mouth: who when He was reviled, did not revile; when He suffered, He threatened not, but delivered Himself to him who judged Him unjustly; who His own self bore our sins in His body on the tree; that we being dead to sin might live unto justice: by those whose stripes you were healed. For you were as sheep going astray: but you are now converted to the Pastor and Bishop of your souls." (I Peter 1:14; 2:12, 16, 19–25)

Another revealed truth of vital importance in the actual religious state of the world is brought before us by this Decree of the Sovereign Pontiff. We refer to the doctrine of the Church on the nature of Original Sin and the duty of being purified from it in the Sacrament of Baptism.

The widespread disregard of this divine Sacrament among those who are separated from the Catholic fold, has reached a height that is hardly conceivable among any people bearing the Christian name. With the command of Jesus Christ before their eyes, which you have heard a few moments ago, many question its worth, doubt its necessity. Many others discard it altogether; while another numerous class neglect it without remorse, who if they would give a moment's thought to the subject could not but know that the doctrine of Baptism was always an article in their Confessions of Faith. If such be the practical unbelief of vast bodies of men in a divine ordinance of the Christian religion, and that ordinance the very first, and in a certain sense, the easiest of all to comply with, we may with grief for such indifference judge what must be the condition of a great portion of the so called Christian world. But this unbelief is only the development of a still deeper error.

The spirit of the age is to take little account of all sin, whether actual or original. With no thought of God's infinite holiness, before whom the angels themselves are not pure: with no sense of the malignity of sin when theologically speaking, even a slight venial fault is in His sight a greater evil than would be the material destruction of the whole world; it is not to be wondered, though it is to be deplored that multitudes both within and out of the Church, live on and sin as though there were no retribution, good or evil, to be expected hereafter. Hence the words of St. Paul: "The sensual man perceiveth not the things that are of the spirit of God: for it is foolishness to him and he cannot understand: because it is spiritually examined." (I Cor. 2:14)

To meet so fatal an error God does not fail to provide a remedy. He has done so in the Dogma of the Immaculate Conception. For this doctrine vividly makes known to us that such is God's abhorrence of all iniquity, that He could not tolerate for one instant, even the appearance of sin in that Virgin who was destined to be the mother of His Incarnate Son when He would descend to save the world. That Mary never committed any actual sin, even the slightest venial fault, has been from the beginning, the faith of the Catholic Church. But now it is moreover certain that not so much as even the shadow of original sin ever dimmed from the first moment of her existence, the perfect purity of her soul.

God worked a miracle of goodness and power to preserve her from the effects of the original transgression: to exempt her from that law by which all who come into this world, are born children of wrath and subject to Satan. The legitimate effect of such a dogma must be to counteract the soul-destroying influences which are always around us, and perchance never more so than at present. It is the doctrine which the spiritual wants of mankind at this moment demand. It holds up to our contemplation a God of infinite purity, in whose sight, were it not for His infinite mercy, no man could stand. It reveals to us His eternal abhorrence of all sin; its hideousness, its enormity. It enforces the unavoidable duty of doing penance, if we would have the faintest hope being saved; It enforces the duty of constant endeavor, constant cheerfulness, humility, watchfulness and prayer: and with these the wisdom of not being without fear for sin forgiven.

The nature of the Sacrament of Baptism, its divine character, origin and efficacy; its necessity for Salvation, the fatal error of unbelief in its regard, the sin of neglecting, nay sometimes, of delaying its reception, all these facts, compared with which, the pursuits, cares, pleasures, riches and honors of this world are shadows; all these heavenly facts are also brought before our minds by this tenet of Mary's Immaculate Conception. For the same God who wrought a wondrous miracle to preserve her from original sin, has wrought another miracle whose elements are His humiliations, toils and sorrows, through more than thirty years; His anguish, tears and blood in Gethsemane and on Calvary, to provide this Sacrament of Baptism for all mankind. Here in these waters of salvation, they are purified, almost as soon as they are stained by sin. Here they are made the children of God, almost as soon as they take their place among the children of men. Here they are enrolled among the citizens of heaven, before they can know that they are for a time, exiles on earth. Here they are saved from the power of Satan; are taken out of his kingdom, and if they die with the robe of their baptismal innocence, they are at once admitted into the choirs of angels to live and rejoice in the presence of Mary, the Immaculate, forever.

No words can describe, no tears can deplore the fatal error of those who believe not, or believing, disregard this holy Sacrament. It is an offense in which the strongest ingratitude, cruelty and unbelief are combined. And this to the dishonor of an ever indulgent and gracious Redeemer, who, clothed with all the attributes of Divinity; as the Incarnate God, triumphant by His own power over death, and now about to ascend in His own right to the highest heavens,—again makes known His most sacred Will and Commandment to those who are to perpetuate His Kingdom among men; nay, to all who will share in His salvation: 'Go ye into the whole world, and preach the Gospel to every creature: He that believeth and baptized shall be saved: but he that believeth not shall be condemned.'

In the midst of such errors and dangers, which need not be exaggerated, for they are evidently great, it is your lot, Beloved Brethren, to be in this world and to have on hand the work of your salvation. A moment of life and all is over. Either the work is done, according to the measure of grace which God has given you, and you are saved: or it is left undone, and you are lost forever. Only the upright and the earnest can realize the value of this moment. For not nearer to certain destruction were the three children in the furnace of the Assyrian King, than are the far greater number even of Christians, every day that we spend in this "free-living, easy-mannered, fair-spoken world." The God who saved them, can and will save us if we do not forsake Him: if in humility, faith and obedience we commend our souls to His protection. And when we name those virtues, we point our the steps by which Mary has risen to that throne, than which there is only one other more glorious in heaven, the throne of the Triune God. That these virtues are the foundation of her glory, we learn from her canticle, the Magnificat; from the inspired salutation of St. Elizabeth, the mother of the greatest of the prophets, and from more than one passage in the life of her Redeemer and ours. Her humility, faith, obedience, repaired the pride, unbelief, disobedience of our first parents; and obtained for Mary that more than angelic purity which gave her strength to crush the Serpent's head, grace to become the Mother of God and Queen of all His elect.

To whom, with more reason, propriety, confidence and veneration can we turn than to a being, whom, from all eternity God has so loved and honored—the advocate of Eve, and therefore the Refuge of all her children—the consoler of him, that was first formed by God, the father of the world, and therefore, the compassionate protector of all his descendants. At the same time no more powerful friend have we with God. The humbler of our chief enemy, Satan, she is in a noble sense, the strength of the weak, the Help of Christians. The overthrow of the apostate angel who is also the spirit of error, Mary has been always regarded as the destroyer of heresies, the guardian of the Faith, the same defender of God's people in the hour of affliction. We only repeat, therefore the counsel of His chosen and most illustrious servants, when we exhort you, Beloved Brethren, to cultivate a tender devotion to the Immaculate Mother of Jesus Christ. Let it be done by all, faithfully and fervently. You can hardly address her in any prayer, salutation or hymn, without uttering the very words which angels and saints have employed before you. No day should be allowed to pass, without some actual proof of your confidence in her protection, of your perpetual joy and gratitude for her Immaculate Conception; and for all the other graces, glory and the power which God has bestowed upon her.

That the Letters Apostolic defining the doctrine of the Immaculate Conception as a Dogma of faith, have been published in our age, is also an event calling for frequent thanksgiving to God and prayer for the prosperity of our Holy Father Pius IX. To have been present on so glorious an occasion; to have taken part therein, as chief pastor of the diocese of Philadelphia, and one of the representatives of the Church in America, is an honor and happiness which my words cannot describe, but for which I return, and forever will return the most humble thanks to our Lord Jesus Christ.

To all the religious societies, to those of the Scapular, Rosary, Bona Mors and the Guardian Angels; to the Sodalities of the Blessed Virgin, originally established in Rome, and now happily found in many parts of our country; to the different Benevolent, Literary and Beneficial Associations, all which we cordially regard as so many means of promoting practical piety, domestic happiness and the general welfare of the Church, we extend our special benediction and earnestly recommend the cultivation of this spirit of filial love and reverence for Mary, the Immaculate, whom says St. Anselm, God has made His Mother that she should be the Mother of all. The same great authority also declares no one who is truly devout to Mary will ever be lost.

On each day of the Triduum, one Mass of the Immaculate Conception either solemn or not, may be celebrated. So those who will worthily approach the sacraments and devoutly assist at the exercises on one of the three days, an indulgence of seven years, and of as many Quadragences, is imparted. They who will assist at all the exercises will gain a plenary indulgence, the usual conditions being fulfilled. These indulgences are applicable to the souls in Purgatory. The Rev. Pastors may adopt such devotional exercises as they will judge best, for this joyful season, and for awakening the piety of the faithful. An evening service, with the Litany of the Blessed Virgin, and the Benediction of the Most Holy Sacrament will, in many Congregations, be suitable.

All will pray for the intentions of our Holy Father, for the welfare of the Church, for the return of peace to the world. And may the Virgin Mother of our Lord and Saviour Jesus Christ, being now more honored on earth, obtain for you and for all mankind an abundant share of those graces and blessings, which will lead you to the possession of the inheritance incorruptible and undefiled, and that cannot fade, reserved in heaven for you.

The Grace of our Lord Jesus Christ be with your spirit, Brethren, Amen.

+ JOHN NEPOMUCEN
Bishop of Philadelphia

October 2, 1859

Grace be to you, and peace, from God our Father, and from the Lord Jesus Christ.

The great and happy progress made by our holy religion in the United States fills us with joy, and we offer continual thanksgivings to the Almighty for the graces which He so abundantly pours out upon our country.

The trials of the young Church of this country were, in the beginning, most severe, and the first laborers were encompassed by poverty and difficulties of every kind; but they confided in God and, through Him, obtained the grace of laboring perseveringly in the vineyard of the widely scattered faithful.

Even at the beginning of this century our Church received notable increase from all parts of Europe; and still every month brings thousands to our shores. In a short time the number of Catholics has grown beyond computation.

We see numbers of churches filled with worshippers, and hundreds of children flocking to our spacious parochial schools. Every year witnesses the opening of new colleges and academies, the erection of asylums, hospitals, and convents. The poor wanderer, far away from the home and scenes of childhood, no longer feels himself a stranger in a strange land, for he beholds on all sides majestic temples before whose altars he can worship his God. Yet whilst religion is thus making rapid strides, there is a great want felt, that of laborers in the vineyard—want which grows more urgent day by day.

It is, indeed, true that during the last fifty years many priests have come to our shores from Europe. They had heard of our spiritual distress; and, actuated by holy zeal and in imitation of the Apostles, they left home and friends to labor in God's house here in America. Many young men, also, not yet in orders, but who had chosen the Lord for their inheritance, found their way to our land, and offered themselves to the Bishops; being accepted, they entered our seminaries, completed their studies, and were admitted to the ranks of the priesthood. In this way our prelates have been able to supply the most important missions with good priests. Since the beginning of the mission-work in our diocese, one hundred and seventy priests have been engaged in it. Of these, forty-seven were native-born, and one hundred and fifty-seven finished their studies in our diocesan seminary. But we cannot depend entirely on such sources. During the last two or three years applications have been less numerous. We shall therefore soon sensibly experience the want of priests; our work will not advance. The clergy are subject to the same evils as their fellow-mortals: sickness and death seek victims among them.

But God, who in His infinite wisdom orders all things well, will provide for our wants. He already points out the way by which we can supply them, viz., by the co-operation of those whose duty it is to instruct you and to sanctify your souls. The way shown us by Divine Providence is the education of our young men to the priesthood in institutions established for this purpose. Through them we shall have constant and abundant sources from which to procure good and able ministers for our holy Church. The lively faith manifesting itself in so many Catholic families, the grandeur and solemnity of our services, the holy influence of religion on our parochial schools, must naturally inspire numbers of our young men with a love for the sacerdotal state. Even during these last years we have perceived in our youth a growing inclination for the priesthood. Year after year, applications are made to us from young men of our diocese to be admitted into different educational establishments with a view to the clerical state. Not many years ago no fewer than twenty were received by us at one time. They have now been studying for three years at the preparatory seminary of St. Charles, Maryland. It gives us great pleasure to be able to state that to their progress in learning, as well as to their good conduct, we can testify.

This is also a manifest sign that Almighty God desires that we should carry out without delay the decree of the Council of Trent, by establishing a preparatory seminary within the precincts of our own diocese. This institution, in connection with our theological seminary of St. Charles Borromeo, will, with the blessing of God and our own co-operation, supply us with pious and learned priests to aid in the fulfilment of our pastoral duties. The holy Council of Trent (Sess. 23, chap. 18) issued the following decree: 'As young men, if not rightly directed, give themselves up to the pleasures of the world and, if not trained from their tender age in piety and virtue, will never submit to ecclesiastical discipline, the holy synod decrees that all cathedral churches are obliged according to their ability to support gratuitously a certain number of young men of the city and diocese, to train them religiously, and to form them in ecclesiastical discipline. The youth who wish to be received for this end must not be under twelve years of age; they must have been born of lawful wedlock; must be able to read and write; and their moral character must justify the hope that they will devote themselves to the service of the Church. Especially should poor children be chosen for gratuitous education. The rich are not to be excluded, though they should be supported at their own expense. The Bishop should divide these young men into as many classes as appears advisable with respect to age, number, and intelligence in ecclesiastical affairs. From these he chooses those who are fit, and again selects others to take their place, so that the institution will continually furnish him servants for the Church. In order that young persons may be better kept in ecclesiastical discipline, they should wear the clerical dress; they should learn grammar, church-music, and other useful sciences; they should, moreover, be instructed in Holy Scripture, and in the homilies of the saints.'

The establishment of these diocesan seminaries according to the plan of the Fathers of the Council of Trent was deemed necessary for the restoration of church-discipline. We doubt not for a moment that this plan will be carried out in our diocese also, and be accompanied by the most gratifying results. The guardianship of parents is certainly the best nursery for good Christians; the blessing of the marriage-sacrament, even under less favorable circumstances, produces more powerful, more efficacious results under the parental roof than the most brilliant scientific educational system in a foreign institution, however richly the latter may be endowed, however distinguished by the learning and talents of its professors. But if Christian youth are to be educated for the service of the Almighty, all contact with what would withdraw them from their holy vocation must be avoided. Parental influence occasionally makes an undue impression on the mind of youth, sometimes turns their thoughts away from the things of God.

It is true, the hearts of these young men are still innocent, yet they are susceptible of good and bad. Their natural waywardness, their want of experience, and the unfortunate striving after the imitation of whatever they foolishly admire in others can very easily tarnish the purity of the soul, sadden the Holy Ghost, and deprive them of the grace of their vocation. It is a great boon which the Church grants to her future servant if she opportunely snatches him from the noxious influences of the world, shelters and fosters him in the salutary atmosphere of her secluded sanctuary, till his character has developed and he has grown up in the wisdom of God.

A period of ten or twelve years devoted to scientific branches, especially ecclesiastical science, qualifies him to instruct the ignorant, strengthen the doubting and wavering, guide the faithful, preach and defend fearlessly the truths of our holy faith.

The character of the priesthood elevates him to, a high dignity, even above the angels, and to this dignity must correspond his virtues that he may be a worthy servant of God, possessed of Christian holiness in so eminent a degree as to be able to discharge the duties of his high office in a manner pleasing to God and salutary to the souls of men.

The time which a seminarian spends at college gives him sufficient opportunity to ascend from virtue to virtue until he reaches the perfection required by the Church of her priests. The Holy Sacrifice of the Mass, meditations in common, prayers daily recited by all, the good example of fellow-students, frequent Holy Communion, and the dwelling under the same roof with our Lord in the Blessed Sacrament, impose upon him the happy necessity not only of avoiding every willful sin, but aid him to prepare his heart for every virtue.

We were therefore highly satisfied when informed last spring that a piece of land with suitable buildings, situated in a healthful region, had been offered for sale. Trusting in God's help and your generosity, we bought it without delay, and made the necessary improvements for the reception of young students. With pleasure we announce for your consolation that there are now twenty-six students and four professors in the institution.

As this institution is connected with our large seminary, we think it advisable to recommend to you their united claims. We do not deem it necessary to exhort you to contribute to them. We know well that our appeal will meet a hearty response, and that every parish priest will do his best to make these establishments successful; neither do we wish to change our plan for raising funds. It has proved itself effective. But we should like to see a more general co-operation on the part of the faithful; therefore we request the reverend clergy to read this Pastoral from the pulpit on the first Sunday after its receipt, and to appoint as many of the faithful as are willing to gather subscriptions, in order that the seminaries may be freed from their heavy debts.

The collection is to continue from October until the middle of November.

Yet, dear brethren, not gifts alone laid on the altar will secure for us good priests, but humble prayer with fasting is necessary.

Particularly during the ember-days should the faithful not omit to pray, to receive Holy Communion, and to practice works of self-denial, in order that the Pastor of our soul may send worthy laborers into His vineyard, and that we may enter undefiled into the possession of the inheritance reserved for us in heaven.

+ John Nepomucene

FURTHER
SUGGESTED READING
on the Life and Teachings
of St. John Neumann

Archival Sources

American Catholic Historical Society of Philadelphia
Budweis Diocesan Archives: *The Rodler Papers*
Redemptorist Archives of the Baltimore Province: *Neumanniana*

Printed Sources

Acta Apostolicae Sedis
Constitutiones Dioecesanae in Synodis Philadelphiensibus
Positio Super Introductione Causa
Spicilegium Historicum Congregationis SSmi. Redemptoris

Books

Berger, Johann, C.Ss.R. *Life of the Right Rev. John N. Neumann.*
    Translated by Eugene Grimm, C.Ss.R., Philadelphia, 1884.
Boever, Richard A., C.Ss.R. *The Spirituality of St. John Neumann,
    C.Ss.R., Fourth Bishop of Philadelphia.* Ann Arbor Michigan;
    University Microfilms International, 1983.

Chorpenning, Joseph F., O.S.F.S., ed. *He Spared Himself in Nothing: Essays on the Life and Thought of John Nepomucene Neumann*. Philadelphia, 2003.

Curley, Michael J, C.Ss.R. *Venerable John Neumann, C.Ss.R.* Washington, 1952.

Dolan, Jay P. *The Immigrant Church*. Notre Dame, 1978.

Light, Dale B. *Rome and the New Republic*. Notre Dame, 1966.

Neumann, John N., C.Ss.R. *Bublische Geschichte des Alten und Neuen Testamentes*. Baltimore, 1849.

——. *Katholischer Katechismus*. Pittsburgh, 1846.

——. *Manuale Devotionis Quadraginta Horarum*. Philadelphia, 1855.

Rush, Alfred C., C.Ss.R., ed. *The Autobiography of St. John Neumann*. Boston, 1977.

Wuest, Joseph, C.Ss.R. *Annales Provinciae Americanae*. Ilchester, Maryland, 1888.

Other Redemptorist Titles
from Liguori Publications...

WITH HEARTS FULL OF JOY
Following Christ the Redeemer
Mathew J. Kessler C.Ss.R., José Antonio Medina S.T.D.

ISBN: 978-0-7648-1911-7

Jesus lived a life of announcing the kingdom of God. Some people converted upon hearing his message and others rejected him. For centuries the Church has proclaimed that the salvation Christ won for us is a gift. But what have we done with that gift? How well do we understand it? How are we living it? *With Hearts Full of Joy: Following Christ the Redeemer* is a book of reflections and questions on the topic of "plentiful redemption," a theme that the Redemptorists, founded by St. Alphonsus Liguori, preached to rich and poor alike.

BLESSINGS OF THE ROSARY
Meditations on the Mysteries
Dennis J. Billy, CSsR

ISBN: 978-0-7648-1941-4

Offering prayerful reflections on each of the twenty mysteries of the rosary along with thoughtful questions that will inspire a richer awareness of God's presence. The reflections in *Blessings of the Rosary* will encourage readers to make the rosary an integral part of their daily devotions. These reflections will be of immeasurable spiritual benefit to individuals and groups engaged in the crucial work of prayer.

**To order visit your local bookstore or call 800-325-9521
or visit us at www.liguori.org.**